The Ways of the Soul

The Ways of the Soul

A Psychiatrist Reflects:
Essays on Life, Death and Beyond

Dr Andrew Powell

muswell hill press

London • New York

First published by Muswell Hill Press, London, 2017.

© 2017 Andrew Powell

www.muswellhillpress.co.uk.

British Library CIP Data available

ISBN: 978-1-90899-523-0

Printed in Great Britain

For my wife Melinda and my children,
Anna, Joshua, Hugo and Flora

Contents

Acknowledgements

I would like to express my thanks to Dr Tim Read for inviting this publication of my written work by Muswell Hill Press. Without Tim's encouragement, I doubt that my papers would have made their appearance as a published volume.

I also wish to record my thanks to Katarzyna Trojanowska for her editorial skills in the revision of this work.

Many of the papers included in this volume were first published elsewhere and I am grateful to the publishers for their kind permission for reproduction here.

I am profoundly indebted to my patients, who have played such an important part in the development of my thinking. Without them, this book would certainly never have been written!

I have been fortunate to benefit from wise counsel throughout the years of my clinical practice – colleagues too numerous to name, but should they find the book in their hands, I hope they will smile in recognition of the part they have played.

My friendships, both personal and professional, have been many and all have helped me to learn and grow in understanding. In particular, I am most grateful for the support of colleagues in the Spirituality and Psychiatry Special Interest Group at the Royal College of Psychiatrists, whose enthusiasm, goodwill and generosity of spirit have made our working together a real pleasure.

We can learn a great deal about life and about ourselves through the therapy that goes on in the seclusion of the consulting room but it is outside, in the company of kith and kin, that we do our real living. Here I pay a heartfelt tribute to my splendid children and grandchildren, whose lives are a constant reminder of the vigour, optimism and loving nature of the human spirit.

Lastly, a special thanks to my dear wife, whose unfailing support, patience and wise commentary have greatly helped in the preparation of this volume.

Foreword

It is only occasionally that you come across a true innovator, one of those people who have a capacity to grasp the moment, understand where it is leading, and then lead the way. Andrew Powell is such a person. We were both psychiatrists at the Maudsley Hospital in London, where I was to specialise in neuropsychiatry and Andrew in psychotherapy. I found psychotherapy difficult to understand. It ranged from Ronnie Laing telling us schizophrenia was down to faulty mothering, to Freudian theory that was revered like a sacred text, while transcendent experiences were regarded simply as neuroses. The psychotherapists lived on the third floor of the outpatient block at the Maudsley. Their day would start at 6am, with psychoanalysis before the daily hospital grind of psychiatric teaching, ward rounds and patients.

So my dealings with Andrew were at the ordinary level of psychiatric diagnoses, medicalisation of the patient and supportive psychotherapy as we were being taught it. Whatever the problem, the Maudsley impressed on its junior staff that the answer lay in the brain, and that was where we should look for the solution.

Andrew left the Maudsley for St. Georges' Hospital and Medical School, I stayed, and he and I followed different paths. But 15 years later, I found myself sitting in a conference listening to Andrew present a paper on 'soul therapy', an unusual topic in those days for a scientific conference. I was bowled over by his humanity, his loving presence, his maturity and his deep insight into who we truly are. Andrew clearly had an understanding of human nature seemingly much deeper than anything that could have been acquired either in standard psychiatric training or from psychoanalysis, and which had the potential to add another dimension to both practices.

In this volume of papers, Andrew gives us a deep insight not only into his own spiritual vision but also into his capacity to understand and help his psychiatric patients by contacting them at some deep, quite different level – the 'soul level'. I was impressed by his facility over the years to draw upon the transpersonal concepts of spirit release, regression analysis and soul growth, and to have seen how his clinical work deepened with his understanding of the spiritual nature of humankind.

Andrew has always had the ability to make his ideas acceptable and trustworthy to his colleagues, and it is a tribute to him that it was no surprise when he prevailed upon a group of us to support him in his application to start a special interest group in spirituality and psychiatry in the Royal College of Psychiatrists. This group has grown rapidly and been wildly successful. I well remember the first meeting, when a fellow psychiatrist burst out with 'This is what I was hoping for when I became a psychiatrist, but never found'.

This series of papers demonstrates Andrew's personal growth and his fine sensitivity for the movement towards spiritual psychiatry that was beginning in the USA but was still nascent in the UK. He has always been at the forefront, and the College meetings of the Spirituality and Psychiatry Special Interest Group are a tribute to his rational eclecticism. I cannot recommend too highly this collection of his papers, which show and reinforce the green shoots of our developing psychiatry, particularly the branch that will finally grow away from the world of brain-based reductionism so unreceptive to the sacred, and into a universe based on love and fully conscious in every atom of its structure.

Peter Fenwick MB, BChir, FRCPsych
Emeritus Consultant, Joint Bethlem and Maudsley Hospitals
Emeritus Honorary Senior Lecturer, Institute of Psychiatry
Psychology and Neuroscience
President, Scientific and Medical Network

Preface

When Muswell Hill Press invited me to publish my papers on spirituality and mental health, this being the first of two volumes,[1] I was both pleased and a bit hesitant to do so because I am aware that others, who are far more knowledgeable, have tapped the same vein.

It could be that over the years my writings have become known as much for my having founded the Spirituality and Psychiatry Special Interest Group[2] (SPSIG) of the Royal College of Psychiatrists as for any merit the papers may have. Therefore, I will start by saying something about the evolution of the group before turning to the theme of these papers and how I came to write them.

The SPSIG provides a forum for psychiatrists who want to put the soul into psychiatry – bearing in mind that the word psychiatry derives from *psyche* (soul) and *iatros* (doctor). I had puzzled for many years over the divide between spirituality and psychiatry. In the history of our profession, spiritual matters have tended to be viewed as being either beyond the remit of mental healthcare, or else coming to the attention of the clinician as a symptom of illness (religious delusions being one such example). The more I thought about it, the more unnatural this division seemed, since a person's spirituality expresses a fundamental aspect of selfhood and personal identity and is thereby deeply engaged in the challenges and stresses of life.

It used to be felt too intrusive to ask patients directly whether they had ever suffered from sexual abuse. Yet we now know that sensitive enquiry into such experiences as part of the psychiatric assessment is not only important to our patients, but also leads to a

---

1. A second volume, *Conversations with the Soul*, is due for publication by Muswell Hill Press in 2018.
2. See www.rcpsych.ac.uk/spirit

better understanding of problems that have arisen and of how best to help. This example might seem a far cry from asking our patients about their spiritual and religious beliefs and practices. Nevertheless, psychiatrists have similarly hesitated to enquire into how such personal beliefs affect our patients' view of themselves and their lives, what impact this might have on falling ill – be it contributory or protective – and how it may influence the kind of help a person is seeking.

Although psychiatric training is not limited to the knowledge base of psychiatry – trainees also learn psychotherapeutic skills, which might be thought to be sufficient to cover the subject of spirituality – both psychodynamic and cognitive training leave spirituality outside the door. It is hardly surprising, therefore, that many psychiatrists remain apprehensive about discussing spiritual matters with their patients. Unprepared for such a dialogue, serious miscommunications can arise. One patient, who happened to be an ordained minister, told me how she had tried to talk with the admitting psychiatrist about the Holy Ghost, only to have it reported in the ward round the next day that she was seeing ghosts!

This institutionalised disregard for spiritual and religious concerns loses us a valuable opportunity to connect with our patients, which has both empathic and diagnostic implications. We know that up to a half of patients turn to their spiritual and religious beliefs to help get them through a crisis but that they do not feel comfortable talking about such things with the psychiatrist.

I will add a personal note here. I have had a lifelong penchant for matters spiritual but during the early years of my career, first in hospital medicine, then psychiatry and subsequently psychotherapy, my clinical work was entirely secular. The psychoanalysis I underwent was likewise secular – I learned a lot about myself but I never saw my spirituality as being part of it. In my early thirties, I became a teaching hospital consultant and my time and energy were spent between building up a regional clinical service and getting on with family life. Some years later, I found myself at a crossroads, with my personal life in disarray. My intuition told me that rather than yet more psychoanalysis, I had better find healing for myself. Consequently, I embarked on a new journey, one that introduced me to the soul in ways that I had never encountered in my church-going youth. I visited healers and began a personal practice of meditation. I turned to reading Carl Jung and the literature on transpersonal psychology.

I was attracted to transpersonal psychology[3] because it aims to integrate the spiritual and transcendent aspects of the human experience with human psychology. In the course of my researches, I gained first-hand knowledge of spirit release therapy and past life regression. I studied anomalous perceptual experiences such as physical mediumship, out-of-body states and the near-death experience. My earlier training in psychodrama came into play as I explored how I could help my patients converse with the soul, find out what it needs and be guided by what it has to say.

This proved to be my point of no return – not that the bio-psychosocial model of care was wrong but for me it was, thereafter, painfully incomplete. I could not imagine working without inward (and often outward) reference to the spiritual dimension.

By the time I felt ready to advocate spiritually informed psychiatry within the profession, I had held consultant and academic appointments in the National Health Service for more than twenty years. I had also come through a major health crisis, one that brought me face to face with my mortality and which spurred me on, given what was then an uncertain future. Suffice to say that in 1999, I felt the time had come to make the move and see if the Royal College of Psychiatrists would support a spirituality and psychiatry special interest group, one where psychiatrists could venture beyond the narrow limits of 'scientific realism'.

With a handful of close colleagues,[4] I set up a working group and we agreed that our remit would be to create a spirituality forum to examine such things as the potential communication gap between patient and psychiatrist,[5] the interrelation of body, mind and spirit, the nature of anomalous perceptual experiences including near-death, mystical and trance states, the difference between healthy and unhealthy religion/spirituality, the place of spiritual values in finding

---

3. Inspired by Jung's writings, transpersonal psychology developed as a movement in the 1960s led by Abraham Maslow, Stanislav Grof, Roberto Assagioli and others. Focusing on development beyond the personal ego, transpersonal psychology sees the self as extending to others, to all humanity and beyond – ultimately being at one with *all that is* (in other words, God).

4. Drs Julian Candy, Larry Culliford, Peter Fenwick, Chris Holman and Professor Andrew Sims.

5. Surveys have shown that while the majority of the general population continue to believe in God or a 'higher presence, or power', less than one-third of psychiatrists and psychologists have such a belief.

purpose and meaning in life; and last but not least, research that was now showing the benefits of spirituality to positive mental health.

Happily, the College gave its support to our proposal and over the 17 years since inauguration, the membership of the SPSIG has grown to more than 3000 psychiatrists. Its website is wholly in the public domain, and publicises programmes and talks, as well as holding an archive of over 200 papers on spirituality written mainly by psychiatrists. Two books on spirituality and mental health have been published by the College[6,7] as well as an information leaflet for service users[8] and guidelines for professional practice.[9]

I have always felt that there is an important subtext to our advocacy of spirituality in healthcare. This is the implicit yet crucial belief that regardless of any other therapeutic intervention, our patients are in need of love. In saying as much, it is important to distinguish between the ego and the soul, a subject about which I write a good deal. Love that serves the needs of the ego is open to abuse in the clinical context. In contrast, love that emanates from the soul is capable only of good, being entirely concerned with the best interests of the other, asking for nothing in return, and bringing equanimity in times of crisis.

This links to a second theme that runs through the papers, the concept of wholeness,[10] which is conspicuously absent from the vocabulary of mental health science.[11] There can be no single definition of what constitutes wholeness of self but at the very least it calls for more than the satisfaction of individual desires and needs. From the start of life, we are in relationship to others. In the words of John Donne, 'no man is an island, entire of itself'.[12] At its most simple,

---

6. Cook et al. (2009).
7. Cook et al. (2016).
8. See 'Spirituality and Mental Health' leaflet. Available at www.rcpsych.ac.uk/spirit
9. Royal College of Psychiatrists (2013).
10. The word 'whole' shares the same root as 'healing' and 'health' (from Saxon *hāl* (healthy, safe), Middle English *hool* (healthy, unhurt), and similarly for *hel* and *heil* in High German and Old Norse.
11. *The Complete Psychological Works of Sigmund Freud* contain over 400 entries for neurosis and none for health.
12. John Donne (1623), *Devotions upon Emergent Occasions and Seuerall Steps in my Sicknes – Meditation XVII.* See Motion (1999: 101).

love is how we connect and without connection there is no life. Hence we 'belong to more than ourselves' – a beautifully concise description of what is meant by spirituality.

No matter how impressive the achievements of technology, the world of human values and meaning lies beyond the reach of science, for science deals with the world of things.[13] How can a psychiatrist help a fellow human being without being concerned with values that guide and illuminate an individual's life's purpose? Unfortunately, the humanities have been largely shouldered out of clinical practice by the onrush of a science that believes it holds the key to human happiness – or at least thinks it knows how to relieve unhappiness. Global prescribing of psychiatric drugs is rising year on year and by 2018 the market is predicted to have reached 77 billion dollars annually.[14]

The medicalisation of human anguish now woven into our culture reflects a society that seems unable to stand back and ask what we are doing to ourselves, the communities in which we live and the natural world. This brings me to a further theme in these papers. What are the assumptions that we make in our post-modern world about the nature of reality? How is it that we are so conditioned by the culture of material realism that many believe that the world of the five senses is all that exists? And what does this pervasive culture of materialism do to the human spirit?

While the human soul can never be destroyed, it is easily denigrated or denied. The consequence is the loss of any deep sense of meaning and purpose and a poverty of spirit that even the most lavish consumerism cannot replenish. While psychiatry is not to be confused with the priesthood, if we confine ourselves to a science-based exchange, we may meet the patient but we will not meet the person, and we certainly will not engage with the soul, so important for the journey of healing and recovery.

I will now turn to the papers, set out here in chronological order, and how I came to write them. All of the papers were prepared for talks given or for journal publication, and therefore written as stand-alone

---

13. For an exposition of this theme that is both profound and eloquent, see Smith (1992).
14. See Dewan (2014).

texts. The papers have been edited for this volume while remaining recognisably the same. The reader who works through them from start to finish inevitably will find a good deal of the same ground being covered, although hopefully from different angles. An alternative would be to dip in as the mood dictates. While I have made revisions, they are for the most part minor ones. I have, however, provided additional references and updates as footnotes where I felt they are required.

Some papers were written with professional colleagues in mind and others were intended for a wider circulation. While the emphasis varies, I have endeavoured to express myself as clearly and with as little jargon as possible. From the outset, I have not disguised my enthusiasm for ideas that I hope may resonate with audiences and readers rather than presenting my views in the balanced way favoured by academic circles.

Lastly, a word about clinical cases. I must record here that I am enormously indebted to my patients who have taught me so much. The case studies included were gathered prior to the 1998 Data Protection Act, which has made them easier to publish than nowadays.[15] Nevertheless, the accounts have been anonymised to protect identities. I should add that some of the vignettes appear more than once, so readers can rest assured they are not suffering from *déjà vu*.

The papers in this volume span the years 1997 to 2005, beginning with 'The Soul of the Newborn Child'. During the previous decade, I had been principally writing about therapeutic group analysis.[16] S. H. Foulkes, who pioneered this treatment approach, contended that: 'it is always the transpersonal network which is sensitised and gives utterance or responds. In this sense we can postulate the existence of a group mind'.[17] This idea greatly interested me, for it seemed to be borne out by my clinical experience working as a group analyst.

---

15. These days, there are formidable obstacles to publishing clinical material, especially in the field of mental health. There have been cases of litigation where a person feels they are recognisable, even though only to themselves, and therefore have challenged the right of publication.
16. Powell (1989, 1991, 1993, 1994).
17. Foulkes (1984: 118).

My involvement with the Scientific and Medical Network[18] during those same years gave me some understanding of how transpersonal phenomena may be accounted for by advances in quantum cosmology. I felt that by using a language that was rooted in science, I would be better able to convey the nature of the transpersonal to colleagues working in mental health. In a more personal sense I was, of course, looking to see how my own lifelong interest in spirituality might be integrated with my work as a psychiatrist and psychotherapist.

I am indebted to Dr Malcolm Pines, then editor of the journal *Group Analysis*, for publishing those early papers, since they were outside the mainstream of group therapy. Did the papers have much influence (beyond my losing some old friends and finding some new ones)? The greatest effect was probably on myself, for I was emboldened to begin writing openly about what most interested me (I have come to think this is generally the best way to write – casting one's bread upon the waters and letting things happen as they will). My hope is that these papers from 1997 onwards, tracing my deliberations, will encourage others both within and outside the mental health profession to reframe the way we think about the troubled mind – how we not only *think* about but also *respond* to the person in crisis. The soul, regardless of what exactly we imagine it to be, is always in attendance. When we engage with another, soul to soul, we draw on a plenitude of love even in the most harrowing of circumstances. There is no better place to start from when making the journey to wholeness, healing and health.

The Soul of the Newborn Child begins with a case report that, if taken seriously, can only be understood on the transpersonal level. The account suggests that the (incoming) soul of the newborn is fully cognisant of all that is taking place, although unable to express this in its embodied form. This same realm of the transpersonal is evidently encountered by survivors of the near-death experience. There are profound implications for the enduring existence of the human soul, as well as the likelihood of reincarnation.

---

18.   See www.scimednet.org

Soul Consciousness and Human Suffering describes how the domain of the soul might relate to the (more familiar) landscape of human depth psychology. Some of the problems that arise when the dimension of the soul is denied or neglected are highlighted, with clinical examples used to illustrate how the soul may be re-engaged and with it, how a renewed capacity for love may emerge.

Beyond Space and Time – The Unbounded Psyche introduces the transpersonal with reference to the work of Carl Jung, which I illustrate with a number of personal and clinical illustrations of synchronicity. Examples are given of past life regression, spirit release therapy and soul recovery and how these may be revealing of the deeper, unbounded nature of space-time.

The Unquiet Self and the Search for Peace looks at meditation both from personal experience and more widely in relation to mental healthcare. A schema is proposed that sees consciousness as inherent to all matter, but which becomes recognisable (to us) with increasing complexity of form. Some of the benefits and dangers of meditation are reviewed, with guidelines for safe practice.

Spirituality and Science: A Personal View summarizes what I take to be the fundamental problem facing psychiatry today – adherence to a biological model of mental illness (rooted in Newtonian science) at the expense of human relationship and connection (intrinsic to quantum modelling). The paradox of wave-particle duality suggests we are intended to experience both Newtonian and quantum perspectives on our journey through life.

Psychosocial Implications of the Shadow explores the nature of human destructiveness, at its worst when ego defences come into play, denying the 'shadow' within the human psyche and instead projecting it out in the world and onto others. I highlight Carl Jung's vision of the inclusive Self, which has the power to overcome the fortress mentality of the ego.

Putting the Soul into Psychiatry describes how the soul came to be elbowed aside by the scientific revolution that followed Newton and Descartes. However, recent advances in science lend credence to the concept of a spiritual universe, one that can be readily accessed in altered states of consciousness. Given the benefits of spirituality to health, I unequivocally argue the case for spiritually informed psychiatry.

GOOD AND EVIL – A PSYCHIATRIST'S PERSPECTIVE draws on case studies to show how the clinician construes 'evil' in terms of psychopathology, for example, as a response to intolerable mental pain. Yet distinguishing between 'good' and 'evil' is the basis of morality and by no means everyone who abuses or murders has a diagnosable mental illness. In wider society, too, the ubiquitous ego defences of splitting and projection provoke violence and stand in the way of humankind's capacity to find kinship with each other.

MENTAL HEALTH AND SPIRITUALITY contends that the scale of mental illness today relates to a society that has largely turned its back on soul values. Notwithstanding, empirical research shows the benefit of a holistic approach inclusive of spirituality. Cure and healing are contrasted with reference to psychoneuroimmunology, altered states of consciousness and transpersonal phenomena. Of the spiritual skills needed by the clinician, the most important by far is the exercise of compassion.

CONSCIOUSNESS THAT TRANSCENDS SPACE-TIME asks the question 'Where is the mind?' and concludes that it is everywhere – a nonlocal quantum field. It follows that in clinical work, 'psi' effects have to be taken seriously, as well as energy depletion and toxic projections that can affect the therapist. On the positive side, a freedom is conferred that allows the patient to engage deeply with experiences that can bring healing, illustrated here by a number of case studies.

PSYCHIATRY AND SPIRIT RELEASE THERAPY returns to the subject of spirit attachment. Shamanic approaches continue in many cultures, including our own. Psychiatry is on uncertain ground here, being founded on scientific realism, which discounts the reality of otherworldly phenomena. A case study of spirit release therapy is included. How can this be understood from the perspectives of psychology or spirituality, or both?

VARIETIES OF LOVE AND THE NEAR-LIFE EXPERIENCE explores the nature of love in illness and health. While the insecure child grows up afraid to love (hence the 'near-life experience') the child who feels loved grows up with love for others. Spiritual love that arises from wholeness of self rests on this foundation. I draw on the Vedic understanding of the chakras to exemplify how such love transcends the duality of the emotions and brings a realisation of oneness.

SPIRITUALITY, HEALING AND THE MIND expands on the archetype of wholeness. Represented symbolically by the mandala, finding wholeness is crucial to the spiritual agenda. Life incurs suffering, and wounds to the psyche are inevitable. Making sense of suffering so as to grow in wisdom and compassion is the goal of individuation. With the healing of wounds comes the freedom to forgive and to love. Such is the aspiration of soul-centred therapy.

DEATH AND SOUL CONSCIOUSNESS recounts my growing interest in the spiritual perspectives of both East and West and how quantum cosmology appealed to me as a bridge between science and mysticism. I highlight the unitary nature of consciousness and associated research into presentiment, psychokinesis, remote viewing and in particular, the near-death experience. I set out my understanding of the soul journey, concluding with two past life regressions of my own, which suggest to me that learning from experience (often through adversity) is part of humankind's continuing evolution of spiritual growth.

SPIRITUALITY AND LATER LIFE – A PERSONAL PERSPECTIVE discusses how the archetype of spirituality may be expressed in secular ideals in the first half of life, while in later life it is more consciously aligned with the sacred. Foreknowledge of death – not so much the fact as its personal meaning – confronts the ego and throws a new light on human folly, one's own not least. Beyond the vicissitudes of the ego, the path to individuation awaits and with it a deepening interest in matters of the soul – hence the value of soul-centred therapy, especially in later life.

References

Cook, C.C.H., Powell, A. & Sims, A. (2009) *Spirituality and Psychiatry*. RCPsych Publications.

Cook, C.C.H., Powell, A. & Sims, A. (2016) *Spirituality and Narrative in Psychiatric Practice*. RCPsych Publications.

Dewan, S.S. (2014) *Drugs for Treating Mental Disorders: Technologies and Global Markets* (BCC Market Research Report PHM074B). BCC Market Research.

Foulkes, S.H. (1984) *Therapeutic Group Analysis*. Karnac.

Motion, Sir A. (1999) *John Donne (1623): Devotions upon Emergent Occasions/ Death's Duel*. Vintage Books.

Powell, A. (1989) The nature of the group matrix. *Group Analysis*, 22, 271–281.

Powell, A. (1991) Matrix, mind and matter: from the internal to the eternal. *Group Analysis*, 24, 299–322.

Powell, A. (1993) The psychophysical matrix and group analysis. *Group Analysis*, 26, 449–468.

Powell, A. (1994) Towards a unifying concept of the group matrix. In *The Psyche and the Social World* (eds D. Brown & L. Zinkin). Routledge.

Royal College of Psychiatrists (2013) *Recommendations for Psychiatrists on Spirituality and Religion* (Position Statement PS03/2013). RCPsych.

Smith, H. (1992) *Forgotten Truth: The Common Vision of the World's Religions*. HarperCollins.

1

The Soul of the Newborn Child

I want to begin with a story once told to Paul Perry,[1] documentary filmmaker and author of a number of books on the near-death experience.

A man had been waiting one night at a bus stop when a car that had gone out of control hit him. The bystanders at the scene thought he had been killed instantly. He was taken to the morgue where he was put in cold storage for 3 days until a post-mortem could be performed. During this time, the man became aware of a pinhole of light. He crawled towards it and through a hole, and found himself on the other side bathed in brightness. He discovered he could 'fly' so he went home to visit his family, where he saw his grieving wife and two small sons. Then he 'visited' the family next door who had a child, born a couple of days before the accident. As it happened, they were deeply distressed by the continuous crying of the baby, who would not stop, no matter how he was comforted.

In this disembodied state, the man found that he could talk to the baby. As he put it, 'No words were exchanged but I asked [the baby] maybe through telepathy what was wrong'. The baby told him that his arm hurt – the man could see that the bone was twisted and broken.

Meanwhile, the pathologist had arrived to do the post-mortem. When moving the body from the cold store, he noticed the man's

First published in *Holistic Science and Human Values* (1997), 3, 110–118.

---

1. The full story appears in Morse & Perry (1992).

eyes were flickering. He ordered the man to be taken to theatre immediately and after emergency surgery the man recovered consciousness. He told his family what had happened when he was 'dead'. No one believed him until he provided details of his out-of-body travels and his knowledge of the baby's fracture. The baby was taken to be X-rayed and was indeed found to have a greenstick fracture of the arm, almost certainly a birth injury.

Such stories are anecdotal, so they get short shrift in our scientific methodology. Nevertheless, taken as it stands, this story is either true or false. Let us entertain the possibility that it is true and without subterfuge.

There are two components to this story that are of interest, each in its own right. Firstly, there is the near-death experience. Much research has taken place over the past twenty years since Raymond Moody's famous compilation of case histories for his doctoral thesis.[2] Some scientists argue that what is being reported are the terminal throes of neural activity in a hypoxic central nervous system. However, the phenomena regularly described with great clarity are in a sequence that, while shaped by cultural factors, carries the same core spiritual revelation and is strikingly invariant.

I refer to the sensation of leaving the body behind, often hovering for a time near the ceiling, sometimes watching resuscitation being attempted, the experience of instant travel to other parts of the hospital or to home, including overhearing family and friends, entering a dark tunnel and floating away from the body with a profound sensation of relief and tranquillity. Then there is the approach of a bright light and often a dialogue with an important other, be it a deceased relative, close friend or higher spiritual being, a kaleidoscopic life review in which the whole of the life with all its deeds, both good and bad, is faced, the awareness of a threshold that once crossed would mean no way back, indeed often a reluctance to return except for the need to complete an important life task, and lastly, the sudden and painful pulling back into the body with the recovery of consciousness.

These experiences are not qualitatively like those in hypoxic or other organic conditions, which are labile and fragmentary. Particularly

---

2. Moody (1975).

striking is the profound and lasting spiritual impact of the near-death experience on the survivor.

Research on the non-local nature of consciousness began in earnest in the 1970s at Stanford Research Institute in Palo Alto, California.[3] Subsequent developments in quantum field theory suggest that consciousness is woven into the fabric of space-time in such a way that far from each of us manufacturing consciousness, it is more probable that we are individually participating in a universal energy field, tapping into it, much as a radio or television set functions as a waveform transducer.[4]

This ties in with the concept that reality is multilayered and that the physical world as we know it, from simple inorganic molecules to the human being, is but one facet of what David Bohm calls the explicate order,[5] arising out of a total vibrational field. Cosmologists have begun to discover just how orderly and coherent this process is turning out to be.

The second feature of the story is even more extraordinary than the near-death experience. It concerns the baby's capacity to communicate the nature of his injury. Even if we accept the primacy of consciousness as some kind of resonating quantum field, how could a newborn baby have this precise knowledge and speak about it?

Our natural incredulity arises from our psychobiological frame of reference. This assumes that we assemble 'reality' from the building blocks of sensory and motor fragments coming together as maturational changes bring about structuring of the contents of the psyche. (On this basis, it is now accepted that the foetus has a rudimentary psychic life, although it follows that it is the more primitive and unformed the further back we go towards the moment of conception.)

If, however, we reverse the usual figure/ground assumption and put mind before matter, then just as the near-death experience is premonitory of a rich and complex life after death, so the story of the baby likewise suggests an existence before birth. Birth and death are no more than the entry and exit points of the physical incarnation of psyche or soul.

3. Targ & Puthoff (1974).
4. Grinberg-Zylerbaum et al. (1992).
5. Bohm (1980).

A further aspect concerns the nature of the space-time dimension inhabited by our bodies, including our central nervous system. In the physical world, perception and cognition depend on mental constructs that compare and contrast. Duality provides the basis for the differentiation of experience – light and shade, good and evil, ignorance and knowledge, inside and outside, then and now, and much more besides, all within the duality of life and death. Even in quantum physics, duality is to be found in particle and wave. The point is that all our empirical research into reality and all that it contains, including the study of the human mind, is mediated by way of this dualistic mental perception.

The infant mind lacks the equipment for complex awareness, thought and communication. However, the baby in the story was not communicating as a neurophysiological organism, nor was the man hearing it as such. It follows that within the dimensional reality in which the communication took place, this was not what we ordinarily think of as a baby doing the speaking.

We cannot speculate beyond a certain point because of the very limits to which I have been referring, but there is no good reason to suppose there is just the one reality that we access with our five senses. Research in mathematics, physics and energy systems suggests that a hierarchy of realities co-exist. Our physical universe, arising from a collision of matter and anti-matter, appears to have been dualistic in nature from the outset, nested within the parameters of space and time. Yet it is perfectly feasible that other vibrational planes should be governed by other rule sets.

The reality consistently described by people who have experienced out-of-body states, while not entirely different from our own, illustrates this difference in rule set. The sense of having a body is retained (although it is weightless) together with continuity of personal identity. There is light and sound, although it is reported that perceptions do not seem to come via the special sense organs. The space-time frame is looser: travel is instantaneous and effected by volition, and time, too, can be traversed in this manner. Communication is telepathic, and infused with a profound awareness of love.

It is generally agreed that science should concern itself with the question 'how' and the humanities with 'why'. Sigmund Freud set out to establish a scientific psychology but did not spare himself the question 'why' in doing so. For example, he asks himself why humankind clings so tenaciously to the belief in God. Freud asserts that we cannot afford to give up the need for an Almighty Father. Why should this be so? The answer given is that humankind craves the security of childhood in the face of knowledge of death and obliteration, which is unbearable to humanity. Heaven is reduced to wish-fulfilment and God to a mere projection.[6]

Freud could not resist asking himself these questions and the answers that he came up with were inevitable, given his psychobiological premise. However, psychology can be founded in psychospirituality equally well. So why not allow ourselves, like Freud, to ask one or two 'hows' and 'whys', bearing in mind what we have been learning from advances in physics?

Quantum theory is shedding new light on the 'how' of consciousness. As to the 'why', since it can be argued that psychophysical consciousness is without end, death is not such a dreadful prospect. We are free to take into account spiritual considerations without dismissing them as defensive rationalisations.

The first question is this: What is the point of being conscious of existing? Traditionally, biologists have regarded consciousness as epiphenomenal, a by-product of neuro-synaptic activity. There is none to start with, then we become self-aware and then, like our physical body, it is all gone. There can be no answer to this question except that it must presumably serve some kind of evolutionary advantage.

In contrast, the psycho-spiritual view is that the mind has access to ultimate reality, if only by a slender thread, and that by means of this perspective we are able to reflect on ourselves and on the miracle of life. Much of the time, we do not bother because we are using the brain, our on-board computer, to negotiate the practical complexities of ordinary life. At other times, our ego keeps the focus exclusively on ourselves. However, when we give ourselves to reflection and contemplation, just as with a hologram in which the part contains the whole, so consciousness opens the limited individual mind to 'all that is'. The small 'self' cognizes the larger 'Self'.

Words cannot adequately convey this experience. Poetry possibly comes closest, along with music and the creative arts. The most immediate and powerful form, 'enlightenment', nirvana or *samadhi*,

---

6. Freud (1927).

as it is variously called, cannot find translation. It has to be 'stepped
down' in such a way as to be talked *about*, for instance, knowledge
that surpasses all facts and the realization of unbounded, selfless love.

Can we frame any of this in more familiar psychodynamic terms?
Over the past half-century, Freud's instinct theory, based on the idea
that the goal of the human organism is self-sufficiency, has been
superseded by object relations theory[7] and not least by John Bowlby's
seminal work on attachment.[8] Not only is the human being driven by
a primary need to relate to the 'other' from birth onwards but the
quality of the early bond that is established, be it anxious or secure,
will mark the whole of that person's life.

From the moment of conception, the fertilised ovum exists in
relation to mother; it is never alone. At first, it is bathed in the secre-
tions of the fallopian tube. Going on to take up residence in the lining
of the womb, it spends the next nine months emotionally and physically attached to mother. After birth, the increasingly complex affective
bond with the caregiver will determine the baby's survival and future
happiness. These biological facts are hardly new. Yet now that we are
learning about the likely holographic structure of the cosmos,[9] it is
time to consider afresh our bond with 'mother' universe.

We are all part of the origin of the universe. Our bodies are made
up of physical matter, which has been recycling through the birth and
death of stars ever since that time. Likewise, our minds have an intimate connectedness with the same source, to which we give the word
God. This is the ultimate and inherent object-relatedness of humankind. As biological parents we are, hopefully, loving guardians of each
life entrusted to our care. However, the child never belongs to the
human parent. We are the occasion of its birth but the true parent is the
cosmos (God) and we are there to safeguard the child's incarnation.

The role of the parent, then, is to support and sustain this new
life so that one day it may begin to experience the stirrings of its
underlying spiritual object relations with the source of all life. Tran-
siently, in young adulthood, this awakening is first manifested in

---

7. Guntrip (1961).
8. Bowlby (1973).
9. See Michael Talbot (1996) for a non-technical introduction to the concept, in
    which our three-dimensional universe is held to be a holographic projection
    of an underlying two-dimensional plane. For an update see Stone (2015).

falling in love. Yet no other human can be God and when the spiritual impulse is denied, for some there will come a restlessness of the soul with the passing years. If psychiatric help is sought (most often for depression), the symptom may not be evidence of pathology but of spiritual homelessness.

To the question I posed earlier, 'What is the point of being conscious of our existence?' the answer I would offer is this: we enter the physical realm seemingly unconscious of ourselves. To begin with, the mind of the newborn baby appears only to be conscious of wonderment, a state of naivety akin to enlightenment, broken at times by incomprehensible distress. Then comes the hard graft, the obstacle course of life, during which consciousness of the self is acquired, being prerequisite for the life tasks that lie ahead. For some people, work, family and social relationships are more than enough; for others, the spiritual longing intensifies and we have no choice but to open ourselves to the divine source of all that is. There is no right or wrong about this, for the blueprint of each life is unique and perfect in its way.

This brings me to a second and bigger question, Why do we exist in the first place? Surely, it would be more comfortable to stay put in the wise and loving world that we hear about in the near-death experience, where there is no death to be feared and no broken bones to be endured.

What appears to happen is that when the soul enters into life, there is a division of sorts; the transpersonal psyche retains its accrued wisdom while the human infant has to start over again. It was famously noted by John Bunyan that being born into a world in which good is paired with evil, joy with suffering, hope with despair and wisdom with folly, all laced with the drama of human emotions, makes a pilgrim of each and every one of us. The challenge is to learn, grow and develop, and feed the soul with the fruits of experience, something that according to Buddhist and Hindu traditions takes many lifetimes.

Within this space-time domain, we are an evolving species nested in an evolving universe. As mentioned earlier, the universe may be better described as a 'holoverse',[10] in which – as with the

---

10.   See *Soul Consciousness and Human Suffering*, this volume, for further description.

hologram – we discern the macrocosm mirrored in the microcosm.[11]
Could it be that we have archetypal knowledge of the Big Bang in
our mythical history of the 'fall from grace', not only projected onto
Adam and Eve but also dramatized in every live birth? Such a fall
from grace is like a fledgling being pushed out of the nest. Only then,
as it falls, does it try its wings in earnest.

According to the Gnostic tradition, the passage of our souls
through life both reflects and enriches the consciousness of the
source of all Creation. Indeed, according to all the religious faiths,
that is what we were made for, why we exist and ultimately where we
are headed. To ensure full immersion in human life and thereby to
grow in knowledge and wisdom from all that is to come, the incarnated mind must be born innocent of experience. We have found out
much about this learning process through the study of developmental psychology, but how might we further advance our knowledge of
consciousness through research into the non-locality of mind, paranormal phenomena, past life regressions, out-of-body experiences
and near-death experiences?

It is common knowledge that we are guilty of projecting all kinds
of imagined things into a newborn baby, especially if it is ours and we
desire to see a reflection of ourselves. Instead, try looking deep into the
eyes of a newborn child, perhaps not your own. You may see a wholeness yet unbroken and a gaze that bears an unspoken wisdom as ancient
as the hills. If, as in the story I started with, you happened to be released
from the constraints of your own body at the time, you might just find
yourself conversing with a mind every bit equal to your own.

References

Bohm, D. (1980) *Wholeness and the Implicate Order*. Routledge.
Bowlby, J. (1973) *Attachment and Loss*. Vol. 1. Hogarth Press.
Freud, S. (1927) The future of an illusion. Reprinted [1966] in *The Standard Edi-
tion of the Complete Psychological Works of Sigmund Freud*, vol. 21 (trans. & ed.
J. Strachey). Hogarth Press.
Guntrip, H. (1961) *Personality Structure and Human Interaction*. Hogarth Press.
Grinberg-Zylerbaum, J., Delaflor, M., Sanchez Arellano, M., et al. (1992) Human
communication and the electrophysiological activity of the brain. *Subtle
Energies*, 3, 25–43.

---

11.   Powell (1993, 1994).

Morse, M. & Perry, P. (1992) *Transformed by the Light*. Piatkus.

Moody, R. (1975) *Life after Life*. Bantam Books.

Powell, A. (1993) The psychophysical matrix and group analysis. *Group Analysis*, 26, 443–468.

Powell, A. (1994) Towards a unifying concept of the group matrix. In *The Psyche and the Social World: Developments in Group-Analytic Theory* (eds D. Brown & L. Zinkin). Routledge.

Stone, M. (2015) There is growing evidence that our universe is a giant hologram. Available at https://motherboard.vice.com/en_us/article/there-is-growing-evidence-that-our-universe-is-a-giant-hologram?utm_source=vicefbus (accessed 27 January 2017).

Talbot, M. (1996) *The Holographic Universe*. Harper Collins.

Targ, R. & Puthoff, H.E. (1974) Information transmission under conditions of sensory shielding. *Nature*, 251, 602–607.

2

Soul Consciousness and Human Suffering: Psychotherapeutic Approaches to Healing

This paper describes a therapeutic approach to working with transpersonal experiences that would otherwise be regarded by many psychiatrists as pathological. A parallel is drawn between psychoanalytic object relations theory and 'spiritual object relations', the latter based on the fundamental premise that mind precedes matter. A number of clinical examples illustrate the importance of working with both psychological and spiritual perspectives, highlighting the need for mental health professionals to be open to the transpersonal frame of reference.

I am taking as my thesis that the experience of wholeness is to be found at the heart of every therapeutic success. What does the word 'wholeness' presuppose? The *Concise Oxford Dictionary* tells us that the root of the word means none other than 'health' or 'healing'. It seems that long before sociologists started debating the meaning of terms like illness and health, we find a simple answer in the history of our language.

The human being has a natural sense of when we are integrated, whole, in harmony with self and, it usually follows, with others as well. We are born with this ancient knowledge, laid down in our

Paper prepared for conference 'Beyond the Brain II – Frontiers in consciousness and healing'. Scientific and Medical Network, Cambridge, August 1997. Published as 'Soul Consciousness and Human Suffering', *Journal of Alternative and Complementary Medicine* (1998), 4, 101–108. Reproduced with permission.

prehistory, and turn to it instinctively throughout our lives. Our ancestors knew without the help of science that wholeness makes for health.

Studies of infant development show that in the state of contentment, which is how a normal baby spends a good deal of its time, the infant spontaneously reaches out to mother with its eyes, hands, mouth and voice, and enjoys an exchange with her in which the mirroring of loving and tender gestures forms a sign language.[1] During this harmonious process, the infant learns to distinguish self from other and to go on to establish its own internal world. We call this extended phase of development the psychological birth of the child and where harmony has prevailed, the result is a flowering of the psyche in which love and joy are free to find expression.

This is how nature and nurture go hand in hand. Adult individuals who are able to respect and value themselves owe much to the internalisation of good parenting that has gone on before. At the same time, those life-enhancing interactions have been laid on a foundation of wholeness of being which was there from birth, indeed from the moment of conception.

There is no reference to wholeness or healing in all of Sigmund Freud's written works. In contrast, Carl Jung was very much concerned with wholeness, seeing it as the developmental task of the second half of life, when strengths and weaknesses can be weighed in the balance, mistakes owned, lessons learned, and the fruits of life's labours harvested.

As with the *ouroboros*, the ancient symbol of the snake with its tail in its mouth, symbols of wholeness are to be found throughout the history of mankind. These are the archetypes of the collective unconscious, the mandala, the Christ archetype, and indeed for each one of us, the individuating Self as archetype, animated by the soul, which Jung called 'the living thing in Man, that which lives of itself and causes life'.[2]

How might the concept of the soul be placed within the earthbound psychology of child development? The patient who comes along suffering the all too frequent twin emotions of self-hatred and

---

1. Winnicott (1960).
2. Jung (1954: 26).

envy of others must surely have once had an experience of wholeness, perhaps only at the very outset but sufficient enough to be left painfully aware of what has been missing ever since. That unfortunate person has suffered a double blow, for not only did the damage inflicted by a childhood of misery and neglect result in a failure to internalise good parenting, it also caused the growing child to lose contact with its original soul nature. Such deeply wounded patients cannot imagine how they will ever overcome the brutality of their own early life experiences.

As analytic psychotherapists, we are often trying to help emotionally traumatized patients to establish what we call healthy internal object relations. This rather ungainly term describes the state of a person's inner world in which the relationships of childhood, with parents and significant others, continue to influence how we think, feel and act. Disruptive or abusive relationships leave the psyche disunited and in turmoil. Treatment is aimed at establishing a new integration of the self through the patient discovering a capacity for trust in the dependability and nurturing of the therapist, a metaphorical return to the breast.

There is, however, a danger of lasting dependency on the therapist, most likely to happen if the therapist joins with the patient in believing that the integration of the psyche that is now being attempted is taking place for the very first time. In this case, the therapist shares in an illusion in which he or she becomes the idealized parent and regression on the part of the patient is liable to occur. Such distortion of reality can be very powerful and beguiling, especially when coupled with constant emphasis on feelings that can only be resolved through the trials and tribulations of the therapeutic relationship.

The situation is quite different if the starting point is to help the patient discover their spiritual birthright of wholeness of being, for while the soul may have been obscured, it cannot be destroyed. The therapist's task is to guide this process of enabling the patient to make contact once again with the enduring nature of their own soul and so to be restored from within.

The approach I describe in my clinical examples is very simple and therein lies its therapeutic strength and immediacy. It is based on the knowledge that the soul finds expression in human consciousness the same the world over, in the evocation of beauty, truth and peace.

When we directly engage the soul, we move to the imaginal space of 'spiritual object relations' – from the attachments of the ego to the attachment of the soul. Here the connection is not with the human other but with the Divine. Since each soul is a scintilla of the Divine, this brings me to a crucial implication of spiritual object relations, that throughout our lifetimes we can connect with each other soul to soul. Most people get a glimpse of this when they first fall in love. The condition is temporary, however, for soon the ego demands of each person come into play and the pleasure in giving is complicated by the need to take. In contrast, soul love gives and receives selflessly. It has the quality of *agape* and because replenishment from the Divine is always on hand, only an open heart is required.

From this metaphysical perspective, our universe can be viewed as one space-time dimension nested within other invisible dimensions that exist beyond the range of our sense perceptions. Mind, and its spiritual essence, the soul, are 'non-material' yet interface with the brain in what is a remarkable evolutionary accomplishment.

I doubt that we will ever entirely penetrate this mystery from within the incarnate life form. What may be less contentious is the idea that mankind is participating in an immense 'holoverse', to use the physicist David Bohm's term, in which the structure of the part always reflects the whole.[3] It would be no surprise, therefore, to find in the spiritual universe the same awareness of relatedness that we know from our experience of the human situation, with one crucial difference – knowledge of the whole and the realisation of oneness. With it comes an experience of serenity, indeed joy that is beyond the reach of the ego.

Clearly, I think Freud was wrong in supposing that our search for the Divine arises merely from a neurotic projection intended to shield us from the fear of death and oblivion. I take the opposite view – that much of the existential loneliness people experience is because of the painful separation from the 'Godhead' from which we come. The therapeutic task is to help bring the mind, by means of active imagination and reflection, to a heightened awareness of that relationship and to take strength and courage from it.

---

3. Bohm (1980). The concept of the holoverse is also discussed in *Putting the Soul into Psychiatry*, this volume.

Before I turn to the experiences of our patients, I need to add a few words about what Jung called the 'shadow'. The term refers to those denied and unwanted parts of the self as contrasted with the 'persona', the face we show to the world to gain us approval. In every culture there is found a shadow aspect, which is dealt with either by repression or split off and projected elsewhere. The Cold War was an example of the Soviet Union and the USA mutually projecting their shadows. We have all come across scapegoating, and if we are honest, we will find that we are generally intolerant in others of what we dislike most in ourselves. This is why our enemies have so much to teach us.

Wholeness and healing call for the shadow to be acknowledged, for the passions of love and hate are twinned in the human psyche. The task is not to disown the shadow but to recognize it for what it is, as part of the self, and to learn how to accept and contain it so as not to hurt others. Then, as the ancient Daoist tradition advises, *yin* and *yang* are in balance and the way is open to living in harmony with oneself and the world.

This challenge to move from conflict to wholeness is not resolved as an abstract proposition but by way of struggling with emotions that are rooted in the body. When we do manage to transcend the pull of opposites that threaten to tear us apart, we can see that *from the point of view of the inviolable soul* there is no such thing as a bad experience. However, the vantage point of the soul is not the same as how we feel when mired in human suffering.

Patients come to us because they have got stuck in the mire of suffering. When analytic psychotherapy enables a patient to find a new understanding within the framework of childhood, family and personal relationships, then a new beginning can be made. This is the bread and butter of clinical practice and it is often sufficient. However, at other times the darkness is so dark and the questions so big that the very meaning of life and death, what it is all for and why we are here, have to be faced head on. Working with soul awareness brings an experience of love and wisdom that makes such anguish the more bearable, and suggests ways forward that may never otherwise have been envisaged.

My personal view is that there is truly no such thing as death; we simply leave the body behind like a suit of old clothes. This belief is based on my own spiritual practice and in recent years also by the many accounts of the near-death experience. However, I am a psychiatrist, not a priest, and in the clinical setting it would be inappropriate to wear my personal beliefs on my sleeve. Instead, when the circumstance calls for it, I might ask a patient if he or she believes that life truly begins with birth and ends with death. Thus far, no one has said with certainty that there is nothing more to life than that.

Here is a clinical illustration of going 'beyond' death:

> Joan came to see me about a year after the death of her husband Ted, having nursed him through a long and debilitating illness. They had been together 40 years and her loss left her grief-stricken. She continually felt Ted's presence around the house, yet the awareness brought only pain. I asked Joan if she thought there could be an afterlife. Yes, she thought there might be, but how could that help her now?
>
> I asked her if she would like to try to make contact with Ted in a way that might bring her peace of mind. At my suggestion, Joan shut her eyes, relaxed, and was encouraged to see if she could 'find' Ted wherever he might be. After a couple of minutes, a faint smile played on her lips. I asked Joan what she saw. She replied that she could see Ted in his cricket whites playing cricket and looking very fit and happy. I remarked that he seemed to be enjoying a game of heavenly cricket! Joan's smile widened and she added that cricket had been Ted's great passion. Then a look of deep sadness passed across her face. I asked whether she would like to speak with Ted. She nodded, so l suggested she walk up to him and see what might happen. After a moment, Joan said that she was now next to him and that he had put his arm around her. What was he saying? He was saying 'Don't worry; everything is going to be all right.' I asked Joan to look around her. Was anyone else present? Then she saw her deceased sister and parents there, smiling and waving to her.

I had encouraged Joan to use her own imagination, better understood here as spiritual insight. I did not know at the outset what would happen. However, I trusted in Joan's capacity to find within and bring to consciousness what she needed for her own healing. Being able to see death not as an ending but as a transition helped her resume life with hope and expectation.

Joan's healing process began readily enough. Yet it cannot be forced, as the following case shows:

> Christine was chronically depressed. Throughout childhood, she never felt valued for her own self. Academic success had temporarily

bolstered her self-esteem but later, when a personal relationship failed, this fell apart. Her emotions froze over and she became profoundly withdrawn.

Christine had described her depression as a black cave. I invited her to close her eyes, go inside and report back with what she could find. After some minutes, she found a pair of steel handcuffs, then a rope and an iron chain. I pressed her to go on looking. After what seemed an eternity, her expression changed to one of concern and I asked her what she had found. It was a little puppy in a dark corner. I suggested she pick it up and hold it to her. With her eyes still closed, she cradled the puppy. What could she feel? She replied that she could feel the puppy's love for her. I urged her to let her own love flow to this puppy and she began to cry. I suggested she found an image for her emotion and she chose a golden heart.

The process can be understood psychologically as the puppy symbolizing the child Christine. She re-discovers and nurtures this child self with which she had lost touch and in doing so discovers that she still has the capacity for love. In terms of spiritual object relations, Christine has reclaimed her soul that had been lost to view in the darkness of her childhood. Looked at either way, what matters is that Christine was supported in following a process that emerged from deep within the compass of the psyche, unlimited in its spiritual dimension yet powerfully expressed in the symbols of everyday life.

Many people are born into situations of great hardship. Yet the burden of misfortune is lessened if we can make sense of it and see it as having some kind of purpose. Finding such an understanding weaves a narrative from the life lived. Here is another instance:

Ann was seen for assessment of depression. She suffered from limb-girdle muscular dystrophy that began when she was a child and was now wheelchair bound. As if that were not enough to bear, her three brothers bullied her relentlessly when she was small. The home life of this entire family was wretched and later her parents rejected her. Ann's cry from the bottom of her heart was 'Why me?'

After reviewing Ann's forlorn past, I asked her to recollect one happy memory and she remembered a visit to the Lake District. By way of her imagination, we 'went there' together. Ann gazed around her, drinking in the beauty of the hills and valleys. I asked Ann to imagine herself as the living spirit of the fell and to tell me what she could see from up there. Rather to her surprise Ann found herself answering that she had been there for thousands of years and seen much of life, people coming and going and many generations of the families living close by. I asked Ann if, with the help of this sacred spirit, we might put an important question to God. Yes indeed.

I now urged Ann to look again for the young girl who had made the visit here all those years ago. Far off, she could see herself once more as that child, being cruelly bullied by her brothers. Could God now answer Ann's heartfelt question 'Why me?' All at once, the answer arose from deep within her. 'You were sent to teach your brothers and your family how to love!'

No one could have been more surprised than Ann to hear this coming from her own lips. Was there anything else she needed to ask? With a flash of anger, she said, 'Then why didn't you stay and take care of me?' The answer came right back at her, with great tenderness. 'I never left you, not for one minute, and I am always with you.'

This story highlights the soul wisdom that is already present in a person if only it can be engaged. When we see that wisdom in action, answering a problem deep within the self, we are moved by its power and authenticity. Such wisdom can as easily be directed towards unresolved problems with deceased persons, as in this case:

Pat came for help having suffered from depression for many years. Since childhood, she had longed for approval but felt she could never please. Her mother would mock and belittle her and Pat was often full of anger that she never dared express.

When her mother died, Pat heaved a sigh of relief thinking she could now get on with her own life. But she found she could not, for her mother's presence was all around and she still seemed to hear her scorning her. Feeling possessed by her mother, as she herself put it, Pat had become suicidal.

I said to Pat that suicide would resolve nothing and that we needed to find a way to help the two of them separate. I invited her to confront her mother in death, as she had not been able to in life. We did this by having Pat visualise her mother facing her, using an empty chair. Pat went right ahead. For the first time she was able to deliver a few home truths and told her mother it was time she got off her back.

I now asked Pat to sit in the empty chair and role reverse with mother. Mum came straight back, saying she had no intention of stopping! She enjoyed hanging around Pat and in any case, she had nowhere else to go.

I asked Mum, through Pat, about the life she had just lived and I learned that her own mother had rejected her from an early age. She resolved to escape from home and took the first man she could to help her get away. However, getting pregnant with Pat when she was 17 ended her hopes of a career and tied her to a man she did not love. Her daughter became the life-long target of her resentment.

I explained to the mother how it would help her to move on, and to look around for someone that might help accompany her on the way. To begin with nobody appeared, so I urged her to look for just one person in her whole life that had shown her kindness. After a long pause, she remembered a Mrs Cox, who had been a nurse staying with the mother's family for a time, and who had made a real fuss over her when she had been a little girl. As Pat's mother recalled Mrs Cox, her face softened and I asked her to try to find her. Then she smiled and said she could now see her, looking just the way she did all those years ago. I asked her to take Mrs Cox's hand and walk towards the light. There was no further protest and she left with her friend. When this was over, Pat looked emotionally drained but at peace. She went back to her own chair and said, 'It feels that she has really gone for the first time.'

The psychodramatic use of the empty chair enabled Pat to ventilate her feelings more powerfully than by telling the therapist *about* mother. Then, through role reversal with her mother, Pat experienced first hand her mother's plight and the unhappiness that underlay her bitterness. Feeling validated, and with deeper understanding, Pat no longer felt in thrall to her mother. In enabling the release of her mother's spirit, Pat was put in touch with her own compassion, which will greatly assist in her healing.

What took place can be understood on two levels. As an exercise in psychodrama, the painful relationship with the mother that Pat was still carrying around inside her was being externalised and addressed. At the level of spirit release, Pat's mother had been truly stuck and needed help to let go and move on.

My last example goes one step further. Helen, in her forties, had suddenly become aware of feeling deeply emotionally burdened. There was nothing she could identify to account for it. All she could say was that she could feel a woman's presence calling out to her in distress.

Helen wanted to understand more about this voice speaking to her from within. Through hypnotic induction, I was able to make direct contact with the woman, Marianne, as she called herself, and this is her story:

> Marianne had lived several centuries ago. Her mother had died in childbirth and she had been brought up by her father who was an impoverished crofter. As a small child, she fell ill and the father, at his wit's end, left her close to death on the doorstep of a convent. The mother superior found the child there and took her in. Marianne was nursed back to health, and although deeply affected by the loss of her father, she grew to love the mother superior, who showed her great kindness. The convent became her home.

> When she was little more than a child, there was a civil uprising and a band of drunken militia broke into the convent. Mother superior insisted that Marianne hide herself and then went out with the other nuns to face the militia. The nuns were all raped and killed. Marianne could hear what was happening and was terrified. Later, she crept out to find bodies everywhere. Weeping, she ran into the nearby woods and there, overwhelmed with guilt at not saving her beloved mother superior, she hung herself. Immediately she found herself, in spirit, back at the convent, unable to leave the scene of the massacre. From that time on, she wandered alone in a state of shock and deeply burdened by guilt, until she found herself attracted to my patient Helen and 'moved in'.

> The therapeutic task was to take this traumatised soul back to her suicide and help her complete the transition to the afterlife. As soon as she crossed over, the first person to greet her was the mother superior. Marianne wept and asked for forgiveness. The mother superior embraced her, saying, 'You have nothing to blame yourself for.' Marianne answered, 'But how can I repay all you did for me?' The mother superior replied, 'I have waited a long time for you to come and you are repaying me now by enabling me to be the first person to greet you.'

> Then Marianne looked round and saw her father. He had died a few years after leaving his child at the door of the convent. Still in anguish as to whether he had done the right thing, he asked her to forgive him. Finally, Marianne's mother, who she had never known, appeared and lovingly greeted her. For the first time this family was complete and reunited.

Marianne never troubled Helen again. The therapeutic effect on my patient was profound, for it also addressed a lifelong concern of her own: feeling that it was dangerous to love without reservation for fear of abandonment. In a letter some months later, Helen wrote that both she and Marianne had been released from what she called 'the trap of abandonment'.

Through witnessing Marianne's reunion, first with the mother superior and then with her parents, Helen could see that no one in Marianne's family had wished to cause hurt and rejection; on the contrary, their love for Marianne was plain to see. In the light of this experience, Helen could now recognise that her own family, imperfect though it may have been, had done its best for her.

I hope that my examples have shown that the therapist does not have to have answers but is there to create the opportunity for patients to find their own answers to the questions that trouble them. When working with the soul, what is required of the therapist is the willingness to consider spiritual reality to be as 'real' as any aspect of life, readiness to work beyond the bounds of the mundane and confidence that our patients hold the key to their own healing. There is no place for self-importance in this. Earth is our spiritual kindergarten and we are all here to learn the same lessons.

References

Bohm, D. (1980) *Wholeness and the Implicate Order*. Routledge.

Jung, C.G. (1954) Archetypes of the collective unconscious. Reprinted [1959] in *C.G. Jung: The Collected Works*, vol. 9, part 1: The Archetypes and The Collective Unconscious (eds H. Read, M. Fordham & G. Adler). Routledge and Kegan Paul.

Winnicott, D.W. (1960) The theory of the parent-infant relationship. In *The Maturational Processes and the Facilitating Environment*. Hogarth Press.

3

Beyond Space and Time – The Unbounded Psyche

I would like to show how therapeutic approaches such as past life regression, spirit release and soul recovery can be used to work with the emergence of material from the Collective Unconscious. In such work, the ordinary limits of space-time are transcended. The pre-eminence of archetypes, synchronicity and the significance of *psi* are discussed in the light of quantum theory and the primary role of consciousness in the collapse of the wave function, extending Jung's own early researches of more than half a century ago.

A good many years back, I was taking part in a group meditation that began with guided imagery. We were asked to imagine ourselves walking in a field in the countryside on a summer day, with birds singing, bees humming and the smell of grass and flowers. Then we were instructed to look around until we saw something of special interest, to go towards it and let the experience take us where it will. This is where it took me:

> I am standing before a majestic and mysterious tree. It has the appear-
> ance of a sequoia (giant redwood) and soars up into the sky. As soon
> as I come close to the trunk, I begin ascending rapidly, as if I am
> going up in a fast lift. I shoot past the top of the tree and suddenly
> find myself scrambling up a rocky outcrop. At once, I know exactly

Paper prepared for conference 'Beyond the Brain III – Does individual identity extend beyond birth and death?' Scientific and Medical Network, Cambridge, August 1999. Published as chapter in *Thinking Beyond the Brain – A Wider Science of Consciousness* (ed. D. Lorimer), pp. 169–186. Floris Books, 2001. Reproduced with permission.

what is going on. This is Arizona, the year is 1848, my name is Tom McCann and I am being hunted by a raiding party of Apache Indians. I heave myself up onto the flat top of the rock. I can hear the Indian braves a short way below and I know they will get to me in a couple of minutes and have my scalp. I pull out of my pocket a worn leather wallet and gaze for the last time with sadness and longing on the picture of my wife and two young daughters. Then I take out my gun, put the muzzle to my head and pull the trigger. There is no sound and no impact. I simply find myself floating peacefully up and away from the body lying on the top of the rock.

At just this moment the person leading the group exercise said it was now time we came back to our bodies. I burst out laughing, for the remark could not have been more apt! The memory of that experience is etched as sharply in my mind now as the day it happened – my first taste of what popularly are called 'past lives'.

Consciously, I had known nothing about this period of American history, but while preparing this paper I looked up a few facts. Eighteen forty-eight is the year the war between the United States and Mexico ended, with the USA seizing control of what are now New Mexico and Arizona. American Indians were given the right to vote but most remained at war with the white man for another 20 years. I also found that the name of the sequoia tree comes from a Cherokee Indian, Sequoya, who pioneered the first written language for North American Indians. Yet, at the same time, the Cherokee were being driven west of the Mississippi by the federal troops of the US army, a shameful chapter of history known as the 'trail of tears' during which more than four thousand Cherokee died of starvation and disease.

Sceptics consider past lives to be nothing but instances of cryptomnesia, the historical facts having been once known and then stored away in the unconscious until they happen to surface later. I would concur, with the proviso that the 'facts' emerge not from the personal unconscious but from the Collective Unconscious as described by Carl Jung. In my case, the guided imagery had set in motion what Jung called 'active imagination'.[1] The alchemical tree, an archetype of transformation, had transported me to the realm of the

---

1.   Chodorow (1997).

archetypes of death and rebirth, in which a stream of images welled up in the psyche over which I had no control.

Jung wrote, 'the Collective Unconscious is anything but an encapsulated personal system: it is sheer objectivity, as wide as the world and open to the entire world. There I am the object of every subject, in complete reversal of my ordinary consciousness, where I am always the subject that has an object'.[2] This fits perfectly with what is found in past lives; the drama takes a course that the ego has no power to change, for things are as they are and the entire script is set out from start to finish. There is no sense of 'me' doing the thinking. Rather, 'it thinks me' – through to the end, when death supervenes and consciousness separates from the physical body.

The archetypes of the Collective Unconscious can never be apprehended directly. They are the *primordia* that give structure and meaning to consciousness through the formation of symbols and images. Symbols and images fall within space-time but the archetypal realm itself does not, for it functions as though time and space as we know them did not exist. Yet we certainly experience archetypal images in an entirely personal way since they are constellated according to the psychic reality of the individual. An example would be the poignant theme of loss in the past life fragment I have just given. The scene affected me deeply, for I had a loss of my own to contend with at that time.

The breakthrough of archetypal material has a profound and often disturbing impact. Take Jung's account of the events that occurred in 1916, immediately prior to his writing of the Gnostic text *Seven Sermons to the Dead* under the mysterious inspiration of Basilides of Alexandria. Jung records:

> 'There was an ominous atmosphere around me. I had the strange feeling the air was filled with ghostly entities.' [He goes on to relate how his children also saw and felt these entities.] 'Then the doorbell began ringing frantically… it was a bright summer day… there was no one in sight… I not only heard it but saw it moving… then I knew that something had to happen. The whole house was filled as if there were a crowd present, crammed full of spirits. They were packed deep right up to the door, and the air was so thick it was scarcely possible

---

2. Jung (1954: 22).

to breathe. As for myself, I was all a-quiver with the question, "For God's sake, what in the world is this?" Then they cried out in chorus, "We have come back from Jerusalem where we found not what we sought." Then it began to flow out of me and in the course of three evenings, the whole thing was written. As soon as I took up the pen, the whole ghostly assemblage evaporated. The room quieted and the atmosphere cleared. The haunting was over'.[3]

Tapping into the Collective Unconscious also gives rise to uncanny coincidences, to which Jung gave the term 'synchronicity'. Jung describes three kinds of synchronistic phenomena.[4] The first is when a psychic event and an apparently unrelated physical event occur in the same place and at the same time. Jung tells of a patient who had just been recounting a dream of a scarab beetle when a scarabaeid beetle tried to fly in through the window of the consulting room.[5] Such strange coincidences are not rare, although we tend to brush them aside. Here is one I remember well from my own experience:

> I was feeling both apprehensive and excited because it was the start of my first day as a hospital consultant. I searched the building looking for my room but when I did find it, the door was locked. I tracked down the Professor's secretary, who took a Yale key off a large ring, which I put in my jacket pocket. It was a big moment for me, for I was now about to take possession of my room. I went back down the corridor and pulled the key out of my pocket. To my astonishment, the shank of the key had bent on itself through ninety degrees. I could not enter my sanctum until I had clamped the key in a doorframe and straightened it out with brute force.

The episode of the key might be interpreted symbolically as reflecting my heightened anxiety on my first day as a fledgling consultant. We no longer have rites of phallic initiation to prepare us for manhood, as did our tribal forefathers! Nevertheless, the classical laws of physics cannot account for the bent key I stood staring at in amazement.

---

3. Jung (1961: 215).
4. Main (1997).
5. Jung (1952: 439).

The large body of evidence for psychokinesis that has accumulated since is still ignored by most scientists, who prefer the comfort of the familiar. Jung showed astonishing prescience when he wrote:

> 'Despite the materialist tendency to understand the psyche as a mere reflection or imprint of physical and chemical processes, there is not a single proof of this hypothesis [...] There is thus no ground at all for regarding the psyche as something secondary or as an epiphenomenon' [and also:] 'Sooner or later nuclear physics and the psychology of the unconscious will draw closer together as both of them, independently of one another and from opposite directions, push forward into transcendental territory, the one with the concept of the atom, the other with that of the archetype'.[6]

Jung's second variety of synchronicity deals with non-local phenomena. Here is an example from my clinical practice:

> I had been supervising a trainee psychiatrist with her first psychotherapy patient, a young woman I shall call Gillian. Gillian longed for closeness but was deeply mistrustful of intimacy. The therapy went well and after a few months, Gillian decided to track down her mother, whom she had never known. She followed up various leads only to discover that her mother had died a year or two earlier. This was a bitter blow but she took it well.
>
> A couple of weeks later, my trainee attended for supervision. She seemed flustered and somewhat embarrassed. She said, 'I want to tell you something, you'll probably think it's stupid of me'. She went on to say that on the previous Sunday, which she had been spending at home with her family, she had suddenly experienced a terrible sadness. It came on inexplicably at three in the afternoon and she could not shake it off. Then at about six o'clock, the feeling vanished as quickly as it had come.
>
> On Monday, she had seen her patient Gillian, who told her that since the time before, she had found out that her mother had been buried in a London cemetery and that on Sunday she had gone there to try to find her. For hours, she had searched in vain but at three p.m., she found the grave, and spent the next three hours crying for the mother she had never known.

---

6.   Jung (1954: 58).

According to Newtonian physics, this exact coincidence of emotions at a distance can only be due to chance. Yet it has been shown that when two people who have empathic rapport are separated and electromagnetically shielded from each other, an evoked electrical potential stimulated in the brain of the first subject is instantaneously mirrored by a spike (transferred potential) in the brain of the second subject. This correlation of brain waves is independent of the distance between subjects and neither can it be accounted for based on information passing from one subject to the other through physical space because it occurs simultaneously.[7]

This takes us to quantum theory and the famous Einstein–Podolsky–Rosen (EPR) thought experiment of 1935. Albert Einstein hypothesized that two particles, which first interacted and were then separated in space, would, in theory, continue to be related even if light years apart by virtue of their shared waveform. Einstein thought this quantum prediction must be patently untrue but in due course he was proved to be wrong. In 1972, John Clauser experimentally showed that arresting the spin of one particle instantly arrested the spin of the other and ten years later Alain Aspect demonstrated that this correlation, a transluminal function, holds true even when once-entangled particles are widely separated in space.[8]

There is a lively debate going on about how non-local effects can take place with large structures like brains. Nevertheless, there is strong empirical evidence that *psi* occurs, as shown in a host of Ganzfeld experiments.[9] In one such experiment, the subject is required to describe a pre-selected target picture or location, unknown to them, which can be hundreds of miles away. Honorton has extensively researched this phenomenon and the findings of his meta-analysis of the research evidence are compelling.[10] Even more extraordinary is the work of Helmut Schmidt demonstrating that subjects show precognition of the target *before* the target itself has been selected.[11] The conventional rules of not only space but also time are violated.

---

7.   Grinberg-Zylberbaum et al. (1992).
8.   See 'Quantum "spookiness" passes toughest test yet', in *Nature* (Merali, 2015).
9.   Radin (1997).
10.   Honorton & Ferrari (1989).
11.   Schmidt et al. (1986).

Jung would have applauded these findings. He was intrigued by instances of synchronicity in which a psychic event relates to a physical event that takes place in the future. Nor are they so uncommon. I vividly recall one instance, which happened to me 20 years ago:

My wife and I were due to drive down from the north of Scotland. During the small hours of the night before the journey, my wife had a fearful dream. In it, we were overtaking on a country road when suddenly a car came speeding head on towards us. She could see clearly that it was a green Austin A40. She awoke just before the impact.

My wife was not given to superstition but so powerful was the dream that she was most reluctant to travel. I reassured her I would drive with extra care and would keep a close look out for any green Austin that might be around! Halfway across the wilds of Sutherland, I found myself stuck behind an ancient tractor on an empty country road. As I swung out to overtake, I remembered the dream and pulled back. The next instant a green Austin, the first car for miles, hurtled round the bend and past us.

To my knowledge, Jung did not describe a fourth category of synchronicity, when a psychic event occurs with the corresponding physical event in the remote past. Yet this is what my patient Alice experienced.

Alice is a 43-year-old woman who came with a 10-year history of sarcoidosis, an autoimmune disease that was causing her to go blind. She was increasingly reliant on her husband, John, to care for her. Theirs was a loving marriage and she said of him with a smile, 'He was a good catch!' Alice's loss of sight was challenging her to try to make sense of her misfortune. Recently she had heard about past life regression and wanted to see if it could provide any clue.

The sarcoidosis had begun with blinding headaches. In the session, we went back to that time when she lay exhausted and crying, holding her head in her hands in a darkened room.

I asked Alice to find words for the terrible pain in her head. If her headache could speak what would it say? She cried out, 'Leave me alone. Let me be free.' I suggested she give in to the longing and see where it took her. Her face relaxed and she lay with her eyes closed and a smile on her lips. At once, she found herself lazing in the warm, calm water of a tropical ocean. I asked her to look around. She could see the sandy shore some way off and beyond that, dense vegetation covering the lower slopes of distant mountains. Next, I asked her to look down at her body. She said with astonishment, 'I'm… like a fish.' Then she exclaimed, 'No, not a fish, I'm a dolphin!' Her expression was one of intense pleasure. I asked if there were any other dolphins nearby. It transpired that this young dolphin had disobeyed her parents and had swum off on her own.

I then asked her to go forward in time to the next important thing that happened. She found herself lying on the sand, unable to move. (Alice's body started making ineffectual jerking movements on the couch.) I asked her to check her body and she became aware of a large hole in her side. Now tears began to trickle down her cheeks. There was no pain but her strength was ebbing. She looked up and could see the prow of a boat a few feet away. Standing on it and staring at her was a fisherman with painted face and body, holding a spear in his hand. Then the boat slid away. As darkness fell, she grew calm. Suddenly she found herself rising up into the sky and looking down, without emotion or regret, at the lifeless body of the dolphin on the beach.

Did she need to face this fisherman who had killed her with his spear? At first, she was reluctant, saying 'It wasn't his fault. He never killed another dolphin'. Then she agreed that it could be important. So, she waited there for a while until his turn came to die and he crossed over. Now she could see the fisherman coming closer. Involuntarily, she found herself going forward and embracing him. I asked her if she recognised him. 'Of course, it's my husband John', she said, beginning to laugh and cry at the same time. 'He caught me and this time I've caught him. We are together and he is here to take care of me!'

The account of Alice's past life as a dolphin has to be taken for what it is, psychic reality, together with the karmic debt that made such good sense to my patient. On the other hand, scientific enquiry into reincarnation has depended on meticulous fieldwork. Professor Ian Stevenson has intensively studied not only historical evidence but also cases of children claiming to remember past lives. Many bear physical birthmarks that correspond to the site of physical trauma in the past life, usually the injury that brought that life to an end.[12]

----

12.   Stevenson (1966, 1997a,b).

Sceptics hold the view that over 90% of information revealed in past lives can be readily accounted for by phantasy but there remains a stubborn minority where the facts defy such explanations. There is the phenomenon of xenoglossy, speaking a language unknown to the subject, which Stevenson has also researched,[13] as well as a number of well-documented case studies that contain obscure but verifiable historical detail.[14] One point at issue concerns the many occasions on which the same famous historical persons have appeared in past life regressions. This raises the possibility that a given past life does not 'belong' to a single person but that just as anyone holding the right key can open the door, a past life is available to all individuals with closely similar sympathetic resonance.

When working transpersonally, the narrative that takes place in the spirit world after physical death[15] often leads to powerful thera-peutic insights, as when Alice recognised the fisherman to be her husband John from their present life. Other times, we find a limbo in which the spirit wanders confused or lost. Here is such a case:

My patient Barbara had recently been visiting a well-known museum and wanted to look at the paintings on the first floor. There was a big central staircase with stairwells on both sides. Halfway up, she started feeling dizzy and could not proceed. Since that time a few months back, open spaces and heights triggered severe panic attacks.

In the session, I asked Barbara to close her eyes and imagine herself back at the bottom of the stairs. She became visibly tense and I asked her to focus on the sensation of fear and go with the feeling to the very first time it happened, wherever that might be.

With some surprise, Barbara reported that she was standing at the bottom of a stone pyramid with big steps leading upwards and a sheer drop on each side. She was wearing rough leather sandals and a long cotton skirt. I asked her what she was doing there. She replied that she was going to be sacrificed by the chief priest. She could see him wait-ing for her at the top of the pyramid, where he would cut her throat.

How had she come to be chosen? This took her back to a scene in the village the night before, when the elders had singled her out and said 'It might as well be her'. She had no relatives to protect her

13. Stevenson (1984).
14. Ducasse (1960), Tarazi (1997).
15. See Newton (1994), Woolger (1999).

and so she was dragged away. I asked her to go back further, to her childhood in that lifetime. She told me her name was Miria. By nature, she was a solitary child, who liked to play alone in the forest. Later, being fiercely independent, she scared away her suitors, which left her with no husband to protect her and no status in village life.

As if in a trance, she now climbed slowly up the pyramid steps. The height made her dizzy. At the top, she was lifted onto a stone slab and the priest raised his sword. Suddenly it was over and she was free. There was no pain.

Miria floated away from the body but remained suspended in a shadowy, featureless world. I asked her to look around and tell me if she could see anyone. Looking down, Miria saw a 5-year-old girl playing alone in the fields behind some houses. As she came closer, she could see that it was Barbara, my patient, when she was a child. Miria felt attracted to the little girl and so she stayed with her from that time on.

From the transpersonal perspective, Miria's spirit had thereafter remained earthbound, finding solace in the company of another child. The attachment only surfaced when the museum steps triggered a resurgence of fear in Miria, which then instantly and deeply affected my patient Barbara.

Once this was explained to Miria, she agreed to leave. I encouraged her to look for the light, and after a short while, she found herself moving rapidly towards it and was gone.

What Barbara had experienced can be understood in a number of ways. It could simply be the emergence of phantasy, constellating the archetypal theme of ritual sacrifice. Alternatively, Barbara may really have been visiting a life she herself once lived, leaving her psyche with a trauma that her body, though not her conscious mind, recalled. Last but not least, had we uncovered the source of a spirit attachment that was afflicting my patient?

With regard to Miria, the transpersonal narrative suggests an earthbound spirit:[16] the traumatic ending to her life, the failure to move on to the light after leaving the body, a resulting limbo state and then attraction to a sympathetic soul, for Barbara too had been a lonely child. There had been no symptomatic disturbance until many

---

16.   See Baldwin (1992).

years later when the museum steps had triggered a breakthrough of Miria's unresolved terror and had rooted Barbara to the spot.

In psychodynamic therapy, terms such as projection and introjection are used as explanatory metaphors. However, the shamanic tradition works literally in taking the movement and attachment of such energies to be real and palpable.

Sally, in her mid-fifties, was suffering from treatment-resistant depression. Her problems had begun in early childhood, which had been blighted with insecurity. When she was seven, she fell into the hands of a fundamentalist schoolteacher, Miss Edwards, who terrified the child with threats of hell and damnation. Sally had recurring visions of flames licking around her bed and the red face of the devil would appear at night and in her dreams.

In adulthood, Sally seemed to overcome these fears, but following major surgery, which left her body scarred, she once again succumbed to these visions, living from day to day in a state of sheer panic.

First, I encouraged Sally to visualise her soul. She located it inside her chest but as a feeble thing, not much more than a glimmer of light. I asked her to look carefully to see if there were any strands or cords running out from it into the darkness. She found such a cord, so I urged her to follow it and see where it led. After a moment she looked up and said she could see Miss Edwards, looking very old but as fierce as ever, holding the end of the cord tightly in her hand.

I then had a frank discussion with Miss Edwards, speaking with her through the agency of Sally. Miss Edwards insisted that what she did was right, the child had to be controlled and if she instilled fear in her, it was for her own good. I pointed out that instead of helping, it had only led to a lifetime of misery and torment. Is this what Miss Edwards as a Christian really intended? She faltered and I pressed home my advantage. She herself would now be nearing the end of her life and soon facing her Maker. How would she be judged? Then Miss Edwards became fearful. She hadn't intended harm and she hoped God would have pity on her. I put it to her that she could start making amends right now by letting go of Sally's soul and giving it back to her. Miss Edwards agreed and let go of the cord. I asked Sally to draw it back into herself, reclaiming the soul as rightfully her own.

Following the session, Sally reported that the red devil had lost his power over her. The next step would be to help Sally find compassion for that child who had lived with so much fear.

These clinical examples have something in common: when we move beyond the constraints of consensual 'reality' and the bounds of physical space-time, we enter a domain in which *all time is now and all space is here*. I want to enlarge on this concept, for it re-instates the 'sixth sense', which for 300 years Western science has discounted and even scorned.

Newton's laws of motion and gravitation, together with Rene Descartes' mind/body dualism, gave rise to a science of material realism that profoundly shapes how we think about the nature of reality. We conceive of an enduring physical universe 'out there', a stage on which our lives are lived and from which in due course we make our exit. This physical realm is held to be the only one, while consciousness is seen as a miraculous by-product of evolutionary biology.

Anyone holding the view that we are eternal souls in physical bodies has been obliged to hypothesise another parallel but non-physical world in which the soul resides. This has led to all kinds of problems, such as where to locate heaven, and why no energy transfer has ever been shown to take place between heaven and earth. On the other hand, the science of material realism has advanced apace, its world firmly bounded by the five senses and all that it contains.

Just when it begins to look like game, set and match to material realism, physicists discover quantum theory, which tells a different story. The wave-particle experiment breaks with 300 years of certainty. Depending on how the experimenter sets up the light experiment, particles become waves and waves become particles. We find we have two realities with equal validity. If two, why not ten? Bosonic string theory argues there must be 26 dimensions, although from the vantage point of our space-time, all but four of them are curled up into a space smaller than a millionth of an inch.[17] Viewed from another dimension, our whole physical universe might look like a mere drawing on a piece of paper!

Electrons are no longer thought of as particles spinning around the nucleus of the atom like a miniature solar system. Instead, the electron is dispersed throughout all of space as a probability wave,

---

17.   Subsequent development of the more fundamental M-theory suggests 11 dimensions. Either way, cosmology no longer treats sense perception as the benchmark from which to argue the (ultimate) nature of reality.

which only collapses into its space-time locale when a conscious observer makes a measurement. Nor can the velocity and position of the electron be known at the same time, for this is a world of uncertainties. There is only a statistical probability that the electron will appear where you expect it to be. It may just materialise hundreds, thousands or even millions of miles away and when it does so, it takes zero time to get there.

Both space and time are thus bypassed. Such fundamental non-locality reveals the breath-taking interconnectedness of the cosmos. The new cosmology sweeps away the old dualism of mind and matter. Amit Goswami names it monistic idealism after Plato, remarking that 'between observations, the electron exists as a possibility form, like a Platonic archetype, in the transcendent domain of *potentia*'.[18] Indeed, all of quantum reality is *in potentia* until consciousness collapses the wave function, at which moment mind and matter arise simultaneously, forming a 'tangled hierarchy' like two sides of one coin. Mark Woodhouse calls this complementarity 'energy monism'.[19] Each individual consciousness is now identified with its own bodily existence in space-time, from which vantage point it goes on to play its own part in contributing to further innumerable collapses of the wave.

We have to conclude that the old-style Newtonian universe is something of an illusion, for there is no such thing as an external world 'out there' that exists apart from consciousness. *Everything is Mind.* We are not part of the universe; we *are* the universe. More extraordinary still, it is we as conscious observers that bring the world of the five senses into being. Along with all creatures of consciousness, we are co-creators of the physical universe!

According to Goswami, the brain-mind, as the two sides of one coin, exhibits both Newtonian and quantum properties. By means of its classical Newtonian function, it performs brilliantly as a measuring instrument, obeying the law of cause and effect, and provides us with a timeline of personal memories and a stable identity. It can do this because the wave function collapses in accordance with the maximum probability (in line with all the countless collapses that have

18.   Goswami (1993: 59).
19.   Woodhouse (1996).

previously taken place). Our physical world has structural stability because the probability wave has been generated by countless individual acts of consciousness pooled together over time. Consequently, you can expect to find your home still standing where you left it when you went off to work this morning. Yet since the wave contains everything *in potentia*, there is no limit to what is possible, however improbable. A mind of sufficient power could collapse the wave uniquely (the Gospels cite Jesus as having miraculously turned water into wine).

The brain-mind's quantum function is one of endless renewal, drawing on a transcendent realm in which everything that has already happened, is happening now and someday will happen, co-exists. The opaque window of space-time obscures from us what ultimately comprises this realm, yet humankind intuitively draws on the archetype of the Imago Dei.[20,21]

In the case histories I have given so far, specific therapeutic interventions were called for but Nature in her wisdom provides a powerful tool for self-help in the form of dreams, as in the following account:

> My patient John had been born into circumstances of great deprivation. Fortunately, he was saved from a life in care by being taken in, aged four, by a neighbour, Bob, who from that time on was father in all but name.
>
> The boy grew into a man and made good. He married, had a family and moved south. Nevertheless, John often went back to see Bob, now ageing and alone but fiercely independent. Then the time came when Bob grew so frail that his neighbours had to come in and start washing and caring for him. Bob couldn't bear it. One day he got himself upstairs to the spare bedroom, lay down with his cap on his head as always, swallowed a lot of tablets and died.
>
> John was devastated at the news. He kept dreaming Bob was still alive only to wake up and find him gone. He fell into a severe depression and was referred for help.

---

20.   Powell (1993).
21.   It has been argued that domains of space-time such as ours arise so that God has the opportunity of manifesting as transcendent rather than being confined to the immanent – presumably a requirement for the full expression of 'all that is' – and reminiscent of the Gnostic view of the part played by humankind in furthering the self-realization of God.

John then told me that just before attending this consultation, something had happened which had 'knocked him for six'. He had dreamed again of Bob but this was different.

In the dream, he 'knew' for the first time that Bob was dead. Yet there was Bob, sitting across from him, large as life, cap on head, just the way he always sat. My patient asked him out-right, 'Bob, are you dead?' Bob answered him as direct as ever, 'Yes!' His next question to Bob was, 'Is there life after death?' Another emphatic 'Yes,' came right back. Then he challenged Bob head on. 'Prove it to me!' Bob pulled out a book that looked like a Bible with detailed drawings in it and, sure enough, the proof was all there.

Then my patient awoke. All day he could intensely feel Bob's presence. He found his emotions welling up and although it was very painful, he could say to me in that first meeting 'I know I'm getting better'.

Thus far, I have drawn on a number of case studies and a modicum of theory to highlight the clinical perspective. When it comes to the fiercely debated question of whether or not our individual identities as we know them continue to exist in other domains, it is worth recalling that looking at things dichotomously is simply the mind-set of classical physics.

There is another way to look at this, not as 'either-or' but as 'both-and' – the equation that lies at the heart of the wave-particle experiment I mentioned earlier.

Within the quantum realm, everything that has been, is now and ever shall be, exists as one coterminous whole. When viewed from the standpoint of the delimited self (as found in the Abra-hamic faith traditions), the quantum realm takes on archetypal personifications that persuade us of the continuity of individual identity in spirit. However, some Eastern spiritual traditions regard attachment to a delimited self as standing in the way of enlighten-ment. 'Awakening' from the illusion of self and object leads to pure awareness of 'being', a paradoxical state beyond duality, in which identity predicated on the attributes of the ego ('me' and 'mine') dissolves away. In that event, there really is no question left to debate.

It makes sense to give weight to both accounts, for they are not mutually exclusive. Indeed, reports by survivors of the near-death experience suggest there are many realms to be visited according to our needs.[22]

Dreams are the royal road to the unconscious, as Freud famously remarked. By way of ending, here is a lucid dream, which took the self-aware dreamer into the role of Creator and then showed him why he could not stay there.

> In the dream, I found myself back at my old school. I decided to go up to the roof so I launched myself into the air and floated gently upwards. Now I was at treetop level and looked down at the woods all around the school. It was crystal clear, like a still autumn day, the sun shining and with the leaves red and gold. I descended some way and floated along, following a path through the woods. Everything was inexpressibly beautiful, more vivid even than in waking life. I somehow knew that I had created this experience and that I could make happen whatever I wanted to happen. It was sheer beauty and perfection. I felt joy, like when you hear beautiful music. At the same time, I had a profound realisation that brought a kind of sadness. I saw that because I could make it all happen without any effort, like being God, I would not be meeting any situations, or other real people, that would really challenge me. There would never be anything to learn and I would always be alone. I found myself longing for that other 'real' world again. Then I awoke.

Pure consciousness is a jewel of infinite beauty, yet we are no less indebted to the physical realm, for the gift of experience is infinitely precious too. The same apple that tempted Eve was later to fall at Newton's feet, and both spirituality and science have been beneficiaries. Nevertheless, we carry great responsibility for what we do with our consciousness, since we can just as easily create hell as heaven. How may we give ourselves the best chance? While we have the inestimable gift of our individual identities within the bounds of

---

22.   One way to consider this is to see 'direct experience' (*samadhi*, nirvana) as opening the mind to the formless realm of pure 'being'. Yet just as a tree bears fruit, through extending into a multiplicity of space-time domains the formless takes form; our physical universe is one such example. See also *The Unquiet Self*, this volume.

space and time, in the quantum realm there is another truth to be discovered: that we are one. If humankind should ever learn that what belongs to one belongs to all, heaven on earth will be assured.

References

Baldwin, W. (1992) *Spirit Releasement Therapy*. Headline Books Inc.

Chodorow, J. (1997) *Jung on Active Imagination*. Routledge.

Ducasse, C. J. (1960) How the case of the search for Bridey Murphy stands today. *Journal of the American Society for Psychical Research*, 54, 3–22.

Goswami, A. (1993) *The Self-Aware Universe*. Putnam.

Grinberg-Zylberbaum, J., Delaflor, M., Sanchez Arellano, M.E., et al. (1992) Human communication and the electrophysiological activity of the brain. *Subtle Energies*, 3, 26–43.

Honorton, C. & Ferrari, D.C. (1989) Future telling: a meta-analysis of forced-choice precognition experiments, 1935–1987. *Journal of Parapsychology*, 53, 281–308.

Jung, C.G. (1952) Synchronicity: an acausal connecting principle. Reprinted [1969] in *C.G. Jung: The Collected Works*, vol. 8: The Structure and Dynamics of the Psyche (eds H. Read, M. Fordham & G. Adler). Routledge and Kegan Paul.

Jung, C.G. (1954) Archetypes of the Collective Unconscious. Reprinted [1959] in *C.G. Jung: The Collected Works*, vol. 9, part 1: The Archetypes and the Collective Unconscious (eds H. Read, M. Fordham & G. Adler). Routledge and Kegan Paul.

Jung, C.G. (1961) *Memories, Dreams, Reflections*. Random House.

Main, R. (1997) *Jung on Synchronicity and the Paranormal*. Routledge.

Merali, Z. (2015) Quantum 'spookiness' passes toughest test yet. *Nature*, 2015, 525(7567), 14–15.

Newton, M. (1994) *Journey of Souls*. Llewellyn Publications.

Powell, A. (1993) The psychophysical matrix and group analysis. *Group Analysis*, 26, 449–468.

Radin, D. (1997) *The Conscious Universe*. Harper Edge.

Schmidt, H., Morris, R. & Rudolph, L. (1986) Channelling evidence for a PK effect to independent observers. *Journal of Parapsychology*, 50, 1–16.

Stevenson, I. (1966) *Twenty Cases Suggestive of Reincarnation*. University Press of Virginia.

Stevenson, I. (1984) *Unlearned Language: New Studies in Xenoglossy*. University Press of Virginia.

Stevenson, I. (1997a) *Reincarnation and Biology: A Contribution to the Etiology of Birthmarks*. Vol. 1. Praegar.

Stevenson, I. (1997b) *Birth Defects and Other Anomalies.* Vol. 2. Praegar.

Tarazi, L. (1997) *Under the Inquisition: An Experience Relived.* Hampton Roads Publishing.

Woodhouse, M. (1996) *Paradigm Wars.* Frog.

Woolger, R. (1999) *Other Lives, Other Selves.* Bantam Books.

4

The Unquiet Self and the Search for Peace

'Fear not that your life will come to an end.
Fear rather that it will never come to a beginning.'

Attributed to Cardinal Newman

I am going to offer a personal perspective on meditation. This will take me to exploring the interface of psychology and spirituality and to consideration of both the dangers and benefits of meditation.

First, what do I mean by meditation? The origins of the word are obscure, coming from the Latin *meditare*, to measure, or from *mederi*, meaning to cure, or perhaps from both. Definitions include thinking carefully about something calmly and seriously, exercising the mind in religious contemplation, simply emptying the mind of thought or preconception, or conversely, concentrating the mind on one single thing (often with the use of a mantra).

The problem with such definitions is that they all refer to an ordinary state of consciousness and meditation is an altered, some would say, an alternative state of consciousness that can be sought through disciplined practice or can arise unbidden. The Chinese are closer to the mark with *mingxiang* or 'trance thinking'.

Paper prepared for conference 'Beyond the Brain IV – Scientific and spiritual perspectives on meditation'. Scientific and Medical Network, Ripon, York, August 2001.

Unforeseen Moments

My first experience of 'meditation' happened entirely unexpectedly. I believe I was 3 or 4 years old. It was a hot summer's day and all the children in the day nursery I attended were in the garden, probably twenty or thirty of us. The garden seemed very big and was surrounded by trees. I know we had been given something to do, searching for grasshoppers I vaguely recollect. Everything was going on as usual. Then I looked up and saw this tree – the picture is still absolutely clear in my mind. It may have been a big horse chestnut, standing there motionless. There could not have been a breath of wind. The leaves shone brilliant green in the sunlight and inside there was deep, dark shade. My gaze was irresistibly drawn into the shade, and then, suddenly, all sound ceased, time stood still, and although it may have lasted for only seconds, it seemed an eternity.

The unexpected and unbidden can be a rare gift. For example, a good friend of mine underwent cardiac bypass surgery. Coming round from the anaesthetic, he was profoundly moved by the sound of the most heavenly music he had ever heard in his life. As he fully awakened, the music faded; but he knew that this music had been celestial, surpassing anything heard on Earth!

When some years later I found myself needing major surgery, I wondered if I might be blessed with such an experience. Instead, I came out of the anaesthetic with the unpleasant hallucination that every time I closed my eyes I felt as though I was standing on my head. It was days before I could get myself down from this peculiar headstand – evidently my world had been turned upside down!

Psychological Considerations

While I make no claim to spiritual pre-eminence, I am interested in what can be called 'spiritual psychiatry', including the interface of the psychological and spiritual with respect to meditation, why we are drawn to it and what we hope to achieve.

Psychiatry is a shadowy place full of confused feelings. A good deal of the time, we endeavour to put people in touch with their emotions, for they often come for help in a state of disconnection, a mechanism that ensures survival but at the cost of real living. Other times, it is a matter of helping people learn how to stand back and make sense of their emotions instead of simply being overwhelmed. At the heart of all this misery, I have generally found a deep yearning for peace and happiness, so often missing from the relationships of daily life.

Psychiatry in general and psychotherapy in particular call for us to reflect thoughtfully and honestly on our fears and desires. Above all, we have to reckon with suffering and what to do about it. If only patient and therapist alike could keep in mind the serenity prayer of Pastor Reinhold Niebuhr:

> 'God, grant me the serenity to accept the things I cannot change,
> The courage to change the things I can,
> And wisdom to know the difference.'[1]

Inevitably, we get our first taste of suffering as babies. The very survival of the baby depends on its relationship with mother. The paediatrician and psychoanalyst Donald Winnicott remarked, 'there is no such thing as a baby',[2] meaning there is always baby plus mother. When mother and baby are one, as when the baby is happily feeding, we can see that the baby is experiencing something akin to bliss. However, this oceanic merging has to be disrupted periodically. The baby gets wind and cries, or mother leaves the room, so that what was unified becomes painfully broken. In small, manageable doses, such suffering is Nature's way of stimulating us into action; otherwise, we would stay on our mothers' laps for life. When the bond is damaged or even broken by premature, enforced separation or abuse, there are profound consequences. The child no longer can trust in the goodness of relationships.

As John Bowlby showed, the more secure the attachment, the more the child can later let go of mother and develop healthy autonomy.[3] On the other hand, a distraught mother may be heard shouting at her toddler that if he[4] doesn't shut up, she'll leave him right there! This threat will subdue him because the idea is so terrifying but the internal

---

1. Sifton (2003).
2. Winnicott (1958: 99).
3. Bowlby (1969).
4. 'He' is used, without prejudice, to denote both male and female gender.

cost will be to foster an anxious attachment. Relationships then become clinging in nature, with over-sensitivity to perceived rejection.

The Mind of the Meditator

I raise these matters because it is important to take into account the meditator's state of mind. What are his hopes, fears and aims? Will the effect of meditation be to bring about integration and wholeness? Alternatively, is he in flight from emotions and challenges that need facing in daily life?

Imagine how secure and anxious personalities might compare when answering a question like 'How should life be lived?' The secure person may answer with a smile, 'To work and play, to explore, to be challenged, to love and raise a family, to take care of others, to express yourself and to be fulfilled'. How about the anxiously disposed? 'To find shelter and safety, steer clear of danger, avoid unpleasantness, to keep well, to find someone to love you and look after you, and so on'. While a secure person is able to take the self for granted, and can turn his attention to other matters, the anxious individual is more preoccupied with safeguarding the insecure self.

Here lies a great irony. As Jesus Christ pointed out, 'I tell you that to everyone who has, more will be given, but as for the one who has nothing, even what they have will be taken away'.[5]

In the sphere of adult human relationships, give love and it comes back in abundance. Go looking for it and you are certain to be disappointed. Only in the spiritual realm can we continue to ask for, and experience, unconditional love.

The Spiritual Realm and the Phenomenal World

I am not attempting to reduce the vast body of knowledge about the human psyche to the one issue of emotional security versus anxiety, but the question is so basic that it is a good place to work from, not least because it can shape how we experience the spiritual realm.

---

5.   Luke 19:26. *The Holy Bible*, NIV.

My own understanding is that we live in a universe in which consciousness is primary and from which matter arises. For 300 years, the Newtonian view of a mechanistic universe dominated scientific thinking, the outcome of which was to regard consciousness as nothing but the by-product of brain function. However, during the 20th century, advances in quantum physics and transpersonal psychology have converged. Spirituality and science are engaged in a new dialogue,[6] one open to the age-old intuition that we are not so much human beings on a spiritual journey as spiritual beings on a human one.

It is also my belief that even while we are living out this incarnation, we remain connected to our source, the Godhead.[7] Many people who have survived a near-death experience tell of the profound realisation they have had that life on earth is 'just visiting'. They report with overwhelming conviction that the place to which they travelled when out-of-body is that place from whence we come and to which we return, the eternal dwelling place of the soul and our true spiritual 'home'.[8]

I have described elsewhere how the mind can take us to 'other worlds' unencumbered by the constraints of space-time, and how the 'new' physics provides us with a compelling paradigm for the interface of mind and matter.[9] This perspective sees the material world as nested within the quantum domain of mind, in turn nested within an ultimate virtual reality, as described by Deepak Chopra.[10]

Consider the well-known Daoist symbol of the *Taiji*, the circle depicting that which is beyond form, giving birth to form (*yin* and *yang*).

4.1 Duality (form) arising from the non-dual (formless).

6. See *Spirituality and Science*, this volume, and Bohm (1980).
7. Powell (1997).
8. Fenwick & Fenwick (1995).
9. See *Beyond Space and Time*, this volume.
10. Chopra (2001).

The symbol characterises both form and movement. Everything in nature follows this law of opposites working together to create a perfect balance. *Yin* and *yang* are expressed as complementary aspects, in both the physical and mental worlds.[11] We construe according to such polarities, for instance, cold/warm, light/dark, male/female, sadness/joy, right/wrong and good/evil. Importantly, *Taiji* is not the source, for it represents the phenomenal world, which according to Taoism[12] arises from *Wuji* – beyond all form. Two and a half thousand years ago the sage Lao Tsu meditated deeply on this mystery, leaving us these words:

'The Tao that can be told is not the eternal Tao.
The name that can be named is not the eternal name.
The nameless is the beginning of heaven and earth.
The named is the mother of ten thousand things.'

Lao Tsu, Tao Te Ching[13]

The composite picture that follows is my understanding of the relationship between the material, quantum and virtual domains, bearing in mind that all such schemas are merely conceptual tools.

In the quantum and material domains of mind and matter, consciousness is mediated by the mind/brain, which bestows on us a wealth of perceptions, cognitions and emotions. No less important, we are given the freedom to act for good or ill.

What we unveil in the quantum domain depends on our own tendencies and desires. As was made clear 2000 years ago: 'Ask and it will be given to you; seek and you will find; knock and the door will be opened to you'.[14] What we find must, of necessity, be coloured by mental projections, for our earthly domain is still one of 'self' and 'other'. Yet this is not mere imagination, for an energetic connection is being established with the quantum domain, giving rise to a

---

11. Guo & Powell (2001).
12. In translation from Chinese, alternative spellings are commonly used: Taoism becomes Daoism, Lao Tsu becomes Laozi and *Tao Te Ching* becomes *Daodejing*.
13. Feng & English (1973).
14. Matthew 7:7. *The Holy Bible*, NIV.

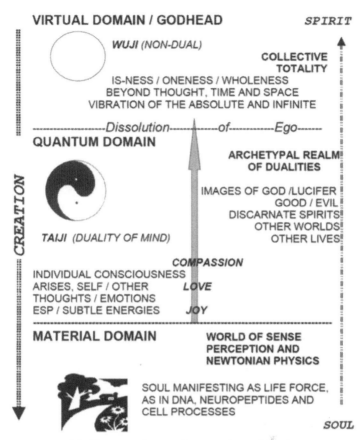

4.2 The conscious universe - three domains.

subject–object complex[15] that constellates as an archetype. Archetypes have both positive and negative poles; an emanation of love calls forth a loving presence, one that can help overcome fear and anger, while negative emotions are more likely to evoke persecutory imagos.

Transpersonal therapists working with *possession states* understand such disorders as resulting from one or more intrusive spirit presences[16] attaching to a person because of vulnerability through

---

15.   Described in quantum mechanics as the collapse of the probability wave.
16.   See *Psychiatry and Spirit Release Therapy*, this volume.

illness, negative self-image, or 'opening' themselves naively to the occult.[17] Consequently, dabbling in psychism, as with the use of Ouija boards, can be a dangerous game. On the other hand, the quantum domain has the power to inspire us with boundless images of divine love, as recorded by the visionary Swedenborg.[18] Here is one such glimpse, by Minnie Louise Haskins, whose little poem 'God Knows' has been a comfort to many a child.

'I said to the man who stood at the gate of the year,
　　Give me a light that I may tread safely into the unknown.
　　And he replied, 'Go out into the darkness and put your hand into
the hand of God.
　　That shall be to you better than a light and safer than a known
way.'[19]

In the map of the conscious universe, the quantum domain is shown positioned between the material world and the Godhead, providing an opportunity for infinite learning on the soul journey. Having the gift of free will is an extraordinary challenge. If we get locked into cycles of fear, anger and retaliation, it becomes very difficult to make progress. Then, according to perennial wisdom traditions, we are obliged to stay in the same class for as many incarnations as it takes to learn the lesson.

Nonetheless, there is a path homewards, and the soul, if we are willing to listen, points the way. Meditation, prayer and contemplation help us attune to the soul and bring us to the threshold of the Godhead; only the ego holds us back.

In the diagram, I have represented the soul as very much part of the embodied self, in Carl Jung's words, 'the living thing in Man, that which lives of itself and causes life'.[20] It is the diaspora of the Godhead, inherent in Creation and now a scintilla within each human being. How it is experienced and expressed depends on the 'level' it is working on. At its most basic and physiological, the soul is busy ensuring the coherence of cellular processes. At the psychological level, it vitalises us with a consciousness of personhood. At the spiritual level, we sense the divine values of peace, purity and love.

---

17.   See Fiore (1987), Baldwin (1992), Lucas (1993).
18.   Swedenborg (2000).
19.   Haskins (1940).
20.   Jung (1954: 26).

In the incarnate state, the unitive vision of the soul is frequently overruled by the strivings of the ego. However, when the ego is stilled, the preoccupation with what is mine and yours, what belongs to self and other, yields to collective consciousness, the species mind of humanity,[21] and ultimately to an all-embracing is-ness/one-ness/whole-ness. As the *Tao Te Ching* suggests, this is beyond words; nevertheless, to put a name to it, I have called it 'spirit'.

Beyond Words

I would like to mention a further experience of my own, 40 years on from that inexplicable childhood reverie. Between times, I had tried yoga and various kinds of meditation but there had never been that absolute shift of consciousness until a 'direct experience', on the third day of a Zen Enlightenment Intensive.

During this retreat, my assignment was to spend every waking minute focused on the *koan* 'What is life?' We were a group of about twelve, working non-stop in pairs. Each person would take their turn speaking for half an hour and then listening for half an hour in silence to the other. The bell would ring, partners would change and then the process would be repeated, hour after hour. By the end of the first day, I was running out of all the imaginable descriptions of 'what is life'.

During the second day, time started slowing down, and I found myself uttering strange half-familiar words as the unconscious disgorged itself. As my intellect ran out of steam, the cracks in my mind grew wider and wider. Then, on day three, and with the same vividness that I remember the tree from childhood, suddenly and without warning everything stopped. I was contemplating an apple, which I held in my left hand, when my mind did a kind of somersault. I was looking at the apple but I was everywhere, which also meant either that there was no 'me' or that everything was me! All was unity, all in its right place, timeless and bursting with is-ness. There was absolute peace, with nothing needing to be done, no action forever. Later, I remember watching a thought unfold like a piece of ticker tape. It 'said' to me, 'Now, for the first time, you know what it is to be conscious without anxiety'.

---

21.   Bache (2000).

Then, after what may have been some minutes – I cannot really say – the whole thing was over. Tears sprang to my eyes and I felt a rush of great emotion – of love and gratitude. I was back in the domain of mind. The experience had been abrupt and very powerful. There was no worship, no Imago Dei, no spiritual path to climb and nowhere to go. It had been more like falling off a mountain! This would seem to be characteristic of Zen awakenings.

Although I am profoundly glad to have had this further timeless experience, when I have felt most beset by adversity I have been drawn to the image of Christ. Here is the shortest and most memorable dream I have ever had.

> I was walking beside a handsome young man, probably about 30 years old. I turned to him and caught a wonderful smile. His eyes were sparkling with liveliness and good humour. No words were needed. The power of his encouragement was immense, and yet delivered with extraordinary tenderness. I immediately awoke and had no doubt that my companion was Jesus.[22]

Emotional Resources and the Spiritual Search

As I outlined earlier, people who have had the good fortune (or karma, as the religions of the East would put it) to grow up in a loving and secure environment are confident in their approach to life. When such people meditate, their natural disposition works greatly to their advantage. Benefits of meditation include:

- SELF-REGARD. Feeling worthy to give and receive love. The right and freedom to engage in relationships both human and Divine.
- PSYCHOLOGICAL STABILITY. Being at ease with oneself. The capacity to engage with the unknown. A relaxed attitude that enhances appreciation of life and readily integrates with the tasks and challenges of day-to-day living.

---

22. For an in-depth study of such dreams, see G. Scott Sparrow (2002) *Sacred Encounters with Jesus*.

- Reality Testing/Secure Boundaries. The capacity voluntarily to enter the 'virtual domain' and return at will. The loss and subsequent recovery of ego are managed with equanimity.
- Gnosis of the Archetypal Realm/Imago Dei. Enhanced spiritual vision. The spur to constructive and compassionate action in the material world.
- Soul Consciousness. A desire to safeguard the soul and deepen understanding. While recognising the material world as the stage for action and experience, never losing sight of the greater whole that lies beyond the confines of sense perception.
- Alleviating Anxiety and Depression.[23] 'Stress' is never the event itself but how we react to it, which is often conditioned by events of the past. Meditation can help maintain equanimity while deepening self-understanding.

In some situations, however, psychological issues may need to be addressed when commencing meditation. For example:

- Fight/Flight Reaction. When this reaction is aroused in someone with a low fear threshold, attention is directed outwards in order to cope with the anticipated threat (real or imagined). In this hyper-vigilant state, soul awareness, which requires calm introversion, may be suppressed. Help is sometimes needed to enable the person to lower their guard and to feel comfortable with – and accepting of – feelings and thoughts that may arise in the course of meditation.
- Idealisation and Disillusion. People who earlier in life have been traumatised or suffered privation may be unable to express anger, since they are left with the fear of yet more punishment. Healthy maturation of the self is then blocked since anger has to be repressed. Instead, there is an idealisation of intimacy that is incapable of sustaining a person through the ups and downs of a relationship. Inevitable frustrations can lead to disappointment and hurt, with a sudden breakthrough of anger, directed either at

---

23. Since this paper was written, mindfulness meditation has become recognised as an approved treatment for anxiety and the prevention of relapse of depression.

the other or towards the self, leading to withdrawal and depression.

The practice of meditation is liable to suffer the same vicissitudes, first of idealisation and then disillusion when the results are slow to come – which they probably will be, since hoping for too much usually results in disappointment. Guidance will be needed to encourage long-term goals and to provide stability when emotions are running high.

- ARCHETYPES ARE INVARIABLY BIPOLAR. By their nature, archetypes are constellated in antithesis. *Yin* co-exists with *yang*. The person whose self is over-identified with pain and suffering needs to be helped to see that there are two sides to the same coin; sorrow and joy are not in opposition but complementary. When the whole coin can be grasped, a new perspective arises that inspires us to overcome the limitations of the ego, and to find acceptance and peace.[24]

Practical Guidelines

How may the unquiet self be best helped along the spiritual path? Here are a few suggestions.

1. If a person's reality testing is shaky, including borderline psychotic reactions, I do not advocate meditation. Life can be soul-centred without trying to enter 'other realms'. Straightforward prayer will do. A good life, lived with generosity of spirit, understanding and courage takes the soul a long way indeed. In these circumstances, soul-centred psychotherapy stands more chance of helping such a person learn to be at peace with themselves and their emotions than meditation *per se*.[25]

2. Where meditation is the chosen path, it is generally best to situate regular practice within a clear framework of spiritual teaching.[26]

---

24. See *Soul Consciousness and Human Suffering*, this volume.
25. See Peck (1978), Moore (1992), Kowalski (2001).
26. Suzuki (1970).

This provides a meaningful and secure foundation for what is to come, connects the person with a like-minded community of others and addresses the frequent problem of isolation.[27]

3. Psychoeducation can be a great help, including understanding how the archetypes of the spiritual domain are coloured by the influence of negative emotions.[28] This is especially likely when the emotions have not been acknowledged and are liable to rebound on the self. The task is not heroically to attempt to defeat one's 'shadow' but to accept it and to treat it with compassion, as one would a wayward child. Then it loses the power to dominate and destroy.[29]

The infant science of psychology has come a long way, but wisdom is timeless. Seven hundred years ago, Julian of Norwich wrote, 'I do not say that evil is praiseworthy but that our Lord's allowing it is praiseworthy. In this his goodness shall be known forever; by his loving kindness and by the power of his mercy and grace'.[30] In other words, we are first given the opportunity to fail. Then, when we fail, however miserably, we can ask for and receive forgiveness. This is very important because depression is fuelled by a self that is unforgiving, especially towards itself. What a revelation to discover that to experience being forgiven unlocks the capacity to forgive, including forgiveness of oneself!

Dating from the 14th century, a profound mystical text known as *The Cloud of Unknowing* contains this excerpt:

'It is the work of the soul that most pleases God… when you first begin, you find only darkness, and as it were, a cloud of unknowing… reconcile yourself to wait in this darkness as long as is necessary, but still go on longing after him whom you love… this work does not take a long time for its completion… it is neither shorter nor longer than a single impulse of your will, the chief part of your soul… for he comes down to our level, adapting his Godhead to our power to comprehend. He cannot be comprehended by our intellect or any man's – or any angel's for that matter. But only to our intellect is he incomprehensible: not to our love.'[31]

---

27.   O'Donnell (1987), Sumedho (1991).
28.   Assagioli (1965), Nelson (1994).
29.   Johnson (1991).
30.   Llewelyn (1980: 14).
31.   Wolters (1978: 61–63).

Closer to our own time, Jiddu Krishnamurti reminds us that the action of love is the one action that has no motive and needs no motive. He writes:

'The mind must be clear, without movement, and in the light of that clarity the timeless is revealed... when the mind is no longer seeking, no longer breeding conflict through its wants and cravings, when it is silent with understanding, only then can the immeasurable come into being... when the mind realises the totality of its own conditioning... then all its movements come to an end; it is completely still, without any desire, without any compulsion, without any motive. Only then is there freedom.'[32]

What benefits are conferred by such freedom? The freedom is from longings that cannot be satisfied and from attachments that serve to bind. Then the unquiet self finds what the world cannot give, the fulfilment of all longing and peace that passes all understanding.

References

Assagioli, R. (1965) *Psychosynthesis: A Manual of Principles and Techniques*. Hobbs, Dorman & Company.

Bache, C. (2000) *Dark Night, Early Dawn*. State University of New York Press.

Baldwin, W. (1992) *Spirit Releasement Therapy*. Headline Books.

Bohm, D. (1980) *Wholeness and the Implicate Order*. Routledge.

Bowlby, J. (1969) *Attachment*. Hogarth Press.

Chopra, D. (2001) *How to Know God*. Rider, Random House.

Feng, G.F. & English, J. (trans.) (1973) *Lao Tsu: Tao Te Ching*. Wildwood House.

Fenwick, P. & Fenwick, E. (1995) *The Truth in the Light*. Headline.

Fiore, E. (1987) *The Unquiet Dead*. Doubleday/Dolphin.

Guo, B. & Powell, A. (2001) *Listen to Your Body: the Wisdom of the Dao*. University of Hawaii Press.

Haskins, M.L. (1940) God knows. *The Rotarian*, 57(4).

Johnson, R. (1991) *Owning Your Own Shadow*. HarperSanFrancisco.

Jung, C.G. (1954) Archetypes of the Collective Unconscious. Reprinted [1959] in *C.G. Jung: The Collected Works*, vol. 9, part 1: The Archetypes and the Collective Unconscious (eds H. Read, M. Fordham & G. Adler). Routledge and Kegan Paul.

---

32. Krishnamurti (1991: 10–11, 60).

Krishnamurti, J. (1991) *Commentaries on Living*. Third series. Victor Gollancz.

Kowalski, R. (2001) *The Only Way Out Is In*. Jon Carpenter Publishing.

Llewelyn, R. (1980) *Daily Readings with Julian of Norwich*. 'Enfolded in Love' series. Darton, Longman and Todd.

Lucas, W. (1993) *Regression Therapy*. Vols 1 & 2. Deep Forest Press.

Moore, T. (1992) *Care of the Soul*. Piatkus.

Nelson, J. (1994) *Healing the Split*. State University of New York Press.

O'Donnell, K. (1987) *New Beginnings*. Brahma Kumaris World Spiritual University.

Peck, S.M. (1978) *The Road Less Travelled*. Arrow Books.

Powell, A. (1997) Birth and death: passwords to the human spiritual encounter. *Network: Journal of the Scientific and Medical Network*, 65, 12–14.

Scott Sparrow, G. (2002) *Sacred Encounters with Jesus*. Sparrow: Thomas More Publications.

Sifton, E. (2003) *The Serenity Prayer: Faith and Politics in Times of Peace and War*. WW Norton.

Sumedho, S. (1991) *The Way It Is*. Amaravati Publications.

Suzuki, S. (1970) *Zen Mind, Beginner's Mind*. Weatherhill.

Swedenborg, E. (2000) *Heaven and Hell* (trans. G. Dole). Swedenborg Foundation.

Winnicott, D.W. (1958) Anxiety associated with insecurity. In *Through Paediatrics to Psycho-analysis*. Tavistock Publications.

Wolters, C. (1978) *The Cloud of Unknowing and Other Works* (anon). Penguin.

5

Spirituality and Science:
A Personal View

British psychiatry has largely focused on the biology of mental disorder, supported over recent years by advances in the neurosciences. There has been a somewhat awkward fit with psychology, since psychology is based on the concept of mind, and how the mind and brain are related is far from clear. The view taken by many is to regard mind as epiphenomenal, on the basis that the brain itself is somehow generating consciousness.

In this model of the psyche, there is no need to postulate a soul. We are nothing but the product of our genes, as Richard Dawkins would have us believe.[1]

Such an assertion comes at the tail end of an epoch that began 300 years ago with the intellectual giants, Rene Descartes and Isaac Newton. Descartes set down a lasting blueprint for science, that he would hold nothing to be true unless he could prove to his satisfaction that it was true. Newton laid the foundation of a mechanical universe, in which time is absolute and space is structured according to the laws of motion, a cosmos of stars and planets all held in place by the forces of momentum and gravitation.

Both Descartes and Newton were deeply religious men. Descartes' famous dictum, 'Cogito ergo sum', led him simply to argue that God had created two classes of substance, a mental world and a

First published as 'Spirituality and science: a personal view' in *Advances in Psychiatric Treatment* (2001), 7, 319–321. Reprinted with permission.

---

1. Dawkins (1976).

physical world, while Newton spent more time engrossed in his alchemical researches than working out the laws of motion. Yet their discoveries led to an enduring split between religion and science with which we live to this day. The Church could no longer claim to understand how the universe worked, for its mediaeval cosmology had been swept aside. As the mental and physical worlds drifted further apart, God became a shadowy figure behind the scenes, whose only function was winding up the mainspring of the universe. In the past 100 years, the science of psychology has redefined the mental world along essentially humanist lines, a mindset that can be traced to Sigmund Freud, who saw religion as a powerful defence against neurosis.[2] Even Carl Jung was careful to stay within the bounds of psychology when defining the soul as 'the living thing in Man, that which lives of itself and causes life'.[3]

Our patients have no such reservations. We know from a survey carried out by the Mental Health Foundation that over 50% of service users hold religious or spiritual beliefs that they see as important in helping them cope with mental illness, yet do not feel free to discuss these beliefs with the psychiatrist.[4]

Need there be such a divide between psychiatrists and their patients? If we care to look at some of the advances in physics over the past 75 years, we find good cause to think again.

In the light of quantum mechanics, Newton's view of a physical world that is substantial, fixed and independent of mind is no longer tenable. For example, the famous wave-particle experiment shows that when a beam of light is shone through a particle detector, sub-atomic packets of light called quanta strike the detector screen like miniature bullets. Change the detector screen to two slits side by side and the light coming through the slits generates a wave interference pattern, just as ripples criss-cross when two stones are dropped side by side into a pond. Particles become waves and waves become particles. Both of these dimensional realities have equal validity and cannot be divorced from the consciousness of the participant-observer. This is but a window onto a greater vista, for current

---

2. Freud (1927).
3. Jung (1954: 26).
4. Faulkner (1997).

superstring theory postulates many more dimensions than our local space-time can accommodate.

No longer is the electron thought of as a particle that spins around the atom like a miniature solar system. Instead, it is conceptualized as 'virtual', being diffused throughout all space in a quantum wave that only collapses as a particle into our physical space-time when the consciousness of the observer is engaged in the act of measurement. Nor can its velocity and position ever both be known at the same time, for when the quantum wave collapses, there is only a statistical probability that the electron will turn up where it is expected. It may just materialise hundreds, thousands or even millions of miles away. When it does so, it arrives at that place instantaneously, transcending the limits of both space and time. Here is what three eminent physicists have to say:

> 'The fundamental process of nature lies outside space-time but generates events that can be located in space-time'.[5]
>
> 'Ultimately, the entire universe (with all its particles, including those constituting human beings, their laboratories, observing instruments, etc.) has to be understood as a single undivided whole, in which analysis into separately and independently existent parts has no fundamental status'.[6]
>
> 'The universe exists as formless potentia in myriad possible branches in the transcendent domain and becomes manifest only when observed by conscious beings'.[7]

When consciousness collapses the wave function into the space-time of our perceptual world, mind and matter arise simultaneously, like two sides of one coin. The brain, of course, is crucial in this; the mind, with its capacity for individual self-awareness, is constellated with each physical self. Consciousness is then perpetuated through repeated further collapse of the wave function. (The process can be compared with the individual frames of a film flowing together to create movement.) In this way, we are continually generating what we think of as 'reality', characterised by memories, our personal

---

5. Stapp (1977: 202).
6. Bohm (1983: 174).
7. Goswami (1993: 141).

histories and an enduring sense of identity. (Fortunately for us, our shared world of sense perception has structural stability, not because it is independent of consciousness but because the probability wave from which it arises has been collectively generated by all conscious beings throughout time.)

Quantum effects show up most readily at the subatomic level, but empirical research into large-scale systems has also demonstrated that mind can influence matter. For example, random number generators have been shown, over thousands of trials, to yield scores correlating with the mental intention of the experimenter.[8] More striking still are those unaccountable events we call miracles. Since the wave function contains, *in potentia*, all that ever was, is and shall be, there is no limit in principle to what is possible. Why should not a mind of such exceptional power as that of Jesus collapse the wave uniquely and thereby turn water into wine?

Evidence for the non-locality of consciousness was first demonstrated over 25 years ago, when it was shown that experimental subjects who are emotionally attuned could synchronize their brain waves at a distance from each other.[9] Remote viewing and precognition have since been firmly established on an empirical basis.[10] The efficacy of prayer has been researched,[11] as have more than 150 controlled studies on healing.[12] Such findings merit the epithet 'paranormal' only if we view them through Newtonian glasses.

Who can therefore say what does not exist in the quantum domain, from the supreme consciousness we call God to those sensed presences (often of the newly departed) that psychiatrists refer to as pseudo-hallucinations, down to unruly spirits that, according to the beliefs of many societies, blight the lives of those they persecute?

When we enquire into the beliefs our patients hold, such matters deserve to be discussed with a genuinely open mind. We do not have the answers and indeed our patients may sometimes be

---

8.   Schmidt (1987).
9.   Targ & Puthoff (1974).
10.   Radin (1997).
11.   Byrd (1988).
12.   Benor (1992).

closer to the truth than we know. Nor are we required to affirm a particular religious or spiritual viewpoint but simply to treat the often strange experiences told us by our patients as authentic. This can sometimes be uncomfortable, for we are trained to judge with confidence the difference between phantasy and reality and to diagnose accordingly. Yet doing so comes a whole lot easier once we concede the limitations of space-time, which we can do by taking an unprejudiced intellectual position or experientially through spiritual practice.

People in sound mental health, who sense that beyond the doors of perception there lies a greater world, can use such awareness to enrich their lives, be it through prayer, mediumship or mystical reverie. Yet where there is mental turmoil, whatever its cause, that same sensitivity can bring profound distress.[13] The stigma that so often burdens our patients is more than the result of social opprobrium. There is often a deep sense of estrangement from humanity and this is something that the psychiatrist who takes into account both science and spirituality can surely help overcome.

References

Benor, D. (1992) *Healing Research: Holistic Energy Medicine and Spirituality*. Helix.

Bohm, D. (1983) *Wholeness and the Implicate Order*. Ark Paperbacks.

Byrd, R.C. (1988) Positive therapeutic effects of intercessory prayer in a coronary care unit population. *Southern Medical Journal*, 81, 826–829.

Dawkins, R. (1976) *The Selfish Gene*. Oxford University Press.

Faulkner, A. (1997) *Knowing Our Own Minds*. Mental Health Foundation.

Freud, S. (1927) The future of an illusion. Reprinted [1961] in *The Standard Edition of the Complete Psychological Works of Sigmund Freud*, vol. 21 (trans. & ed. J. Strachey). Hogarth Press.

Goswami, A. (1993) *The Self-Aware Universe*. Putnam.

Jung, C.G. (1954) Archetypes of the collective unconscious. Reprinted [1959] in *C.G. Jung: The Collected Works*, vol. 9, part 1: The Archetypes and the Collective Unconscious (eds H. Read, M. Fordham & G. Adler). Routledge and Kegan Paul.

Radin, D. (1997) *The Conscious Universe: The Scientific Truth of Psychic Phenomena*. Harper Edge.

---

13.   See *Soul Consciousness and Human Suffering* and *Beyond Space and Time*, both this volume.

Schmidt, H. (1987) The strange properties of psychokinesis. *Journal of Scientific Exploration*, 1, 103–118.

Stapp, H.P. (1977) Are superluminal connections necessary? *Nuovo Cimento*, 40B, 191–204.

Targ, R. & Puthoff, H.E. (1974) Information transmission under conditions of sensory shielding. *Nature*, 251, 602–607.

6

Psychosocial Implications of the Shadow

The aim of this paper is to give a psychotherapeutic account of humanity's seeming compulsion to turn against its own kind as a species and commit endless self-harm. My perspective has been shaped by working for 30 years with individuals, families and groups who have sought psychotherapy to extricate themselves from patterns of destructive behaviour and the misery that goes with it. The consulting room may seem a long way from the killing fields of humankind. Nevertheless, as the twig is bent, so grows the tree. Society mirrors the mental turmoil in each one of us. Only through raising the level of consciousness of humanity, which also means becoming aware of the shadow carried by humankind, will there be any possibility of peace on earth.

The Beginnings of Culture

I will start by observing that on the one hand we are as gods, while on the other hand we are very much animals. Our gift of consciousness, which transcends the animal world, has to live with a brain and body geared to the evolution of the hunter-gatherer and the basic survival mechanisms of fight or flight. This is hardly surprising when we consider how recently language and culture have evolved.

It is thought that *Homo erectus* first appeared some 1.5 million years back. A milestone achievement around 300,000 years ago was

Paper prepared for the Jupiter Trust, Oxford, 2001. First published in *Holistic Science and Human Values* (2003), 6, 26–42.

learning how to harness fire. Not only did this enable food to be cooked, it also protected against wild animals. Our progenitors could relax in safety, in tribes or clans around the fire, and begin the process of socialisation and culture. As little as 150,000 years ago, the blink of an eye on the evolutionary timeline, *Homo sapiens* discovered the miracle of language.

The Mind of the Infant

How does the infant mind start to form? To begin with, the mind has no constructs with which to organize information arising from the world of sense perception. A baby's experience of consciousness may well be something akin to what sages and mystics know to be 'the ground of all being'. A sublime expression of this state of wonder is found in the cantata 'Dies Natalis', which is set to the 17th-century words of the poet Thomas Traherne:

'Sweet Infancy
O hevenly Fire! O Sacred Light!
How fair and bright! How Great am I
Whom the whol world doth magnify!
O hevenly Joy!
O Great and Sacred Blessedness
Which I possess!
So great a Joy
Who did into my Arms convey?'[1]

The infant mind very soon begins to be structured by experience. Pleasure, and pain too, initially mediated by body sensations but then extending to the mental world, shape the behaviour of the little person. Without mother (or the caregiver), the child would be in acute danger of physical or mental catastrophe.[2] The good mother keeps traumatic impingements to a minimum, but to some extent they are part of life. Colic, chafed skin, bumps on the head; how does the child manage these inevitable traumas? In fact, children

---

1. Finzi (1939).
2. Winnicott (1962).

can cope remarkably well with all manner of adversity provided they feel inwardly secure. Anxiety and discomfort can be tolerated when experience has taught them it will not be forever, and when help is on hand, best of all, a parent's love and concern.

What happens when that same child grows up in a world that presents serious threats to its survival and where there is little comfort? The child dares not express healthy aggression because if it does, it will be punished. As it happens, the worst form of punishment is not a physical beating but threat of abandonment. The crucial developmental step taken by the higher mammals and primates in particular is the intimacy and duration of the parent–infant bond. Many parents have no idea of the emotional impact of shouting 'You do that again and I'll leave you right here!' The fear of abandonment will lead the child to suppress all their anger and grievances while submitting passively to any amount of abuse, just so long as they are not thrown out.[3]

The child has to find a way to get rid of psychic pain so that equilibrium can be restored to the ego. This is carried out by a variety of psychological defence mechanisms,[4] best collectively understood in terms of specific coping strategies. The more disturbed the childhood, the more the defences come to dominate emotional life, although anyone is liable to take refuge in defence mechanisms when sufficiently threatened.

Ego Development

Every growing child learns how to protect its sense of personal identity. Two early markers of a child's ego development are worth noting. One is the ability to say no, which comes well before the child learns to say yes. This is a crucial step, for the child is establishing a sense of its own, separate being. The other milestone, which holds lifelong significance, is the discovery of the personal pronoun, 'mine' – coming way ahead of 'ours'. Unfortunately, 'mine' is turning out to be a four-letter word with devastating implications for human society.

---

3.   Bowlby (1973).
4.   Freud (1936).

The advent of the human ego is a two-edged sword. Without it, there could be no development of will, no mastery of the environment and no spur to emotional and intellectual growth. The ego ideal[5] first arises in the child based on love and admiration for its parents. Later, however, a prohibitive function is acquired due to the internalising of parental injunctions ('I said no!'), which Freud called the superego.[6] Having a conscience means learning to set limits for oneself as a self-governed individual with a capacity for moral introspection.

At the same time, this separation of self from 'other' presents an existential challenge for every child; where there is emotional instability, healthy competitiveness can easily turn into destructive rivalry, admiration into envy and need into greed. These negative developments arise when the child continues to experience a core sense of threat. One need look no further than the school playground. Unless a protective and respectful culture has been established by the teachers (and for which parental support is also needed), we find the same struggle for dominance that William Golding wrote about so chillingly in *Lord of the Flies*.[7]

Defence Mechanisms

Everyone has defence mechanisms on board. They are like trip switches in an electrical circuit; overload triggers the switch instead of burning out the circuit. A vulnerable and insecure child with a fragile ego cannot tolerate fluctuations in emotional tension, instead relying heavily on defence mechanisms for protection. By contrast, the more love, security and understanding that have been given to a child, the greater the stability and resilience of its inner world. Accordingly, it learns to handle emotions with confidence and not to anticipate disaster. Defence mechanisms still come into play in the event of major trauma, but the ups and downs of daily life can be managed well enough.

---

5. Jacobson (1964).
6. Freud (1923).
7. Golding (1962).

Numerous defences have been identified but I need only describe the key ones here.

Repression

Repression is the defence most people have heard of. A traumatic event gets split off from consciousness and buried, out of sight and out of mind. However, it is still there 10, 20, 50 years on, and for so long as it lies concealed, the imprint of the trauma remains as powerful as the day it was laid down. We see this with childhood sexual abuse, where terrifying flashbacks may occur for the first time during lovemaking in adulthood. Yet the problem may be compounded by the unconscious choice to submit to an abusive adult relationship. It often transpires in such cases that deep down, the child was left with guilt and shame, or a sense of badness, and years later unconsciously selects a partner on the basis of 'I'm not worthy of more' at best and 'I deserve to be punished' at worst. The reality we half expect is usually the one we create for ourselves.

Splitting and Projection

We often see parents aiding and abetting their children in the defences of splitting and projection in small ways. A child trips over a chair and starts to cry. 'Naughty chair', says the grown up and even gives the chair a smack. The child is comforted, since it obviously must have been the chair's fault and the child is not to blame. The problem has been *split off* and *projected* into the hapless chair, a device that does no harm to a healthy toddler and its self-esteem, which had momentarily collapsed.

Projection is not necessarily defensive. We know that what we see is always coloured by how we feel, for the world is not a thing apart but part of us. We do not see things as they are, we see things as we are.[8] When we project love, we can find beauty in all of Creation. There is no splitting, for we are happy to feel ourselves in harmony with Creation. However, when we project anger, we turn against the world and its contents. Me good, chair bad! Splitting

---

8. Nin (1969).

enables a person to feel virtuous while putting the bad feeling out-side of them, where it can be kicked, smashed up, run away from or enjoyed by watching it on television – an ideal outlet for Schadenfreude.

Children begin making categorical judgements about good and bad when still very small. Parental input is needed to soften the harshness of those early judgements and this is where the action of love helps the child learn that justice needs tempering with mercy and grandiosity with humility.

A hallmark of pathological splitting at work in the adult is that such persons hold their opinions with absolute certainty. Ambivalence has to be avoided at all costs in case it leads to inner confusion. Developing a capacity for ambivalence requires us to tolerate con-flicting impulses, feelings and ideas, for example, selfishness and gen-erosity, love and hate, right and wrong. The problem has to be owned and a more mature solution found. This can mean bearing with frus-tration and loving others (and oneself too) despite human faults and failings. As a developmental achievement, ambivalence gives us the capacity for introspection and depth of personality. Where would Shakespeare be without it!

Unencumbered by introspection, people prone to splitting often make charismatic, if immature, leaders because of their conviction in themselves and the absolute rightness of their view of the world. The enemy 'out there' is ruthlessly attacked and any attempt at concilia-tion is seen as a sign of weakness and scorned. If an enemy cannot be found, one will have to be invented. This leads to paranoia, the Cold War mentality, circumstances in which even to question authority of the leader is tantamount to an act of treason.

Manic-Defence and Idealisation

The combination of self-idealisation and denigration of other is known as manic-defence; the need for power and triumph over oth-ers is understood psychoanalytically as a defence against helplessness and depression.

An alternative way of dealing with weakness and vulnerability is to attach yourself to someone you see as all-powerful and who can be made the object of idealisation. Yet if that person should let you down, the fall from grace is precipitous and he or she is now dis-missed as either a fool or a knave. Immediately the search is on for a new hero and saviour. The hallmark of this dependency situation is the expectation of getting rescued from without, rather than learning how to rescue oneself.

Mutual Projection Systems

Splitting of the ego can take place on its own, as in multiple personality disorder, but usually goes hand in hand with projection.[9] Earlier I gave the example of the child and chair, but people attract projections too. Hate, for instance, can bind a couple as powerfully as love. People ask, 'Why not leave?' as if it was the obvious thing to do. But who, then, would be left to hate? You might discover it was yourself you hated all along and end up contemplating suicide (paranoia and depression are two sides of one coin, depending on whether the hostility is directed outwards or inwards).

Sometimes projection systems are both mutual and complementary. Take, for instance, the husband whose wife gets depressed. Until they are seen together, the wife would seem to be the one needing treatment. Closer investigation shows that the husband's anxieties and fears are inadmissible because he was brought up never to show vulnerability. Unconsciously, the wife takes on the role of the carrier of these emotions for both of them, for she, let us say, was brought up to believe that the woman must give support to the man. Therefore, she projects the inadmissible aspect of herself, her own strength, into her husband, where it fortifies his self-esteem. Sometimes such relationships work out well enough. However, when the roles become fixed, there is usually trouble, since neither of the couple are being wholly themselves.

Identification With the Aggressor

In the blackboard jungle, a child perceived as weaker than others is fated to be bullied, often ruthlessly. On investigation, the same unconscious processes of projection and splitting are found to be driving the behaviour of the bullying child. Anna Freud named this defence mechanism identification with the aggressor. Such a child

---

9.   Klein (1957).

comes from a disturbed background and he or she has experienced what it means to be a victim. Now there is a chance to turn the tables: the child takes on the characteristics of the abuser, relishing the feeling of power. But what is to be done now with the split-off victim aspect, which has never known love and sympathy? The bully must get rid of this Achilles heel at all costs, so the object is to find someone weaker, into whom this hated aspect of the self can be projected and then attacked 'out there', in the other. We call this scapegoating, but in its more malignant expression it can lead to murder.

Such is the danger when, for defensive purposes, the 'other' is treated as alien to the self. It highlights the need for parents and teachers to encourage the child in developing the capacity for empathy, to become aware of what is going on in the mind of the other. As a species, we are fortunate to be hard-wired for this kind of learning, known as 'theory of mind'. Some children are less fortunate; for example, those living with autistic-spectrum disorder, which presents a major problem in understanding how another person thinks and feels. Consequently, the world of the autistic child is profoundly self-centred.[10]

Blindness to the feelings of others can also arise when defence mechanisms habitually control the psyche. Humans then show no compunction in seducing, bullying or manipulating others into doing what they want. Very few people actually see themselves as bad, yet splitting of the ego can lead to bizarre situations as, for instance, with those mass murderers who would seem nevertheless to have been conscientious and loving parents.

Denial

This brings me to the last term I want to include, the defence known as denial. Facts may be staring a person in the face, yet what they signify cannot be grasped. Some patients really do not want to face that they have cancer. The unexpected death of a loved one is another case in point – the shock is so overwhelming that the defence cuts in and the person simply cannot take in the bad news. Such denial

---

10.   Baron-Cohen et al. (1999). Autistic-spectrum disorder is not to be confused with psychopathic personality, in which intellectual empathy may enable highly manipulative behaviour without a trace of emotional empathy.

is usually temporary. In other situations, like admitting responsibility for genocide, the denial may be lifelong and buttressed by all manner of justifications and rationalizations. Should such denial break down, the outcome can be fatal. Franz Stangl, who had been commandant at Treblinka, was later interviewed by Gitta Sereny weekly over a period of one year. In the last interview, he admitted to some degree his responsibility for the mass murder of 900,000 Jews. Nineteen hours after this last interview, he died from a heart attack.[11]

Human Society and the Unconscious

I have been illustrating how the pathological use of defence mechanisms can operate in the individual case. Now let us look at some of the consequences for human society.

When we consider groups, we see the collective emergence of the same mechanisms that apply to the individual. However, the group situation adds a new dimension and to enlarge on this, I want to include the mechanism Freud called 'transference'.[12]

Transference refers to the way in which we unwittingly transfer the emotions we have felt towards key persons in our formative years onto other people and into other situations. Typically, it is not uncommon for someone with a domineering father to have difficulty, years on, with the boss at work, since unresolved rebellious emotions surface and get in the way of a good working relationship. A child who never felt sure of the parent's affection may be left excessively anxious to please when grown up. Children in a family who had desperately to compete for the parents' love may have trouble with poor peer relationships later, since rivalry rather than co-operation still feels like being the only way to succeed. These unconscious patterns surface because the group situation activates the archetypal constellation of the family.[13]

Just as with the saying 'blood is thicker than water', when there is an external threat, people will set aside their differences to join

11.   Sereny (1974).
12.   Freud (1920).
13.   Foulkes (1964).

forces against the common foe, like a family under threat. The leader of the group becomes the object of intense transference projections, for he or she now carries the 'ego-ideal' for all, be it cause or crusade, religious uprising or political ideology.[14] Special sanctions are dispensed in the name of the cause, such as giving orders to kill other people. The 'us and them' dynamic, lurking only just beneath the surface at the best of times, becomes legitimised, while propaganda ensures that the enemy is thoroughly vilified. (The armed forces know how dangerous it is to allow fraternisation, for this can undermine the willingness to kill.)

Once the rules of normal civilized behaviour have been suspended and killing is approved, a profound taboo has been lifted; little wonder that rape and other atrocities are commonplace in war. In some indigenous cultures, it is believed that taking a life is strong magic against losing your own. This would be another example of manic-defence, in which the person triumphs over death by projecting his own fear of death into the enemy, where it can be exultantly 'killed'.

The larger the group, the more individual identity is swept aside.[15] Football matches are a case in point. Group cohesion is vested in the favoured team – a secular ego ideal that for some is as powerful as any religion. Having such opportunities to unite with fellow man can be a powerful antidote to living in a society where so many feel alienated and estranged.

Because transference reactions have their roots in the hopes and fears of childhood, they tend to be extreme in character, inherently unstable, riding on a wave of emotion and not much amenable to reason. Politicians know how fickle the mood of the electorate can be and how suddenly disillusionment can set in. Democracy may be a wonderful thing, but the world over, leaders and led get caught alike in the dynamics of the dependency relationship. Every child needs guiding and protecting. Yet as the child grows, it resents being controlled, as the idealisation of the parent is replaced with a more realistic perception of the parent's fallibility. Parents are usually hurt by this biting of the hand that feeds, just as politicians usually end up

---

14.   Freud (1921).
15.   Kreeger (1975).

feeling wounded by the slings and arrows of the electorate. With the family of origin, one solution (favoured in the West) is to leave home. In a totalitarian state, there is no escape; the solution is literal repression, while an attempt is made to expunge individual memories by re-writing social history. In a democracy, we elect a new government every few years and with the help of splitting, projection and idealisation, flagging optimism is periodically revived.

The Dominance of Emotions Over Intellect

In the evolution of civilisation as we know it, war has played a central, and perhaps indispensable, part. Until now, the planet has been sufficiently large, and the weapons of mankind sufficiently limited, to allow each nation to go on behaving as if it were the epicentre of the world. Yet, even the most rudimentary knowledge of geography and history shows this to be an egocentric prejudice.

This ego-centred perspective is mirrored at every level of social structure, in each community, family, couple, down to the individual self. A profound discrepancy exists between emotional reality and intellectual comprehension. For instance, study of the earth's ecosystems clearly shows that to survive as a species, we urgently need to devote ourselves to caring for our planet, which means confronting the problems of overpopulation, pollution, deforestation, arms proliferation, conflicting ideologies, and social and racial injustice. Yet, from the emotional standpoint, we have not advanced much beyond the world of the child, which experiences itself as the centre of all things. This is the field of action of our ego defences, which develop in the early years long before the intellect is able to grasp the meaning of the big picture. Nor can these defences be simply extracted from the human ego, for they are deeply woven into the ego's limited view of self-in-the-world. This is why it is so important that we become aware of them.

Good and Evil

The developmental psychology I have outlined so far does not address the question of good and evil. Indeed, psychology claims to be a science supposedly independent of moral value judgements, seeing good and evil as best left to philosophers and theologians to argue about. In fact, psychology has all sorts of built-in assumptions about what is good and bad, usually implied by integration of the psyche (good) versus fragmentation (bad), as well as placing a value on the importance of truthfulness, the relief of suffering and the goal of happiness, to name but a few.

Since we live in a time when whole countries are being castigated as 'the axis of evil', I had better offer my own understanding of good and evil before I discuss the psychology of the shadow any further. I do not think psychology needs to stand back from the question of good and evil. In our world of sense perception, structured by space and time, polarities characterize our every experience. This is embodied in the ancient Chinese symbol of the *Taiji*, where *yin* and *yang* entwine within the circle that represents *Wuji*, the formless infinite.[16] The complementary nature of *yin* and *yang* arises with every manifestation of form. Dark is dark only because it compares with light; inside is contrasted with outside; bigness with smallness; more abstractly, pleasure compares with pain and love with hate. We know good because we know evil too.

Material realism, which has been firmly in the driving seat for a couple of centuries, sees the ethics of good and evil, like everything else in consciousness, as simply a by-product of brain activity. It follows on this basis that God exists only because we invented 'Him' as purely a projection of the ego ideal of goodness. We can then be comforted for eternity by an imagined good and loving parent. At the same time, by means of splitting and projection, we invent the Devil so that we can keep the badness outside.

While Freud has taught us a great deal about defence mechanisms, applying such a reductionist approach to spirituality is seriously outdated. Instead, we have a new cosmology derived largely from quantum physics during the past century that suggests that we live in a multidimensional cosmos. Comprising an unimaginably vast hologram,[17] our physical universe unfolds in the dimensions of what

16.   Guo & Powell (2001).
17.   Talbot (1991).

we know as space-time. Since the process is not static but flowing, the physicist David Bohm used the term 'holomovement'[18] to describe this flux between the hidden and the revealed, what he called the implicate and explicate orders.[19] Since a hologram contains the whole within the part, it follows that humankind carries and faithfully reflects the image of the greater whole. On this basis, what we experience as consciousness is nothing less than the reflection of a self-aware universe.

The most radical claim of quantum theory is that the action of human consciousness, through what is known as 'the collapse of the probability wave', physically materializes our universe of space-time and everything it contains.[20] If so, this is a great undertaking on behalf of Creation, in which we, along with all advanced life forms, are instruments of the supreme consciousness we call God.

Living in Our Own Shadow

If humanity is an instrument of the Divine, how come folly and wisdom exist cheek by jowl? Why, indeed, should the impact of hatred and violence be allowed to jeopardise our very existence? Our history suggests that *Homo sapiens* is still at a very early stage of evolution. Just as Neanderthal man was superseded by *Homo sapiens*, one may hope that the next stage, if humanity survives that long, will be the emergence of *Homo spiritus*.[21] However, we are not there yet; too much of our consciousness is deployed in fight/flight mentality. While there are many who lead good lives, conducted according to the spiritual values of concern, kindness and compassion, many others are caught up in the ego defences that I have enumerated, leading to self-survival in the short term but jeopardising the long-term future of humanity.

Herein lies a deep ethical quandary, for there can be no solution to injustice through repression of violence, or retaliation. However

---

18.   See also *The Soul of the Newborn Child*, this volume.
19.   Bohm (1980).
20.   Goswami (1993).
21.   Bache (2000).

much the retaliatory strike is seen as a lesson in deterrence and a rid-
ding of evil, the act of retaliation draws the offender and the one
offended against into the same behaviour. Where there was one bully
in the playground, now there are two. How could any real progress
ever result? Nor is overcoming these ego defences easily achieved.
First, by their nature, they work through the unconscious so that they
fly in the face of reason. Second, a vicious circle is invariably established; interactions based on threat and counter-threat intensify the
operation of defences. Maintaining the ego ideal means having right
on one's side. How else could one man's terrorist be another man's
freedom fighter?

Bringing the Shadow to Light

Carl Jung was deeply concerned with how humankind likes to
maintain its sense of goodness, what he called the persona, at the
cost of getting rid of the unwanted aspects of the self, which he
grouped together and called the shadow. Psychoanalysis had mapped
the structure of the ego and its defences, in particular, how split-
off emotions get projected onto others, but until Jung, no one had
grasped the implications for humanity. Jung saw with dreadful
clarity how the collective shadow falls on humankind and spares
no one.[22]

Jung concluded that unless a way could be found to integrate the
shadow within the psyche instead of unconsciously projecting it,
humankind would be forever doomed to act out the shadow's
destructiveness in all arenas of life, personal, national and international. Jung saw this maturational task as the crucial challenge for
humankind. He called the process 'individuation' in the sense of
becoming indivisible, a unity, and thereby whole. Jung believed that
this potential is found not in the ego but in the Self, which he
described as 'not only the centre but also the whole circumference
which embraces both conscious and unconscious; it is the centre of
this totality, just as the ego is the centre of consciousness'.[23] This

---

22. Jung (1961).
23. Jung (1943: 41).

means that healing, which comes from wholeness, can never be accomplished merely by the activity of the ego. Only the Self, embracing the psyche of both the individual and the collective, holds the key. Jung saw that the Self has the power to accept and contain the internal splits and factions within the psyche because its primary concern is with totality and completeness. From the perspective of the bigger picture, the squabbles of the ego can be managed as you would manage an unruly child.

There are three implications. The first is that the shadow can be lived with as part of oneself, indeed as part of one's humanity, instead of being inflicted on others. We do not have to remain victims of childhood when we see the disposition of the ego from the perspective of the Self.

The second is that individuation is not merely an intellectual exercise but a path of transformation for the emotional and spiritual development of the psyche. Overcoming the limitations and distortions of transference-driven emotions means to become self-sovereign and to experience real freedom.

The third is that the collective aspect of the Self is more than interpersonal; it is transpersonal – making one creature of all humankind. Jung has written 'what was divided on a lower level will reappear, united, on a higher one'.[24]

All great leaders of spiritual and peace movements have expressed these characteristics of the greater Self. They are unconcerned with the accomplishments of the personal ego; on the contrary, their guiding light is humility and compassion. They are indifferent to their own status while dedicated to the welfare of others. They eschew all violence. They give love without reserve, unconditionally, and inspire love in return.

As to hypothesising about the exact balance of good and evil, such leaders do not spend a lot of time philosophising. If the drama being played out on the world stage is such that some humans are bent on destruction, even more reason to throw your weight behind creativity. If there is a collision of values, be steadfast in holding to one's own without standing in judgement over the other.

---

24. Jung (1941: 189).

The Ethic of Interconnectedness

Change through acceptance of self and of other is hard for most of us since our reflex mode to threat as an emergent species is defence and attack. So what does acceptance actually mean? It does not mean condoning behaviour we believe to be hurtful and harmful. It *does* mean recognising that not only do we need to share the same planet, the same air, the same water; we also participate in the same unitary consciousness of the greater Self.[25] Acting out the impulse to destroy makes absolutely no sense once we have grasped this essential point.[26] When we put aside the fortress mentality of the ego and see how the Self extends to comprise one living, sentient consciousness, to shoot another is only to shoot oneself in the foot. This realisation brings the ego and the Self into line; individuality and commonality are understood to be complementary. As Carl Rogers pointed out, 'what is most personal is most general'.[27]

If humankind is to have a future, a quantum shift from the ego and its defences to the Self and its inclusive vision is urgently required. What will happen to the shadow? It will always be acted out in the playground of childhood, since the ego must have its day. Yet retrieving the shadow is the object lesson of spiritual education. Owning the shadow does not make a person into a murderer. To the contrary, we are helped to find compassion for those who take life – and never realised it was their own they were taking.

References

Bache, C. (2000) *Dark Night, Early Dawn.* State University of New York Press.
Baron-Cohen, S., Tager-Flusberg, H. & Cohen, D. (1999) *Understanding Other Minds: Perspectives from Autism and Cognitive Neuroscience.* Oxford University Press.
Bohm, D. (1980) *Wholeness and the Implicate Order.* Ark.
Bowlby, J. (1973) *Attachment and Loss.* Vol. 2: Separation: Anxiety and Anger. Hogarth Press.
Finzi, G. (1939) *Dies Natalis* [CD]. EMI, CDM7.63372-2.

---

25.   Lorimer (1990).
26.   Walsch (1998).
27.   Rogers (1989: 27).

Foulkes, S. H. (1964) *Therapeutic Group Analysis.* George Allen & Unwin.

Freud, S. (1920) Beyond the pleasure principle. Reprinted [1955] in *The Standard Edition of the Complete Psychological Works of Sigmund Freud*, vol. 18 (trans. & ed. J. Strachey). Hogarth Press.

Freud, S. (1921) Group psychology and the analysis of the ego. Reprinted [1955] in *The Standard Edition of the Complete Psychological Works of Sigmund Freud*, vol. 18 (trans. & ed. J. Strachey). Hogarth Press.

Freud, S. (1923) The ego and the id. Reprinted [1961] in *The Standard Edition of the Complete Psychological Works of Sigmund Freud*, vol. 19 (trans. & ed. J. Strachey). Hogarth Press.

Freud, A. (1936) *The Ego and the Mechanisms of Defence.* Hogarth Press.

Golding, W. (1962) *The Lord of the Flies.* Faber and Faber.

Goswami, A. (1993) *The Self-Aware Universe.* Putnam.

Guo, B. & Powell, A. (2001) *Listen to Your Body: the Wisdom of the Dao.* University of Hawaii Press.

Jacobson, E. (1964) *The Self and the Object World.* International Universities Press.

Jung, C. (1941) Paracelsus as a spiritual phenomenon. Reprinted [1968] in *C.G. Jung: The Collected Works*, vol. 13: Alchemical Studies (eds H. Read, M. Fordham & G. Adler). Routledge and Kegan Paul.

Jung, C. (1943) Individual dream symbolism in relation to alchemy. Reprinted [1953] in *C.G. Jung: The Collected Works*, vol. 12 (eds H. Read, M. Fordham & G. Adler). Routledge and Kegan Paul.

Jung, C. (1961) Confrontation with the unconscious. In *Memories, Dreams, Reflections.* Reprinted [1993], Fontana.

Klein, M. (1957) *Contributions to Psycho-analysis.* Hogarth Press.

Kreeger, L. (1975) *The Large Group – Dynamics and Therapy.* Maresfield Reprints. Karnac Books.

Lorimer, D. (1990) *Whole in One.* Arkana.

Nin, A. (1969) *The Diary of Anais Nin 1939–1944.* Brace and World.

Rogers, C. (1989) *The Carl Rogers Reader* (eds H. Kirschenbaum & V.L. Henderson). Howard Mifflin.

Sereny, G. (1974) *Into that Darkness.* Andre Deutsch.

Talbot, M. (1991) *The Holographic Universe.* HarperCollins.

Walsch, N. (1998) *Conversations with God* (Book 3). Hampton Roads.

Winnicott, D. W. (1962) Ego integration. In *The Maturational Processes and the Facilitating Environment.* Hogarth Press.

7

Putting the Soul into Psychiatry

To throw some light on how the soul came to be left out of psychiatry in the first place, I will begin with a bit of history. Then I want to say something about recent developments in physics that have revolutionised how we think about consciousness, time and space. I will take up the implications for the envisioning of soul, and how altered states of consciousness provide us with some valuable insights. Finally, I will refer to the empirical evidence now correlating spirituality with mental health, and why we need to be able to bring discussion of spiritual concerns into the consulting room.

A Historical Perspective

In the West, we tend to forget that our world-view of what constitutes 'reality' is not something absolute but the product of our cultural history, one to which, until quite recently, the great nations of the East remained largely indifferent. I will begin with Pythagoras, the Greek philosopher of the 5th century BC, the same century, incidentally, that introduced the Buddha to India and Laozi to China.

Pythagoras was a dualist, holding that mind and body co-exist but that neither could be explained in terms of the other. He firmly believed in the eternal nature of the soul and is said to have recalled an earlier incarnation as Euphorbus, a warrior in the Trojan War.

Paper prepared for the joint conference of the Section of Psychiatry of the Royal Society of Medicine and the Psychiatry and Spirituality Special Interest Group of the Royal College of Psychiatrists, 'The place of spirituality in psychiatry', Royal Society of Medicine, London, 14 May 2002.

He and his students carried out pioneering arithmetical studies, which they saw as unveiling the principle of proportion, order and harmony throughout the universe. With extraordinary prescience, they considered Earth to be a globe revolving along with the other planets around a central fire, the sun.

Some 200 years later, Aristotle emphatically rejected the views of Pythagoras, convinced that the earth was at the centre of the universe. Aristotle also claimed that there is nothing in the intellect that was not first in the senses, so that his notion of soul comes much closer to what our science of psychology calls the mind.

The legacy for the Roman Catholic Church was 'pick and mix', commending Aristotle's geocentric cosmology as 'the handmaiden to the Queen of Sciences, Theology' while espousing the dualist, Pythagorean view of body and soul.

The first challenge to this doctrinal position came in the 15th century from Copernicus, whose studies led him to conclude, like Pythagoras, that the Earth revolves around the Sun. However, it was Galileo, 100 years later, who posed a far greater challenge, since his findings were based on the newly discovered power of the telescope. In 1632, Galileo was put on trial and sentenced to life imprisonment.

It was to be 50 years more before science burst its bonds due to the magisterial work of Isaac Newton, who became the Lucasian professor of mathematics in Cambridge at the age of 27. Over a 30-year period, he transformed the understanding of the physical universe through his studies on optics, calculus and the laws of gravitation and motion – concepts we live with to this day.

It is less well known that Newton's alchemical researches inspired his great discoveries. He described his method as first, mystical intuition or insight into implicate truth; second, mathematical intellection, to prove, express or explicate the implicate understanding; third, experimentation, in order to demonstrate and verify the proof. Newton asserted truth to be the offspring of silent, unbroken meditation. For Newton, there was no schism between the spiritual and physical universe for he believed that the physical world had been created by, and was a profound testimony to the work of, God.[1]

---

1. In the *General Scholium of the 2nd Edition of the Principia* (1713), Newton writes of God that 'He is eternal and infinite, omnipotent and omniscient;

A few words must be said about the other giant of the early Renaissance, Descartes. Descartes revived the Aristotelian principle of scepticism, which argues that nothing can be held to be true until one is absolutely certain of it. He concluded that the one thing he could not doubt was his own existence. It led to his famous dictum *cogito ergo sum*, 'I think, therefore I am'.[2] This in no way distanced Descartes from God, for he went on to apply the deductive method of science as follows: to be capable of so perfect an idea as God means that such an idea could not have been caused by anything with less perfection than God himself. Therefore, argued Descartes, the two classes of substance, body and mind, must both have been created by God.

Unfortunately, Newton's scientific discoveries were seized upon by the Age of Enlightenment as an opportunity to jettison spiritual reality in favour of equating reality with the physical universe. Descartes' discoveries were similarly hijacked. Man's intellect became the new icon and only empirical science was held to be truly revealing of the nature of reality.

The dire consequences of this outlook reached its heyday in the 20th century with logical positivism, which deemed that any utterance that could not be confirmed or disconfirmed by sensory experience must be rejected as meaningless. Everything beyond the world of sense perception, including God, spiritual values and transcendental strivings, had to be discounted. Alfred Ayer, the leading philosopher of logical positivism, said of his own near-death experience, 'My experiences have weakened, not my belief that there is no life after death, but my inflexible attitude toward that belief'.[3] It seems that in

---

that is, his duration reaches from eternity to eternity; his presence from infinity to infinity: he governs all things, and knows all things that are or can be done… He endures forever and is everywhere present; and by existing always and everywhere, he constitutes duration and space… He is all similar, all eye, all ear, all brain, all arm, all power to perceive, to understand, and to act; but in a manner not at all human, in a manner not at all corporeal, in a manner utterly unknown to us'. Quoted in Burtt (1923: 257).

2. First written by Descartes in 1637 as 'Je pense, donc je suis' in *Discourse on the Method*, first paragraph, fourth part.

3. Ayer's experience was due to cardiac arrest (Ayer, 1988). (Ayer later concluded that if there is life after death, however unlikely, it would be more likely to take the form of reincarnation than resurrection.)

the light of his experience, Ayer was at least willing to admit to a very small degree of doubt.

We are now living in a post-modernist culture, which holds that there are no absolute, enduring values found in 'Nature', 'Truth' or 'God'. The revolution in science that Newton started has given us a world filled with extraordinary technology and a great deal of knowledge about the physical universe. Yet just as that paradigm shift was resisted in time, so has it been with the 'new physics' of the 20th century.

The Second Revolution in Science

I am referring to the vast implications that flow from advances in relativity theory, quantum physics and cosmology. There are at least three reasons why the paradigm shift has met with such resistance. Firstly, so long as the world is viewed through Newtonian glasses, the new findings are deeply counter-intuitive. Secondly, a lot of reputations and research rests on maintaining the Newtonian paradigm. Lastly, the new science carries profound implications for the nature and purpose of existence – what I would call its spiritual significance.

Here are some headline implications of the new physics, many of which I have detailed elsewhere.[4]

- The Newtonian world of sense perception, of solid objects and space, appears to exist in its own right, a cosmic stage on which we make our entrance and exit. Yet matter is energy, objects are not solid and space is not empty.
- The illusion of separateness, which is the template for Newtonian physics, is a phenomenon of sense perception (cf. show five fingers and they are visibly separated until the hand comes into view).
- Our space-time dimension is but one of many, nested within a plurality of other dimensions. Sub-atomic particles are not confined to our universe – they are believed constantly to flit in and out of other universes too.

---

4. Powell (1993, 1994). See also *Beyond Space and Time*, *The Unquiet Self* and *Spirituality and Science*, this volume.

- To speak of sub-atomic 'particles' is really a misnomer. As far as we can tell, they are more like minute strings, from which matter emanates like music. The Universe is like a symphony and the laws of physics are its harmonics.
- The eleventh dimension is thought to be infinitely long but existing only about one trillionth of a millimetre distant from every point in our four-dimensional universe. It is right next to our skins and within it exist an infinite number of parallel universes, some with laws of physics, time and space like ours, and others completely different.
- Through the agency of our special sense organs, we experience consciousness to be located in the body, somewhere between the ears and behind the eyes. This has to be a spatial illusion, since it has been demonstrated that consciousness is 'non-local'.
- Consciousness is primary. The brain does not generate consciousness. Rather, consciousness is 'downloaded' by the brain, which apprehends it much as a radio converts radio waves into audible sound. No theory has provided a convincing explanation of how consciousness, being non-physical, could be created by the physical brain. Imaging studies have been used to support this notion, but all the data can equally well be regarded as correlation effects between neuro-synaptic activity and the ambient field of consciousness.
- Mind and brain are complementary. Viewed as a Newtonian instrument, the brain functions as an object in space-time, in which the law of cause and effect holds true. The mind, the seat of consciousness, has quantum properties, functioning both in and outside of space-time.
- Space-time itself is the product of consciousness, the outcome of what is known in quantum physics as the collapse of the probability wave. Not even a tiny particle such as an electron exists as such until it is measured. Up to that moment, it is in the 'virtual state'. The conscious act of measurement precipitates the electron into space-time. Even then, its speed and momentum cannot be simultaneously measured; there is inherent uncertainty and nothing is fixed.
- Everything within space-time intimately relates to everything else by means of quantum entanglement. Two photons that once shared the same quantum field remain connected forever. Separated by a metre or a million miles, it is all the same; stop the spin

of one and the spin of the other will instantly stop likewise. This is not information travelling from one particle to the other even at the speed of light but a field change, taking place all at once outside of space-time.

- So-called 'paranormal' events defy the laws of Newtonian space and linear time, yet are within reach of the mind, especially when the signal-to-noise ratio is amplified by stilling the mind and reducing sensory input.
- There is a robust database of verified paranormal findings both naturally occurring and experimental. These include precognition, telepathy, remote viewing and healing by means of prayer.

Such discoveries suggest a figure-ground reversal; the Newtonian world-view is valid but we must not mistake the part for the whole. Suppose that we never went out at night and only saw the world in the light of the sun. We would not know the night sky, or suspect the presence of worlds beyond our own.[5]

Spirituality and Psychology

If we can overcome these limitations, we have a new vision of reality in which science and spirituality spring from the same source. I am not speaking here of religion. In the West, the Church has largely treated spirituality as synonymous with religion, but it is not the same thing. Religion is a way of structuring and supporting the human impulse to transcend material reality. Religion provides community, ritual and solace, as well as enriching our world with literature, art, music and architecture. Nevertheless, doctrinal assertions about the nature of God are man-made. In contrast, I am talking about the spirituality that expresses itself naturally, arising as scintilla of that supreme consciousness, the source of life, which traditionally we call God.

I shall be using the term soul to describe that quotient of the Godhead[6] that enlivens each human being. It is not a question of

---

5. See Bache (2000: 5).
6. The concept of Godhead is discussed in more detail in *The Unquiet Self*, this volume.

'having' a soul, but of 'being' a soul. There is no conceit attached to regarding all persons as divine beings, for this has nothing to do with ego. We might as well be humbled when we consider the hand of which we are so many billion fingers.

Science asks the question 'how?' and this is a very important line of inquiry, for we do need to find out all we can about the biological substrate of mental disorder. Nevertheless, finding meaning in life is a function not of the brain but of the mind. It depends not on the 'how' but on the 'why'. This is where a century of psychological research comes in and we might reasonably ask if enough of the 'whys' have been asked and answered. In my view, the answer is no. Having worked for 25 years as a psychotherapist, I do not underestimate the value of psychological insight. Yet for some people, the big questions about the ultimate meaning and purpose of life are of fundamental importance. They need addressing for what they are, not by re-casting them within a psychodynamic/developmental frame of reference.

Again, our culture has set the limits on what is legitimate inquiry. In this case, Sigmund Freud was bent on providing a model of the mind in which everything could be accounted for by the epic struggle of the human ego sandwiched between birth and death; God in His heaven was a necessary illusion to avoid facing the finality of death.[7] Carl Jung challenged this assumption, but the scientific climate of the 20th century ensured that Jung's approach, and later transpersonal schools of psychotherapy, never gained much purchase in mainstream healthcare. Behavioural and cognitive treatments are post-modern approaches, tools for re-structuring thought, which avoid questions that could distract from the task of 'getting on with life'. They lend themselves to goals and measurements and do not require either therapist or client to have to tolerate uncertainty, bear with the unknown or seek ultimate meaning.[8]

This is somewhat ironic for psychiatry, since the word 'psyche' comes from the Greek, meaning soul.

---

7. Freud (1927).
8. This paper was written before mindfulness meditation became recognised as an approved treatment for anxiety and the prevention of relapse of depression. Although provided as a secular therapy, the experience of meditation brings the opportunity for spiritual inquiry in those persons so inclined.

The Holoverse and Humanity

If we are thinking of exchanging the materialist world-view for a participative, cosmological spirituality, we might reasonably want to know more about what we are letting ourselves in for.

It looks increasingly as though the universe is structured like a giant hologram, or 'holoverse', as it has been called, so that the whole is always contained in the part, no matter how small.[9] There follows an important implication: by looking within the self – so long dismissed by science – we extend our ability to discern more of the whole. When it comes to our capacity for love, we make direct contact with a universal emotion of infinite amplitude. From the transpersonal perspective, this means nothing other than to harness the subtle energy of love for the benefit, and self-realization, of the individual, group, society, nation and planet.

Such a statement is no grandiose delusion. Neither does it gloss over suffering. Impacts of unimaginable force are inherent in Creation. Some cosmologists are now suggesting that our universe arose from a collision of two parallel universes existing in five-dimensional space, the impact creating a sea of quarks, electrons, protons, photons, and other subatomic particles.[10] Then our baby universe had to contend with the implosion of matter and anti-matter; only a small preponderance of matter over anti-matter by one part in a billion ensured its survival. This drama of colliding forces typifies our human psychological disposition too, as first told in the story of Adam and Eve. Out of conflict come birth, life, and death. In the ensuing play of emotions, each is paired with, and in a sense defined by, its opposite: thus, good and evil, hope and despair, sorrow and joy, and last but not least, there is love and its sworn antagonist, fear.

It seems all experience must be lived and harvested, the suffering we inflict on others and go through ourselves, as well as the reparation we make and our search for goodness, beauty and truth. We could be forgiven for feeling hopeless about the human condition but there are some grounds for optimism if we keep the whole picture in our sights.

---

9.   Talbot (1991).
10.   According to the Ekpyrotic model of Paul Steinhardt et al., an application of M-theory in which two boundary 'branes' collide. See Cowen (2001).

Cosmology suggests that there is a primal thrust towards life. What began as stardust assumes ever more complex forms, resulting in species like our own, with the biological means to support consciousness. This is the anthropic principle, which argues that the attainment of consciousness such as ours was in the blueprint from the very start.

In this evolutionary development, a quantum shift in consciousness is needed to break through the primitive fight/flight mentality of the species, one that brings about a collective realisation of wholeness, of interdependence and of underlying unity. From this arises 'the golden rule', which asserts that since we are one, to harm another is to harm oneself. Astronauts come back deeply moved by seeing 'spaceship Earth' from afar; the oneness of our little planet is so very striking. The task before us, individually and as a species, is really to grasp the unity of life, and so to make sense of all our lives within the greater whole.

We may feel this intuitively but I also want to mention a few key areas of transpersonal research into consciousness.

Altered States of Consciousness

The near-death experience has been reported the world over, regardless of race, colour or creed. Some 10% of people who clinically 'die' suffer cardiopulmonary arrest and are subsequently resuscitated, and report a complex sequence of events of which they have been subjectively conscious throughout.[11] These have been attributed by some scientists to the terminal throes of neural activity in the brain. However, this is unlikely for two reasons; the first is that the near-death experience takes place while the electroencephalogram (EEG) is electrically silent.[12] The second is that the account given is complex and follows a well-recognised sequence. Unlike the fragmented and confused images that are seen in organic and hypoxic conditions, the near-death experience conveys enormous power, clarity and vision.

The 'full' near-death experience includes an out-of-body experience that may begin with looking down at the attempted resuscitation

---

11.   Bailey & Yates (1996).
12.   Parnia et al. (2001).

with extraordinary detachment, then travelling at speed through a tunnel or vortex and approaching a bright light, meeting deceased friends and relatives, encountering a higher or divine presence, being taken through a life review, being shown the reason for coming back and, hardest of all – for this means leaving one's 'true home' – returning to the body. Most survivors of a near-death experience are profoundly and permanently changed. For the great majority, there is no more fear of death. With the return comes a new and deep appreciation of life, beauty and the knowledge that the only true purpose in life is to love.[13]

A second area of research concerns past life regression.[14] The 'past life' is experienced in real time, there is no sense of contrivance and no amount of wishful thinking can change the script. The therapist is able to take the client through the events of that lifetime as if they were scenes from a video recording, and sometimes even switching entirely from one life to another. Most important is the experience of exiting that life by completing the death and leaving the body, which has much the same quality as a near-death experience. It frees the client from the emotional impact of the trauma of death and allows the life just lived to be reviewed from 'the other side' with greater wisdom and compassion.[15] Although critics have dismissed 'past lives' as due to cryptomnesia, some cases have stood the test of historical veracity, and there have been reported cases of xenoglossy.[16,17]

A third area of research is the out-of-body-experience. Such experiences include travelling to distant locations and gathering information that can later be corroborated, bi-location (a person manifests in one place while residing in another place or country at the time), and journeying to the realms of the *bardo*[18] or spirit world. There is a large literature on out-of-body-experiences; the painstaking work of Robert Munroe over 40 years is among the best.[19]

---

13. Fenwick & Fenwick (1995).
14. Lucas (1993).
15. Woolger (1987).
16. Xenoglossy: speaking or writing a language the person claims not to know and which could not have been acquired by natural means.
17. Stevenson (1984).
18. The after-death state: an intermediate realm prior to rebirth, according to the teachings of Tibetan Buddhism. See Evans-Wentz (1960).
19. Munroe (1994).

Fourth is the concept of reincarnation. For over 40 years Canadian-born psychiatrist Ian Stevenson compiled field research on reincarnation,[20] including cases of young children who claimed to have been a member of another family living elsewhere and to have died in traumatic circumstances. When taken to that former home, the children were able to identify members of the family and cite the family history. According to Stevenson, the location of birthmarks on a number of the children's bodies correlated with the known site of gunshot wounds on the deceased.[21]

Lastly, we have what the Church calls the 'ministry of deliverance' and what in transpersonal therapy is known as 'spirit release'. This is dealing with the problem of interference by entities that have attached to humans. The Church treats these entities as demonic; spirit release therapists are more likely to identify them as discarnate (deceased) souls in need of loving but firm guidance – when helped to let go and move on, they usually do so willingly.[22]

One further feature of the transpersonal domain I want to mention concerns 'healing'. As I reported earlier, from the quantum standpoint our physical separateness is a perceptual illusion. The bio-energy field, also known as the aura, is ubiquitous throughout Nature; we are constantly immersed in each other's energy fields.[23] This helps to make sense of how healing might work, for healers enter a subtle but distinctive (non-egoic) altered state of consciousness when they give healing without physical touch. There is evidence from more than 150 controlled studies on plants, animals and humans that healing has a significant effect in over 50% of the studies.[24] Under laboratory conditions, healers have been shown to accelerate the growth of yeast cultures, the germination of seeds and the rate of wound healing, to name but a few. Distant healing has also been researched in a randomised controlled trial of patients being treated in a coronary care unit, a study that has been subsequently replicated.[25] The group prayed for had fewer deaths, needed less intubations, ventila-

---

20. Stevenson (1966).
21. Stevenson (1997a,b).
22. See Sanderson (1998).
23. Hunt et al. (1977).
24. Benor (2001).
25. Byrd (1988), Harris et al. (1999).

tion and drugs, had less pulmonary oedema and there were fewer episodes of cardiopulmonary resuscitation.

The origin of the word 'healing' is wholeness. The effect of mental breakdown is invariably to feel shattered and the need to feel whole again is crucial to recovery.[26] Healing is mediated by empathy, a heartfelt understanding of the other and the desire to be of help. It means entering another's world with sensitivity to, and respect for, the beliefs and values of the person in need. This takes me to the importance of spirituality in the clinical setting.

Spirituality and Soul

In its broad definition, spirituality is that which makes life meaningful and purposeful. It calls for a perspective on life that goes beyond one's own small being – the ego is obliged to step out of the way. For psychiatrists inclined towards material realism and who therefore believe consciousness to be merely the product of brain activity, the empirical research correlating spirituality with mental health should nevertheless be of interest in its own right.

There is, however, a cognitive bias to overcome. Firstly, psychiatrists are not the norm they might suppose they are. Gallup polls show them to be at least twice as unbelieving of matters spiritual and religious as the general population.[27] Secondly, in the materialist culture of 'we are nothing but our genes', the focus in psychiatry is on neuroscience. Thirdly, psychiatrists, like most people, are uncomfortable with not having answers to searching questions.

Yet when psychiatrists engage their patients with open minds, and when the patient senses that the psychiatrist is genuinely concerned to help them make sense of the deepest questions of life and death, spiritual disclosures are often readily forthcoming. Being familiar with transpersonal concepts helps the psychiatrist with this. Since nothing need be ruled out as impossible, the experiences the patient brings can be worked with as authentic and meaningful.

-----

26. See *Soul Consciousness and Human Suffering*, this volume.
27. Shafranske (2000).

We cannot say anything with certainty about the nature of the soul since it is shaped by culture and belief. How it is perceived depends also on one's state of mind. In ordinary consciousness, the soul is experienced as the spiritual attribute of the self. In altered states of consciousness the soul may become permeable and unbounded, engaging with an archetypal world populated with wrathful and beatific spirits. Beyond that, and transcending the individual perspective, there is a merging with collective consciousness, in which all the joy and pain of humankind is laid bare.[28] Lastly, in mystical rapture, or *samadhi*, there is dissolution of the ego and an ensuing oneness that no words can describe.[29] This is the experience of non-duality – absorption into the Godhead.

Whether we see the soul as being on an evolutionary journey or already an essence of perfection depends on the perspective we are taking, since perception of linear time is a function of the ego. This may hold the answer to a seeming paradox. Given that we are here, embodied and in consort with time, it makes sense to envision the journey. Nevertheless, we may allow that beyond this domain of space-time, we are woven into a tapestry of cosmic simultaneities in which past, present and future are enfolded as one.

Future Directions

This paper has ranged far and wide in advancing the view that spirituality is intrinsic to life itself. Given that a person's spiritual resources are especially important in times of stress, how may we help our patients to feel able to explore their spiritual values and beliefs in the clinical setting?

This is not difficult and can be done in a simple, practical and impartial way. Here are some areas of enquiry:

- What is the patient's spiritual/religious background?
- Are spiritual/religious beliefs supportive and positive, or anxiety provoking and punitive?

---

28. Bache (2000).
29. See *The Unquiet Self*, this volume.

- What role did spirituality/religion play in childhood, and how does the patient feel about that now?
- What role does spirituality/religion play now in the patient's life?
- Is religion/spirituality drawn upon to cope with stress? In what ways?
- Is the patient a member of any religious community, and is it supportive?
- What is the patient's relationship with their clergy like?
- Are there any spiritual/religious issues the patient would like to discuss in therapy?
- Do the patient's spiritual/religious beliefs influence the type of therapy he or she would be most comfortable with?
- Do those beliefs influence how the person feels about taking medication?

Other areas of concern include distinguishing between spiritual emergency and mental illness. Not being mutually exclusive, this can be a matter of fine judgement. Then there is the important question of liaison with chaplaincy and spiritual/religious support networks, so often excluded from acute psychiatry.

In the Royal College of Psychiatrists, the Spirituality and Psychiatry Special Interest Group is submitting detailed proposals for training that we hope will be taken on board, for we are concerned to make this a major educational initiative in UK psychiatry.[30]

Putting the soul into psychiatry is not an esoteric undertaking. In the clinical setting, it means being open, interested, asking the relevant questions and letting the answers come naturally. Behind those simple enquiries lies the breath-taking story of Creation, of the birth of consciousness and of enduring spiritual values and aspirations. Psychiatrist and patient are both making their journeys through time and space, on different paths maybe, but heading in the same direction. As long as we are mindful that the journey is not the destination and that finding the right question matters more than

---

30. For a full update (2017) on the work, papers and publications of the Spirituality and Psychiatry Special Interest Group to date, see www.rcpsych.ac.uk/spirit

coming up with the right answer, we have much to learn from each other along the way.

References

Ayer, A. (1988) 'Postscript to a post-mortem'. *Spectator*, 15 October, 205–208.

Bache, C. (2000) *Dark Night, Early Dawn – Steps to an Ecology of Mind*. State University of New York Press.

Bailey, L. & Yates, J. (1996) *The Near Death Experience*. Routledge.

Benor, D. (2001) *Healing Research*. Vol. 1: Spiritual Healing: Scientific Validation of a Healing Revolution. Vision Publications.

Burtt, E.A. (1923) *The Metaphysical Foundations of Modern Physical Science: A Historical and Critical Essay*. Kegan Paul, Trench & Trubner.

Byrd, R.C. (1988) Positive therapeutic effects of intercessory prayer in coronary care unit population. *Southern Medical Journal*, 81, 826–829.

Cowen, R. (2001) When branes collide: stringing together a new theory for the origin of the universe. *Science News*, 160, 184–186.

Evans-Wentz, W.Y. (1960) *The Tibetan Book of the Dead*. Oxford University Press.

Fenwick, P. & Fenwick, E. (1995) *The Truth In The Light*. Headline.

Freud, S. (1927) The future of an illusion. Reprinted [1961] in *The Standard Edition of the Complete Psychological Works of Sigmund Freud*, vol. 21 (trans. & ed. J. Strachey). Hogarth Press.

Harris, W.S., Gowda, M., Kolb, J.W., et al. (1999) A randomised controlled trial of the effects of remote intercessory prayer on outcomes in patients admitted to the coronary care unit. *Archives of Internal Medicine*, 159, 2273–2278.

Hunt, V., Massey, W., Weinberg, R., et al. (1977) *Project Report: A Study of Structural Integration from Neuromuscular, Energy Field and Emotional Approaches*. Rolf Institute of Structural Integration.

Lucas, W.B. (1993) *Regression Therapy – A Handbook for Professionals*. Vols 1 & 2. Deep Forest Press.

Munroe, R. (1994) *Ultimate Journey*. Doubleday.

Parnia, S., Waller, D., Yeates, R., et al. (2001) A qualitative and quantitative study of the incidence, features and aetiology of near death experiences in cardiac arrest survivors. *Resuscitation*, 48, 139–156.

Powell, A. (1993) The psychophysical matrix and group analysis. *Group Analysis*, 26, 449–468.

Powell, A. (1994) Towards a unifying concept of the group matrix. In *The Psyche and the Social World* (eds D. Brown & L. Zinkin). Routledge.

Sanderson, A. (1998) Spirit releasement therapy in a case featuring depression and panic attacks. *European Journal of Clinical Hypnosis*, 4, 190–205.

Shafranske, E.P. (2000) Religious involvement and professional practices of psychiatrists and other mental health professionals. *Psychiatric Annals*, 30, 525–532.

Stevenson, I. (1966) *Twenty Cases Suggestive of Reincarnation.* University Press of Virginia.

Stevenson, I. (1984) *Unlearned Language: New Studies in Xenoglossy.* University Press of Virginia.

Stevenson, I. (1997a) *Reincarnation and Biology: A Contribution to the Etiology of Birthmarks.* Vol. 1. Praegar.

Stevenson, I. (1997b) *Birth Defects and Other Anomalies.* Vol. 2. Praegar.

Talbot, M. (1991) *The Holographic Universe.* Harper Collins.

Woolger, R. (1987) *Other Lives, Other Selves: A Jungian Psychotherapist Discovers Past Lives.* Bantam Books.

8

Good and Evil – A Psychiatrist's Perspective

Good and evil describe the best and worst in *Homo sapiens* since the species became socially evolved. The two words epitomise the judgement we make about human behaviour that defiles or upholds civilization and the values we hold most dear.

How do we reach those uncompromising and absolute judgements? Mostly by way of what we call 'right' and 'wrong', a framework of beliefs that are culturally sanctioned and that, by adulthood, are woven seamlessly into our personalities. As children they are impressed upon us first by our parents, and then by teachers and our great social institutions. We soon learn that some actions are praiseworthy and others blameworthy. Finally, the great majority of us reach a kind of endpoint when it seems we really do know what is good and what is evil.

How might a psychiatrist add to this age-old debate that has exercised the minds of so many great philosophers and theologians? For one thing, psychiatrists do sometimes have to deal with behaviour that would popularly be called evil, yet they must not call it such, and better still, must not think of it in that way. Our profession aims to enable us not only to remain objective in the face of deviant human behaviour but also to try to make sense of it from a psychological perspective, not least when so much of it appears at first sight to be inexplicably destructive.

Paper prepared for 3rd Mental Anguish and Religion Conference, 1 July 2002, Institute for Mental Health, London.

Further, when there is a serious risk of harm to self or other due to mental disorder, psychiatrists have the power to deprive an individual of their freedom under mental health legislation.[1] This is an ethical tightrope; whether someone is deemed mad, bad (or both) can be of utmost significance, not just for the patient but for family, carers and the community. We have only to look at how psychiatry was used as an instrument of the State in the former Soviet Union to see where it can lead.[2] There are occasions, however, when the psychiatrist must be prepared to intervene and to this extent the psychiatrist can never be neutral, for he or she is on the side of life.

Psychiatric Case Studies

To put in context what I want to say, I'll begin with a few brief case studies.

> Julie suffered from depression. Her childhood had been blighted by physical and sexual abuse. In adulthood, Julie's relationships were chaotic; her behaviour swung from being painfully inhibited to outbursts of aggression and sexual provocation, especially when she had been drinking.
>
> One day she came to my clinic at the hospital with a carving knife and threatened to kill me. There was no doubt she meant it. She was disarmed and put in a secure unit. Her countenance was regal, stony hard, without a shred of remorse. She said 'They can lock me away for a hundred years, I don't care'.

Julie's behaviour is not hard to understand. The consequence of her traumatic childhood was a borderline personality with impaired reality testing. When Julie became emotionally aroused, she would be flooded with scenes from childhood, not as memories to be recalled but experienced in the here-and-now of life itself. In Julie's mind, the psychiatrist had become confused with her father (technically known as a delusional transference) and in that state Julie could undoubtedly have killed.

---

1. For example, the Mental Health Act 1983 in England.
2. Bloch & Reddaway (1985).

The case illustrates the value of finding meaning in what superficially might seem incomprehensible. While Julie's behaviour cannot be said to be good, neither does it make sense to call it evil. Consider another example:

> Some years ago a male patient walking down the corridor of a psychiatric hospital suddenly took out a knife he was carrying and stabbed a social worker, who collapsed and died. It turned out this patient was psychotic and hearing voices commanding 'kill, kill' and so he did.

The psychiatric diagnosis was schizophrenia and although the causation of schizophrenia remains an enigma, we can regard the sufferer with compassion when there are so many other signs of a mind that is not in possession of itself. Far from exercising volition, the person is usually harassed mercilessly by voices and bizarre ideas that dominate their mental life. I think it is fair to put aside the intent of evil in cases such as these.

Mental illness is not always deemed to be responsible, as in this case, which I remember well from my early days in psychiatry:

> A consultant colleague and I were assessing a man in prison on remand for murder. The accused had found his wife at home with another man, who fled the house. The aggrieved husband ran into the kitchen, selected a large knife and followed his wife's lover into the street. The other man was trying to start his car to get away. Unfortunately the driver's window was down, and he was stabbed in the chest. He got the car going but died at the wheel a few hundred yards down the road.

From the psychiatric point of view, if it could be shown that the homicide had taken place while the balance of mind was disturbed, the charge would likely be reduced to manslaughter. But on questioning, this prisoner was having none of it. He and his family worked a ride in a funfair and in this small community he had been publicly shamed. Now his pride had been restored to him. 'Doctor', he said, 'there's nothing wrong with me. If it happened again, I'd do it again!'

Although we cannot condone the killing, albeit a crime of passion, most of us would not call this man evil; we can have some empathic identification with his hurt and rage. He is not so different from us, perhaps more in degree than kind. But what about the following example?

> My patient Shirley was referred because of repeated admission to hospital with abdominal pain for which no physical cause was found. When she eventually confided her history, it transpired that she had been systematically abused as a child by the next-door neighbours. The husband and wife would ply her with sweets and then 'play games', which consisted of tying up the little girl and then forcing her to have sex with them. Not until Shirley was in her teens did she finally get away.
>
> Shirley began making good progress in psychotherapy. Then she came to a session almost mute and shaking with fear. She had met this same man in the street, the first time in 10 years. He said just three words to her, 'Come with me', and like a lamb to the slaughter she followed him home where he raped her again.

It is not uncommon to find that perpetrators of abuse continue to hold such power over their victims. The anger that I felt towards the man was intense – anger, incidentally, that the patient could not feel – and to use the word evil for the abuser's behaviour may not be far off the mark. No less an exemplar than Jesus, speaking of children, said 'If anyone causes one of these little ones – those who believe in me – to stumble, it would be better for them to have a large millstone hung around their neck and to be drowned in the depths of the sea'.[3]

Take, for instance, this patient referred to me after a conviction for serial child sexual abuse:

> John had a dreadful childhood, during which he had been frequently sexually abused. He submitted to the abuse in fear and confusion but later came to enjoy it, since it offered (however perversely) a degree of intimacy.
>
> John was concerned that I should know he never did any harm to his young charges. 'They enjoy it, just like I did. It never did me any harm'. He couldn't really see what all the fuss was about. 'It's not as if I'm a bad person', he said. This man lived in a grossly impoverished mental world. All his emotions were centred on his compulsive paedophile activities, for the only relationships he could form were with children, tracking them down, grooming them and then seducing them, one after another.

---

3. Matthew 18:6. *The Holy Bible*, NIV.

Just a handful of cases such as these serves to show why a term like evil, at first sight so seemingly self-evident, begins to break down into complex subsets of meaning once the motives become intelligible. It also explains why people who commit murder may not see themselves as bad – the end is felt to have justified the means.

I remember the forensic psychotherapist Dr Murray Cox speaking of a man he had been seeing in Broadmoor.[4] When the patient was asked why he had killed, the answer came right back, 'I took a life because I needed one'.[5] This can be understood as a concrete, psychotic statement having a certain logic to it. Another serial killer would cut open the abdomens of his victims in order to put his hands into the warm viscera. He explained that it was the only time he could feel close to another human being.

Sometimes we find a split in the psyche so that the same person who kills can go home and be a loving parent, husband or wife. Such dissociation may be partial or complete, as in this case of multiple personality (dissociative identity disorder)[6] referred to me:

> Jean was being assessed for psychotherapy. She was desperate for help, since an 'alter' personality would take over during 'absences' and create havoc. Jean had been told that this alter, named Sylvie, was very aggressive. Sylvie came through during the assessment interview and had only one thing to say, which she put very bluntly. If anyone gave Jean psychotherapy to stop Sylvie, Sylvie would kill the therapist, because she had no intention of being got rid of.
>
> The problem was reported to Jean, who was also concerned about the danger, and supportive therapy was arranged, the aim of which would be to see whether Jean and Sylvie might learn to co-habit with less disruption.

Again, what might have otherwise looked like senseless violence turned out to have a motive – in this case the fear of being annihilated. To kill or be killed is one of the most basic of human survival reactions.

---

4. Broadmoor Special Hospital, a high-security psychiatric hospital for criminal offenders in the UK.
5. Cox (1982).
6. First made famous by novelist Robert Louis Stevenson (1886) in *The Strange Case of Dr Jekyll and Mr Hyde*.

In the comfort and security that many of us enjoy, it is easy to imagine we would be beyond such primitive behaviour, although we can be surprised at ourselves! In 1981, rioting broke out in the neighbourhood of Brixton, London. At the time, I was living nearby and from my garden I could see the billowing smoke and flames. The air reverberated with angry shouts, screams and police sirens. On the radio, I heard that rioters were massing and were heading for the road where I lived. In a split second, everything changed. I rushed about the house looking for a weapon to defend my home and young family. I found an axe and waited inside the front door, prepared for the worst. Fortunately, I waited in vain, since the rioters took a different route. Nevertheless, it was a great lesson to me. I had been accustomed to regarding myself as a tolerant, liberal-minded psychiatrist, and within a few minutes I had turned into someone prepared for extreme violence.

How easily we shed our capacity for dispassionate concern when we ourselves feel threatened! I once asked Dr Cox how he was able to work as a psychotherapist with convicted child murderers only a few miles from where he and his young family lived. He said without hesitation, 'Because there is a 15-foot high wall around Broadmoor!'

Psychiatrists inevitably have to deal with people who have become a law unto themselves, either because of mental illness or 'personality disorder'. The diagnosis of personality disorder can have prognostic value as well as suggesting particular therapeutic approaches. Yet such a diagnosis is as much social and political as it is medical, for it sets human conduct against moral judgements about what constitutes mature, civilised behaviour. We should remember that the 19th-century definition of psychopathy was moral insanity. Psychiatry still bears the burden of that definition to this day. Many psychiatrists are appalled by the new draft mental health bill being currently debated in parliament that will compel people diagnosed with personality disorder who are considered potentially dangerous, yet who have committed no crime, to be treated and even detained against their will.[7]

---

7. The subsequent 2007 amendment to the Mental Health Act of 1983 now provides for Community Treatment Orders when deemed necessary. If treatment is refused, a patient can be compulsorily recalled to hospital.

In summary, I am suggesting that:

1. Evil as a moral concept has to be set aside in the assessment and treatment of mental disorder, including personality disorder.
2. This is not to deny that evil exists and that evil people may be suffering from mental disorder.
3. Where mental disorder is diagnosed, the focus of the psychiatrist must always be therapeutic. Risk assessment requires that dangerous or destructive behaviour is objectively evaluated, but this can be done without moral censure.

Mass Killing

In contrast to murder, defined as the unlawful premeditated killing of a human being by another and generally punishable by a life sentence or death, killing in war is legitimized and even rewarded. There is not much point in treating war as psychopathological, since in war the whole nation is identified with the norm of killing. None the less, the psychology of our extraordinary destructiveness as a species deserves to be examined.

It has been said that if you give a person a gun, that person may kill dozens, but if you give a person an ideology, that person may kill countless thousands. The 20th century has seen more bloodshed than in all the previous history of mankind. Eight million people died in the First World War. In the Second World War, the loss of life was ten times greater.

In the passage that follows, we find a terrible perversion of the 'will to power'.[8] Nietzsche may have proclaimed that 'God is dead' but the Third Reich found in Hitler a new god.

> 'Only when the time comes when the race is no longer overshadowed by the consciousness of its own guilt, then it will find internal peace and external energy to cut down regardlessly and brutally the wild shoots and to pull up the weeds. Conscience is a Jewish invention. It is a blemish like circumcision'.

> *Excerpt from Mein Kampf by Adolf Hitler*[9]

---

8. Nietzsche (2012).
9. Quoted in McIntosh (1999: 32).

Psychoanalytically speaking, such manic omnipotence is based on the paranoid defences of splitting and projection. All that is most painful to recognise and own about the self (individual and collective) is split off and projected into the other, in this case the Jews, who became the epitome of everything evil – what psychoanalysts call 'the bad object'. Then the 'true' German nation, now free of its contamination, could be experienced as virtuous, heroic and free from guilt.

Yet when the split is operating at a societal level, every nation justifies its own actions as necessary. Take, for example, Sir Arthur Harris Travers (Bomber Harris, as he was known), who in response to the Blitz on London ordered the firebombing of Cologne. It was the beginning of a strategy of carpet-bombing that culminated in 1945 in the destruction of Dresden, with the death in one night of over 135,000 civilians. Harris was subsequently decorated with the Knight Grand Cross of the Bath. In Germany to this day, many hold him accountable for war crimes against humanity.

Genocide

The term 'genocide' was adopted by the United Nations General Assembly in 1948 and is defined as the crime of destroying, or committing conspiracy to destroy, a national, ethnic, racial, or religious group.

Examples of genocide in recent history include the massacre of 300,000 Chinese in Nanking by the Japanese in 1937, the death of over 1 million in the Gulag under Stalin's reign of terror, the murder of some 6 million in the Holocaust, over 30 million deaths in China during the Chairmanship of Mao Zedong, the deliberate starvation that killed more than 1 million in the Nigerian–Biafran war of 1969, the slaughter of 300,000 Ugandans by Idi Amin during the 1970s, the massacre of around 3 million Cambodians by the Khmer Rouge, the Iran–Iraq war in the 1980s, which saw the use of nerve gas and in which 1 million died, and the Rwandan civil war of 1994, with 500,000 deaths. Closer to home, we have seen the Balkans war, with ethnic cleansing resulting in over 150,000 deaths and more than 3 million refugees.

The danger in talking about genocide is that it allows decent folk to distance themselves from these 'crimes against humanity'. But where does war end and genocide begin? We in the democratic West are implicated in millions more deaths. The Korean War is a case in point. By 1953, 8 years after the partitioning of Korea by the United States and the USSR, the USA and 19 other nations, including Britain, were supposedly defending South Korea against communist North Korea. Three years on, the death toll had risen to 3 million and the war ended in stalemate. Vietnam was another casualty of ideology, with 2 million Vietnamese killed, a further 3 million wounded and with 12 million refugees.

Nor can we in the West wash our hands of the Arab–Israeli conflict. When the United Nations divided Palestine, which had been under the British mandate, into a Jewish state and an Arab state, the Arab–Israeli war of 1948 that immediately followed resulted in 750,000 Palestinian refugees.

Last and not least, what kind of moral responsibility should Britain take for the Indo-Pakistani crisis? This goes back to 1947, when the Raj was disintegrating in the face of internal dissent. When Britain partitioned India, creating the Muslim state of Pakistan, both sides claimed Kashmir, as Mahatma Gandhi had predicted. Three wars have already been fought over Kashmir and now that both states have nuclear weapons, any future war could be catastrophic.

These brief excursions into history may seem a long way from psychiatry, and perhaps they are. But I am attempting to show that the moral fine-tuning we indulge in, making distinctions between war, genocide, culpable homicide and legitimate self-defence, are as nothing compared with the disastrous psychology of a species that defines itself by means of nationhood and territorial greed, the consequence of which has been the death of over 150 million of its own kind in less than one century.

The Endpoint of Indifference

To habitually kill, or to be party to such killing, requires a total detachment from those being killed, as if disposing of an inferior species. Not only did the SS guards at Auschwitz rapidly become inured to extermination, but the Jewish *kapos*, who were told that their lives would be spared if they cleaned up the gas chambers, had no choice but to do the same or they would go mad with horror. A chilling indifference sets in, a state somewhere between life and death. T.S. Eliot puts it this way:

> 'There are three conditions which often look alike
> Yet differ completely, flourish in the same hedgerow:
> Attachment to self and to things and to persons, detachment
> From self and from things and from persons; and growing between them, indifference
> Which resembles the others as death resembles life,
> Being between two lives – unflowering, between
> The live and the dead nettle.'
>
> *From Little Gidding (1944)*[10]

Indifference is found when the psychopathology has become habitually and completely split-off and disowned.[11] So let us look at what lies behind this terrible mask, for even the most monstrous Nazi was once a child like any other.[12]

The Psychological Origins of Love and Hate

The infant is born with an innate capacity for responsiveness, for harmonious interchange and contentment. Provided its needs are met, the infant's incipient sense of wholeness is characterised by a delight in its own being. We see a happy and contented child.

Yet to be subject to the flesh also means to know suffering, as the Buddha pointed out, and from day one the infant has to contend with bodily processes that will bring distress, even in the best of families. At such moments, the pristine psyche of the infant is

---

10.   Eliot (1944: 40).
11.   As in the case of Franz Stangl, commandant of Treblinka death camp. See *Psychosocial Implications of the Shadow*, this volume.
12.   Adshead (2002).

overwhelmed by painful arousal and the intrinsic biology of the fight/flight reaction takes over. Since there is nowhere to fly, the fight mentality kicks in. Consequently, the breast-feeding scenario can be one of bliss or torture, for the nipple can become in turn the object of love and hate.

These two contrasting experiences, of joy, our spiritual birthright, and suffering, unwelcome companion to the embodied self, will be re-visited by the growing child over the coming years in a thousand different ways. Two very different outcomes are possible. When the child's caregivers sustain it with love, the capacity for joy becomes 'object-related'; the child learns the meaning of trust and love for others. At the same time, it discovers that anger is not a catastrophe but an emotion that can be contained, or channelled positively. A capacity for healthy ambivalence develops, so that conflicting emotions can be managed and digested without the uncontrollable impulse to action. The child learns to show empathy, as it imaginatively identifies with the feeling states of others, and a growing capacity for generosity and gratitude reflects its pleasure in a sense of wholeness of self.

On the other hand, when a child is repeatedly overwhelmed by anger or fear, the effect is a shattering of the stability and coherence of its inner world. The child survives by encapsulating and splitting off these emotions from consciousness. When such uncontained emotions do surface, they get projected outwards, on to others, individually or collectively, as described in the case of the Nazis' hatred of the Jews. A person can feel righteous (note how Hitler, in *Mein Kampf*, disposes of conscience) since the blame lies elsewhere.

This dynamic of victimisation arises when the shadow aspect of the self is denied.[13] Healthy integration of the psyche would mean owning one's shadow instead of projecting it, but instead a perverse restitution of the self is attempted. The wisdom saying of Jesus, 'Do to others as you would have them do to you'[14] translates into, 'As others have done to you, now do the same to them'. Revenge is intoxicating, and the wounded self exults in triumph over the other. This is

---

13. Jung (1948).
14. Luke 6:31. *The Holy Bible*, NIV.

the psychology of hate. Using terms like 'axis of evil' makes it possible to dehumanise the other while letting it be known that one's own self is innocent and good. It is the ultimate statement of otherness, of 'not me'. Indeed, the commonplace use of words like terrorism spares us from seeing the world through the eyes of our adversaries.[15]

There is a whole range of psychological defence mechanisms that bring about this detachment of self from other in the struggle for personal survival. Depending on the nature of the threat, they have evolved for the purpose of conferring protection on self, family, clan, community and country.[16] Such ego-driven defences secure only a temporary reprieve. Attack inevitably leads to counter-attack and domination is followed by rebellion, a cycle that frequently escalates, since the original grievance is soon supplanted by a host of further injustices.

Fortunately, the psychology of hate is more or less balanced by the psychology of love, or else the human species would not have survived this far. In contrast to the primitive defences of splitting and projection, there is a more benign development by way of what has been called 'the depressive position'[17] or 'the stage of concern'.[18] During childhood we develop the capacity to see that those we sometimes hate are also those we at other times love. Then there is concern for the love object that has been under attack, a capacity for healthy guilt and remorse develops and with it, the desire to make reparation. More mature and resilient relationships can develop, based on trust and goodwill.

---

15. Attitudes have further hardened in the West with the destruction being wrought by ISIL (Islamic State of Iraq and the Levant) and the carnage of ongoing sectarian war throughout much of the Middle East.
16. See *Psychosocial Implications of the Shadow*, this volume.
17. Klein (1957).
18. Winnicott (1963).

In summary, I would conclude from this second part of the discussion that:

1. Evil is destructiveness that arises from the impact of pain, a retaliatory strike that has its roots in unconscious processes.
2. Evil is the consequence of the primitive defence mechanisms of denial, splitting and projection that are self-serving and ruthless.
3. The pleasure derived from the act of evil is based on triumph over the other – the hapless recipient of the unacknowledged projections.
4. Relinquishing these primitive mechanisms is an urgent evolutionary challenge, one on which our survival as a species depends. This can be achieved only through the action of love, which recognises and forgives the imperfections of both self and other and which leads to the realisation that ultimately 'All is One'.

Good and Evil as Religious/Spiritual Concepts

The major religions abstract *evil* and *good* from their circumstances and treat them conceptually as standing in opposition. That this should have happened is not surprising since they are primordial archetypes configuring human consciousness. Eating of the tree of knowledge of good and evil is in the blueprint for *Homo sapiens* and our minds have been perfectly designed to put us through this most exhaustive test.

The faith traditions of the East and West offer different ways of going about it. The Pauline view, which became the established Christian doctrine, is that God incarnated only in the person of Christ, and therefore only through Christ can Man be redeemed. As to the nature of good and evil, St. Augustine argued that since God must be good, the cause of evil has to be found in the free will of human beings, which entitles them if they so wish to turn away from God. Evil is therefore the absence of good. How could God permit such a thing? Since it is in the nature of goodness to give of itself, says St. Augustine, and since God is infinite, this must include the possibility of self-negation.

This conjures up a world divided against itself, battle lines drawn between the powers of light and darkness, one in which for there to be a heaven there must also be a hell.

The early Christian Gnostics believed that Christ, the divine spirit, inhabited the body of the man Jesus and that the same divine spirit lies within every human soul. They saw no need for Christ to atone for the sins of the world, nor for a physical resurrection, since the spirit is eternal. Christ was revered as the preeminent wisdom teacher, there to guide every human being who sets out on his or her spiritual journey. This is closer to the Buddhist view of (karmic) self-determination. It also held a powerful appeal for Carl Jung, who saw in the problem of good and evil the greatest opportunity for achieving wholeness of the self by means of healing the split in the psyche.[19] He called this process individuation. Jung held that transcending the ego and discovering the totality of the greater Self in its collective as well as personal meaning holds the key to the transformation of human consciousness.

Jung drew notably on the ancient Chinese teachings of the Dao,[20] in which the Universe, physical and spiritual, is maintained through a perfect balance of nature's energies, described as *yin* and *yang* and illustrated by the symbol of *Taiji* (below).[21] This is no ordinary duality, for *yin* and *yang* 'create, contain and restrain each other. Neither possesses any quality or identity save as the complement of the other'.[22] Such duality holds true at every level, from the balance of the masculine and feminine in the human psyche to the cosmic cycles of creation and destruction of the physical universe.

8.1 Duality (form) arising from the non-dual (formless).

---

19. Jung (1939).
20. Dao and Tao are used interchangeably, as also are Laozi and Lao Tsu, and *Daodejing* and *Tao Te Ching*.
21. Guo & Powell (2001). See also *The Unquiet Self*, this volume.
22. Rose (1999: 85).

The circle that begets *yin* and *yang* is the universal symbol for undifferentiated totality, which in the Daoist tradition is called *Wuji*. In Sanskrit it is known as the mandala.[23] In the Gnostic tradition, too, God is represented by the circle that has no circumference and whose centre is everywhere.

According to Jung's psycho-spiritual formulations,[24] the transformation of the psyche can only be achieved through the acknowledgement and integration of opposites. The dark is as necessary to the light as the light is to the dark. Further, within *yang* is to be found the seed of *yin* and within the *yin*, the seed of *yang* – the dark is always in the light and the light in the dark. The Daoist view is that what we call evil (seen as an entirely human construct) is really a misnomer for the disharmony that arises when *yin* and *yang* are out of balance. The art is to remain supple, unresisting and aligned with the flow of Nature. Two and a half millennia ago, Lao Tsu, the great Daoist sage, wrote:

'A man is born gentle and weak
At his death he is hard and stiff.
Green plants are tender and filled with sap.
At their death they are withered and dry.
Therefore the stiff and unbending is the disciple of death.
The gentle and yielding is the disciple of life…'

Lao Tsu, Tao Te Ching[25]

The Axis of Good and Evil

The striving of the human ego has been a driving force in the evolution of the species, enabling the development of will and personal identity. Unfortunately, the drive to be 'top dog' has engendered a social psychology fixated on blame, in which the collective shadow is projected into 'otherness' – whether ethnic, racial, cultural or national – where it can be fought with counter-ideology and, if needed, with guns and bombs. This kind of behaviour has had its uses in the earlier

---

23. See *Spirituality, Healing and the Mind*, this volume.
24. Jung (1935).
25. Feng & English (1973).

tribal history of humanity but now threatens to destroy the world. How else might evil be managed? Jung says by learning to observe the shadow within, knowing it for what it is and acknowledging its existence in every human being. In standing back from it, there is no compulsion to identify with it; then one does not have to act it out. On the contrary, when acknowledged, the shadow is a great teacher, since it puts us all on a level as human beings, with much to learn, including humility.

Before the language of psychology (viz. projection) had been invented, Jesus made the same point in these words: 'How can you say to your brother, "Brother, let me take the speck out of your eye", when you yourself fail to see the plank in your own eye?'[26] Our endeavours are more likely to bear fruit when we stop telling others what is good for them and concentrate on setting a good example.

The teachings of Jesus are deeply counter-intuitive. 'But I tell you, do not resist an evil person. If anyone slaps you on the right cheek, turn to them the other cheek also. [...] Love your enemies and pray for those who persecute you'.[27] From the Gnostic perspective, we each become the Christ to the extent we genuinely find this humility and compassion within us.

Buddhists, for whom non-violence is a precept, undertake the spiritual practice of Tonglen, in which the anger, fear, pain and hatred of others is breathed in and love is breathed out and offered in return.[28] All great spiritual teachings are based on humility; they help us to see the same flaws in ourselves that reflect our common humanity. 'Like me, like me!' says the Buddhist under his breath when encountering the 'evil' in another.

I am of the view that the challenge of evil is a necessary spur to the spiritual evolution of humankind. The emotions of childhood first awaken us to a duality in which love is the goodness and hatred is the evil. Before long, our ego instincts come to equate goodness with personal survival, and evil with the threat to life. Yet if we stop there, in a world centred only on self-survival, we turn our backs on the spiritual universe, one that invites us to break free of the confines of the ego and find *self in other*. When we do transcend the ego's

---

26. Luke 6:42. *The Holy Bible*, NIV.
27. Matthew 5:39, 44. *The Holy Bible*, NIV.
28. Rinpoche (1992).

preoccupation with itself, we find the most extraordinary thing: awaiting us, beyond the duality of good and evil, is perfect peace.

References

Adshead, G. (2002) *Capacities and Dispositions: Reflections on Good and Evil from a Forensic Psychiatrist.* Available at: http://www.rcpsych.ac.uk/spsigarchive

Bloch, S. & Reddaway, P. (1985) *Soviet Psychiatric Abuse: The Shadow over World Psychiatry.* Westview Press.

Cox, M. (1982) I took a life because I needed one: psychotherapeutic possibilities with the schizophrenic-offender patient. *Psychotherapy and Psychosomatics, 37,* 96–105.

Eliot, T.S. (1944) *Four Quartets.* Reprinted [1999], Faber and Faber.

Feng, G.F. & English, J. (trans.) (1973) *Lao Tsu: Tao Te Ching.* Wildwood House.

Guo, B. & Powell, A. (2001) *Listen to Your Body: The Wisdom of the Dao.* University of Hawaii Press.

Jung, C. (1935) Psychology and alchemy. Reprinted [1953] in *C.G. Jung: The Collected Works,* vol. 12 (eds H. Read, M. Fordham & G. Adler). Routledge and Kegan Paul.

Jung, C. (1939) Conscious, unconscious and individuation [and] a study in the process of individuation. Reprinted [1959] in *C.G. Jung: The Collected Works,* vol. 9, part 1: The Archetypes And The Collective Unconscious (eds H. Read, M. Fordham & G. Adler). Routledge and Kegan Paul.

Jung, C.G. (1948) The Shadow. Reprinted [1959] in *C.G. Jung: The Collected Works,* vol. 9, part 2: Aion (eds H. Read, M. Fordham & G. Adler). Routledge and Kegan Paul.

Klein, M. (1957) *Contributions to Psycho-analysis.* Hogarth Press.

McIntosh, W. (1999) Compelling vice. *Parabola,* 24, 29–34.

Nietzche, F. (2012) *Beyond Good and Evil.* Spastic Cat Press.

Rose, K. (1999) Have no twisty thoughts. *Parabola,* 24, 81–86.

Rinpoche, S. (1992) *The Tibetan Book of Living and Dying.* Rider.

Stevenson, R.L. (1886) *The Strange Case of Dr Jekyll and Mr Hyde.* Reprinted [2013], Usborne Publishing.

Winnicott, D.W. (1963) The development of the capacity for concern. In *The Maturational Processes and the Facilitating Environment.* Hogarth Press.

9

Mental Health and Spirituality

The historical divide between religion and science has had profound implications for the world we live in, culminating in a 20th-century culture modelled on a Newtonian mechanistic paradigm of reality. Yet there need be no such enduring split, for advances in quantum physics, which are profoundly changing our thinking about the universe and the nature of reality, bring an opportunity to reconcile science and spirituality in ways that could not have been imagined 100 years ago.[1]

In this climate of change, and with the millennium fast approaching, a Spirituality and Psychiatry Special Interest Group was established at the Royal College of Psychiatrists.[2] In launching the group, I had been inspired by the work of the late David Larson, a leading American psychiatrist in the field of health and spirituality. In the USA, with the support of the John Templeton Foundation, modules on spirituality have been introduced in over a hundred medical schools. In this country we have just one to date, pioneered by John Swinton at Aberdeen University.[3] Swinton's work has been groundbreaking in the UK and the Special Interest Group strongly supports this kind of development in the medical undergraduate curriculum.[4]

Paper prepared for the College of Psychic Studies, London, 27 September 2002.

---

1. Powell (1993, 1994).
2. Since the Special Interest Group was founded in 1999, the membership has grown to over 3000 psychiatrists. See www.rcpsych.ac.uk/spirit
3. Swinton (2001).
4. Progress in the UK since 2001 has been slow and medical schools have not followed the example set by American universities. See Harbinson & Bell (2015).

Our primary aim is to support teaching on spirituality and mental health for psychiatrists in the UK. Psychiatrists are not given guidance about how to handle spiritual matters when they arise in the consultation, and because they feel unskilled, the tendency is to gloss over such matters. Yet we know from service user surveys that many people going through acute mental distress turn to their spiritual and religious beliefs to help them cope.[5]

The Context of Mental Illness

The scale of the global challenge posed by mental illness has been highlighted by several studies.[6] About one adult in ten is affected (450 million worldwide) accounting for over 12% of the global burden of disease and rising. In Europe and the Americas, the burden of mental illness is over 40% of the total burden of disability.[7] What can this epidemic mean?

Psychiatry, the study and treatment of mental illness, has developed in the West as a specialty of medicine. Like most of Western medicine, it is wedded to the paradigm of the body as a marvellous kind of machine under the direction of the brain. The neural activity of the brain is thought to generate consciousness, while emotional stresses have their impact by directly influencing brain chemistry. Since all mental function is considered a product of brain chemistry, it follows that what we call the mind must be produced by the brain.

Such a view has no place for the metaphysical soul: before each of us was born, there was nothing, and when we die, consciousness is snuffed out forever. This does not preclude a spirituality based on the desire to do good and to act with compassion. However, the mechanistic world-view sees each human being as a little ant, wandering onto a gigantic stage set. Who or what created the stage set is a puzzle for which the culture of modern science has no answer.

The greatest minds have always known better than to be limited by such material realism. For instance, Isaac Newton himself

---

5. Faulkner (1997).
6. Desjarlais et al. (1995), Murray & Lopez (1996), WHO (2001).
7. WHO (2001).

described his method as mystical intuition, or insight into implicate truth, which he then validated using mathematics. Newton asserted Truth to be the offspring of silence and unbroken meditation. To his way of thinking, there was no schism between the spiritual and physical universe since he believed that the physical world had been created by, and was a profound testimony to, the hand of God. René Descartes, who has been unjustly accused of being a materialist, had an equally deep belief in the workings of the Divine.[8]

The physicalist interpretation of the universe according to science is not wrong. The error is to mistake the part for the whole. Science is simply a tool, a means of gathering certain kinds of knowledge according to the capacity and limitations of the instruments used. Unfortunately, as spiritual values have receded under the onslaught of consumer-led materialism, scientific technology has become the new god – a god that always tantalises and never fulfils.

Take, for example, the extraordinary statistic of mental illness contributing 40% of the burden of disability in Europe and the Americas. When for so many people the established faiths seem to be divorced from the reality of daily life, is it surprising that they should take their loss of meaning and purpose to the psychiatrist's consulting room? To treat every situational crisis as a spiritual one would be misguided. Yet beneath the difficulties relating to partners, parents, families, children and the workplace, there is often a painful lack of, and searching for, core spiritual values. Sometimes it takes a breakdown to find them.

It is a fact that the majority of people coping with mental disorder do turn to their spiritual and religious beliefs to help them pull through. For instance, in one survey of psychiatric patients, over half went to religious services and prayed daily, and over 80% felt that their spiritual beliefs had a positive impact on their illness, providing comfort and the feeling of being cared for and not alone. Yet over one-third of them did not feel able to discuss such matters with their psychiatrists.[9] Perhaps their intuition was correct, for other research shows that whereas in the general population over 80% have belief in God or a higher power, around only a third of psychiatrists and

---

8. See Agostini (2015) and Cottingham et al. (1985: 205).
9. Lindgren & Coursey (1995).

psychologists hold such beliefs.[10] The danger here is that psychiatrists may think they represent the norm.

Empirical Research Into Spirituality and Health

Health, according to the Constitution of the World Health Organization, is 'a state of complete physical, mental and social well-being [...] not merely the absence of disease [...]'.[11] The WHO also states:

> '[The] health professions have largely followed a medical model, which seeks to treat patients by focusing on medicines and surgery, and gives less importance to beliefs and to faith – in healing, in the physician and in the doctor–patient relationship. This reductionism or mechanistic view of patients as being only a material body is no longer satisfactory. Patients and physicians have begun to realise the value of elements such as faith, hope and compassion in the healing process'.[12]

The healing process applies to mental and physical afflictions alike. In 2001, *The Handbook of Religion and Health* was published.[13] This was the culmination of a decade's work investigating the relationship between religion/spirituality and a wide range of physical and mental health conditions, covering more than 1200 studies and 400 research reviews. A 60–80% correlation between religion/spirituality and better health was found in the areas of prevention, recovery and coping ability in a wide range of conditions, including high blood pressure, cerebrovascular disease, heart disease (including substantially increased survival in the elderly after heart surgery), immune system dysfunction (increased survival time in AIDS patients), improved coping with cancer (in one study, 93% of cancer patients said that their religious lives helped sustain their hopes), in living with pain

---

10.   Bergin & Jensen (1990).
11.   Preamble to the Constitution of WHO as adopted by the International Health Conference, New York, 19 June – 22 July 1946; signed on 22 July 1946 by the representatives of 61 States (Official Records of WHO, no. 2, p. 100) and entered into force on 7 April 1948.
12.   WHO (1998).
13.   Koenig et al. (2001).

and disability, and in smoking prevention. Not least, there is a striking correlation with longevity. One longitudinal study of over 21,000 US adults has shown that after controlling for other factors, attending religious services more than once-weekly increased the lifespan by an average of 7 years for Whites and 14 years for African Americans.[14]

Many of these areas of research have been based on standard research methodology, using controlled trials and statistical data analysis. A good example has been the effect of intercessory prayer on patients in intensive care units, a double-blind trial that yielded a statistically significant result in which the prayed-for group of patients recovered with fewer complications.[15]

Cure vs. Healing

It is gratifying to find such positive correlations between spirituality and health. However, they overlie a deeper conceptual issue concerning spirituality in medicine. I referred earlier to the paradigm of the body as a machine. This derives from the concept of the universe as mechanical – a world-view that began 300 years ago and still holds sway. It is true that when bodily functions break down, symptom clusters emerge that indicate the dysfunction of component parts, rather like a car engine developing a fault. The notion of cure comes from this way of thinking, and in some cases is readily applicable. Surgical interventions fit the model best – an arthritic hip can be replaced, the aorta patched, a liver transplanted. All of this nicely fits with the 'disease model'. Less successful is the application of the disease model to psychiatry. While neurological, genetic or other biological factors are responsible for a minority of disorders, most mental distress has more to do with the problem of being human than with any underlying physical causation. Yet the search for cure continues unabated, with research almost all focused on biological causation.

In general, Western medicine holds to the view that its limitations will be overcome as our knowledge of the workings of the body steadily improves. For instance, with chemotherapy many cases of

14.   Hummer et al. (1999).
15.   Byrd (1988), Harris et al. (1999).

childhood leukaemia can be cured. Yet it has to be admitted that in adulthood, and increasingly with the passing years, most diseases resist cure. Drug treatments generally have side-effects and a metal hip joint is not the same as one made of bone. Yet the word 'cure' has a magical ring to it, often used to depict an idealisation of health, a magic wand to wave, in a culture that believes fearfully that life ends with death. Accordingly, all kinds of heroic medical interventions are sanctioned, hence the quip 'the operation was successful but the patient died'. This uncomfortably reminds us that there is always a person who is suffering from the cancer, the arthritis or the liver failure. The person is not the disease, just as the driver is not the car.

When we talk of illness as opposed to disease, we are describing the response of that person to a disease process, a response that varies enormously according to temperament, circumstance and the emotional attitude held by the individual. Take the avoidance of pain, for example, widely fostered by pharmaceutical companies promoting popular analgesics. Rather than 'attacking' the headache with a pain-killer, it would be better to ask oneself why the headache has come on. Often it is due to fatigue or stress, an urgent plea by the body for rest.[16] In such cases, responding to this plea will relieve the symptom and although it may take a little longer, instead of symptom suppression, the body has been encouraged to heal.

The essential point to make about healing is that the process concerns wholeness (the root of the word 'wholeness' comes from *hal*, *hel*, or *heil* in Saxon, High German or Old Norse, meaning health or healing).[17] This calls for a different focus – moving from the mechanistic viewpoint to a holistic approach that sees the self as arising from an intimate relationship of mind, body and spirit. Nor can the self be taken in isolation, for it has to be understood as a social reality too, one that delineates each person in a matrix of relationships.

From the holistic perspective, the term disease is best used to mean *dis*-ease,[18] a lack of harmony or balance within the human being. Healing, therefore, has to address the whole organism, from intracellular structures through to organ-specific functions.

---

16.   Guo & Powell (2001).
17.   See *Soul Consciousness and Human Suffering*, this volume.
18.   The etymology of 'disease' is Old French *desaise*, meaning 'lack of ease'.

Holism and Research

I want to highlight the field of psychoneuroimmunology since it promises a revolution in medicine over the next 100 years.[19] For example, research has shown that stress depresses immune function, whereas a person's religious/spiritual beliefs will protect it. Recent laboratory findings include:

- A rise in salivary IgA levels (a marker of immune function) in students watching a film about Mother Teresa, compared with students watching a war film.[20]
- The levels of serum interleukin-6 (IL-6, a powerful mediator of the inflammatory response) in subjects regularly attending religious services is nearly 50% lower than in non-attendees.[21]
- In a study on HIV-positive gay men, spiritual and religious practices and beliefs were associated with higher CD4+ cell counts (active in up-regulating the immune response) than in the control group. On the other hand, high stress levels increase the progression of the disease fourfold.[22]
- In a study of women with breast cancer, the importance of religious or spiritual expression correlated positively with natural killer cell numbers (active against tumours and infective microbes), T-helper cell counts and total lymphocyte activity.[23]

In clinical practice, stress has been shown to be linked with the occurrence of respiratory infections, influenza, herpes virus,[24] delayed wound healing,[25] psoriasis, overactive thyroid function, diabetes, rheumatoid arthritis and relapse in multiple sclerosis.[26] In the mental health field, where stress is common to every kind of breakdown, the extraordinary protective effects of religion and spirituality

---

19. Koenig & Cohen (2002a).
20. McClelland (1988).
21. Koenig et al. (1997).
22. Woods et al. (1999).
23. Schaal et al. (1998).
24. Cohen (2002).
25. Koenig & Cohen (2002b).
26. Koenig & Cohen (2002c).

are now just beginning to be recognised. For example, as Larson & Larson[27] describe:

1. DEPRESSION: overall, some 25% of women and 12% of men suffer major depressive disorder during their lifetime. However, people with a spiritual or religious affiliation are up to 40% less likely to get depressed than those who do not have such an affiliation. Further, when they do get depressed, they recover faster. Where psychotherapy is offered, those receiving religiously orientated therapy sensitive to their religious beliefs score best on post-treatment measures.[28]

2. DEPRESSION AMONG THE MEDICALLY SERIOUSLY ILL: depression affects up to 35% of this group of patients. One study using multi-dimensional measures showed that for every 10-point increase in the intrinsic religion score, there was a 70% increase in the speed of remission from depression,[29] while another study has shown that the more severe the disability, the stronger the protective effect of religious commitment.[30]

3. SUICIDE: adults aged over 50 who have never participated in religious activities are four times more likely to die by suicide than those who do. This holds true after having adjusted for other variables.[31] Religious commitment among teenagers significantly reduces the risk of suicide.[32]

4. SUBSTANCE ABUSE: religious/spiritual commitment correlates with lower levels of substance abuse – the risk of alcohol dependency is 60% greater when there is no religious affiliation.[33] In one study of opiate withdrawal, 45% of participants in a religiously orientated programme remained drug-free at one year compared with 5% in a non-religious treatment programme.[34] Concerning alcohol abuse, those who seek help from Alcoholics Anonymous, which is spiritually orientated and invokes the help of a Higher Power, are most likely to remain abstinent after inpatient or outpatient treatment.[35]

27. Larson & Larson (2001).
28. McCullough & Larson (1999).
29. Koenig et al. (1998).
30. Koenig et al. (1995).
31. Nisbet et al. (2000).
32. Stein et al. (1992).
33. Miller (1998).
34. Desmond & Maddox (1981).
35. Montgomery et al. (1995).

Studies such as these tell us that there is far more to the pathogenesis of mental illness than can ever be accounted for by the biological sciences.

Diagnostic Considerations

Although most mental illnesses have no identifiable organic basis, in the expectation that perhaps one day the cause will be pinpointed, we have an immensely complex system of diagnosis, which is firmly rooted in medicine. The diagnostic manual used worldwide since 1992 is the ICD-10.[36] First published in the 1960s, ICD has been refined many times since.

Even though the underlying pathology may not be understood, reaching a diagnosis is important when it reliably indicates the prognosis and points to an appropriate tried and tested treatment.[37] The two most severe mental illnesses, schizophrenia and bipolar disorder, are widely managed with medication. Misdiagnosis can lead to tragic outcomes in both conditions and making the diagnosis based on a clear operational definition is important. Yet this indebtedness to the medical model raises as many problems as it solves. Take the following category listed in ICD-10: F23.0, acute polymorphic psychotic disorder without symptoms of schizophrenia. To quote:

'[...] hallucinations, delusions and perceptual disturbances are obvious but markedly variable, changing form day to day or even from hour to hour. Emotional turmoil, with intense transient feelings of happiness and ecstasy or anxieties and irritability, is also frequently present. [...] This disorder is particularly likely to have an abrupt onset [...] and a rapid resolution of symptoms; in a large proportion of cases there is no obvious precipitating stress'.

Compare this with schizophrenia (F20) and we find that the picture is much the same except that for schizophrenia, symptoms have to

---

36.   *The International Classification of Diseases*, a standardized diagnostic tool published by the World Health Organization. The tenth edition was published in 1992.

37.   The danger is that ICD-based diagnoses continually reinforce the disease model, to the benefit of the global pharmaceutical industry. Given this scenario, it is hardly surprising that research on healing has attracted little interest.

have been present for more than one month and have a pattern of consistency about them – a less labile and more fixed clinical picture.

This exemplifies how the agitation of a full-blown spiritual crisis can be confused with the onset of an illness like schizophrenia. Research suggests that vulnerability to schizophrenia may have many factors: genetic, traumatic, neurodevelopmental, nutritional and psychological. Yet we simply have no idea how many people who first present with a spiritual emergency may be helped, with the right kind of psycho-spiritual understanding and therapeutic input, to recover without acquiring a diagnosis of schizophrenia.

The psychiatrist Stanislav Grof, a pioneer in transpersonal psychology, worked extensively in this area.[38] It is clear that the management of a full-blown spiritual emergency can be a round-the-clock task, with skilled input over days and sometimes weeks. Regrettably, there is currently no such treatment resource either in the USA or the UK.

Well beyond the bounds of mainstream psychiatry, one transpersonal approach which has been used with some success in the treatment of hallucinations[39] is known as spirit release (or depossession). Take, for example, the work of the Nowotny Foundation. Karl Nowotny was a well-known Viennese psychiatrist who died in 1965. In after-death communications which appeared in the automatic (trance) writing of the medium Grete Schröder, Nowotny claimed that many people presenting with first-onset psychosis are suffering from 'spirit attachment'.[40] He advised that all the patient's resources have to be mustered so that negative influences are resisted with a determined act of will, during which time Nowotny and his team in

---

38. Grof & Grof (1991).
39. The term 'hallucination' is used in psychiatry to describe a perception in the absence of an external stimulus that has the quality of real, vivid and substantial sensory impression. Perceived in normal waking consciousness, a true hallucination is experienced as entirely 'real' and as having objective presence.
40. Nowotny (1995). Spirit release therapists view certain kinds of mental disorder as caused by 'earthbound' spirits of the deceased that have failed to progress to the 'light' and which remain in the vicinity of this world. Unlike exorcism, which treats such attachments as demonic and attempts to expel the spirit forcefully, spirit release therapy aims compassionately to free the attached spirit so that it can continue its onward journey and thereby the sufferer can be restored to health.

the spirit world work for the healing of the discarnate attached spirit. This needed to be coupled with a vigorous psycho-spiritual educational programme to protect against further 'psychic attack'. Nowotny warned that if the attachment persists, personal will is eroded and the subsequent disintegration of personality makes it all the harder to address later.

In the UK, the Spirit Release Foundation, founded in 1999 by psychiatrist Alan Sanderson, brought together practitioners in the field.[41] Many employ the 'interactive' approach,[42] which enables what is, in effect, a psychotherapeutic encounter with the 'attached spirit' through the agency of the patient.[43] Other practitioners are 'intuitives', also known as mediums, who use clairvoyance or clairsentience.

What kind of interface might such approaches have with orthodox psychiatry? Let us turn again to ICD-10, this time to the entry for trance and possession disorders (F44.3). These are classified as disorders in which:

> '…there is a temporary loss of both the sense of personal identity and full awareness of the surroundings; in some instances the individual acts as if taken over by another personality, spirit, deity or "force". Attention and awareness may be limited to, or concentrated upon only one or two aspects of the immediate environment, and there is often a limited but repeated set of movements, postures, and utterances.'

The entry goes on to say that only trance disorders that are involuntary or unwanted, and that intrude into ordinary activities by occurring outside (or being a prolongation of) religious or other culturally accepted situations should be included here. This is a fair point to make but it leaves open to question whether factors of social convenience should define pathology. Many mediums have initially resisted their calling because they knew it would change their lives for ever.

A further issue is that trance states occurring in the presence of other conditions are regarded as abnormal, for instance, after

---

41. Since 2011, the Spirit Release Forum (www.spiritrelease.org) has provided further information, training and a list of registered practitioners.
42. See Fiore (1978), Baldwin (1992), Lucas (1993).
43. An example is given in *Psychiatry and Spirit Release Therapy*, this volume.

head injury, epilepsy or in conjunction with schizophrenic or bipolar disorder. Yet the onset of extra-sensory perception after suffering a head injury has been well documented. David Morehouse, a leading participant in the US military Stargate remote viewing programme, began his work after being struck in the head by a bullet.[44]

For people with clairvoyant abilities, seeing a psychiatrist carries the risk that their psychic abilities, if disclosed, will be seen as a feature of illness. Yet psychiatrists are trying to do a very difficult job and live with the constant awareness that their patients may do harm to themselves or others. They dare not take risks with their patients, for in the event of a critical incident the judgement of society comes down on them like a ton of bricks. It is hardly surprising that in upholding the mores of society on the one hand while adhering to the prevailing science of material realism on the other, psychiatrists generally steer clear, in public at least, of topics like extra-sensory perception.

Spiritual Skills

Privately, a good many psychiatrists do witness events that leave them wondering about the further reaches of consciousness. Yet even with colleagues, they may hesitate to speak about such things for fear of professional censure. From the outset, therefore, we made it clear that in the Spirituality and Psychiatry Special Interest Group we would listen with respect and without censure to each other's opinions and experiences, while encouraging everyone to speak from both heart and mind. We understand the need to talk the language of ICD within the profession at large; it is our *lingua franca* and necessary for everyday clinical practice. However, in the meetings of the group we place diagnosis within a larger frame of reference, namely, the spiritual dimension that attends the lives of our patients and ourselves. Sometimes we find that this is what our patients want and need to talk about.[45]

---

44.   Morehouse (1996).
45.   Culliford (2002).

As clinicians, we should be always concerned to relieve suffering whenever we can. Suffering arises when we have to endure pain, mental or physical, that seems to be without meaning or purpose. Bringing the 'bigger picture' into the consultation opens up looking at the problem of suffering from a different vantage point. It is important to stay within the framework of a person's beliefs if they belong to an established faith tradition, but sometimes discoveries are made that are spontaneous and deeply meaningful during the course of a consultation. The key to working in this way is extraordinarily simple. It requires only that the psychiatrist shows genuine interest in, and respect for, whatever the patient ventures to confide.[46] One person's subjective reality is no less and no more valid than another's when helping search for meaning in life. It is true that there can be serious difficulties when a person's reality badly clashes with consensus reality. Believing yourself to be Jesus does not mean that you are going to be able to walk on water – you could well drown! At the same time, current research into paranormal phenomena[47] is turning what was previously regarded as apocryphal into empirical scientific data, so we should keep an open mind on all occasions.

The task for the psychiatrist is not to assert the supremacy of his or her own world-view but to help the patient find a way to live with themselves and with the world, even when the patient's beliefs and values might appear to outsiders to be highly idiosyncratic. Such beliefs (sometimes classed as delusions) can be explored in terms of hopes and fears that have a universality of meaning. What is life for? How do we understand good and evil? Why must we suffer? What happens when we die? Such fundamental questions tend to get pushed aside by the pressures of everyday life. When someone has a breakdown, these questions loom large, and if the psychiatrist is not afraid to enter into the dialogue, a deep contact is made. This can be crucial if a breakdown is to have the chance of turning into a breakthrough.

---

46. See *Spirituality and Science* in this volume.
47. See Radin (1997).

Healing and Healthcare

Spiritual awareness needs to be the cornerstone of psychiatry.[48] In addition to the biological, social and psychological aspects of mental healthcare, the spiritual dimension brings to our patients the prospect of healing. We know from surveys that patients are asking for this.[49] Chaplaincy is an important liaison resource, but there will be times when it falls to the doctor, nurse or carer to respond. Unfortunately, in the modern world we find ourselves up against a social and cultural divide, deeply ingrained, which finds little or no place for healing in mainstream healthcare. Yet the surge of interest in complementary and alternative medicine based on a holistic approach indicates a change in the climate of our times. People are voting with their feet; by 1997, over 40% of consumer expenditure on health in the USA was on complementary and alternative medicine (CAM).[50] In the UK, it was shown that by 1999, the one-year prevalence of use of CAM had risen to 20%,[51] a figure that continues to grow.[52]

Mental illness always produces fragmentation of the psyche and for any real recovery, healing must be helped to take place. Healing begins with the offering of love, a word that does not figure nearly enough in the lexicon of psychiatry. Compassionate love – spirituality in action – can only do good and mixes well with all other treatments that may be required. Psychiatry, more than any other branch of medicine, cannot afford to do without it.

References

Agostini, I. (2015) Descartes's proof of God and the crisis of Thomas Aquinas's Five Ways in early modern Thomism: scholastic and Cartesian debates. *Harvard Theological Review*, 108, 235–262.

Baldwin, W. (1992) *Spirit Releasement Therapy*. Headline Books.

---

48. See *Putting the Soul into Psychiatry*, this volume.
49. Mental Health Foundation (2002).
50. Eisenberg, et al. (1998).
51. White (2000).
52. For update, see Posadzki et al. (2013), showing that by 2011, one-year prevalence had increased to over 40%.

Bergin, A.E. & Jensen J.P. (1990) Religiosity of psychotherapists: a national survey. *Psychotherapy*, 27, 3–7.

Byrd, R. (1988) Positive therapeutic effects of intercessory prayer in a coronary care unit population. *Southern Medical Journal*, 81, 823–829.

Cohen, S. (2002) Psychosocial stress, social networks and susceptibility to infection. In *The Link between Religion and Health – Psychoneuroimmunology and the Faith Factor* (eds H.G. Koenig & H. J. Cohen). Oxford University Press.

Culliford, L. (2002) Spiritual care and psychiatric treatment: an introduction. *Advances in Psychiatric Treatment*, 8, 249–261.

Cottingham, J., Stoothoff, R. & Murdoch, D. (transl.) (1985) *The Philosophical Writings of Descartes*, vol. 1. Cambridge University Press.

Desjarlais, R., Eisenberg, L., Good, B., et al. (1995) *World Mental Health: Problems and Priorities in Low Income Countries*. Oxford University Press.

Desmond, D.P. & Maddox, J.F. (1981) Religious programs and careers of chronic heroin users. *American Journal of Drug and Alcohol Abuse*, 8, 71–83.

Eisenberg, D., Davis, R., Ettner, S.L., et al. (1998) Trends in alternative medicine use in the United States, 1990-1997: Results of a follow-up national survey. *JAMA*, 280(18), 1569–1575.

Faulkner, A. (1997) *Knowing Our Own Minds*. Mental Health Foundation.

Fiore, E. (1978) *You Have Been Here Before*. Ballantine Books.

Grof, C. & Grof, S. (1991) *The Stormy Search for the Self – Understanding and Living with Spiritual Emergency*. HarperCollins.

Guo, B. & Powell, A. (2001) *Listen to Your Body: The Wisdom of The Dao*. University of Hawaii Press.

Harbinson, M. & Bell, D. (2015) How should teaching on whole person medicine, including spiritual issues, be delivered in the undergraduate medical curriculum in the United Kingdom? *BMC Medical Education*, 15, 96.

Harris, W.S., Gowda, M. & Kolb, J.W. (1999) A randomised controlled trial of the effects of remote intercessory prayer on outcomes in patients admitted to the coronary care unit. *Archives of Internal Medicine*, 159, 2273–2278.

Hummer, R., Rogers, R., Nam, C., et al. (1999) Religious involvement and US adult mortality. *Demography*, 36, 273–285.

Koenig, H.G., Cohen, H.J. & Blazer, D.G. (1995) Cognitive symptoms of depression and religious coping in elderly medical patients. *Psychosomatics*, 36, 369–375.

Koenig, H.G., Cohen, H.J., George, L.K., et al. (1997) Attendance at religious services, interleukin-6, and other biological indicators of immune function in older adults. *International Journal of Psychiatry in Medicine*, 27, 223–250.

Koenig, H.G., George, L.K. & Peterson, B.L. (1998) Religiosity and remission of depression in medically ill older patients. *American Journal of Psychiatry*, 155, 536–542.

Koenig, H.G., McCullough, M.E. & Larson, D.B. (2001) *Handbook of Religion and Health*. Oxford University Press.

Koenig, H.G. & Cohen, H.J. (2002a) *The Link between Religion and Health – Psychoneuroimmunology and the Faith Factor*. Oxford University Press.

Koenig, H.G. & Cohen, H.J. (2002b) Psychological stress and autoimmune disease. In *The Link between Religion and Health – Psychoneuroimmunology and the Faith Factor*. Oxford University Press.

Koenig, H.G. & Cohen, H.J. (2002c) Psychosocial factors, immunity and wound healing. In *The Link between Religion and Health – Psychoneuroimmunology and the Faith Factor*. Oxford University Press.

Larson, D.B. & Larson, S.S. (2001) The patient's spiritual/religious dimension: a forgotten factor in mental health. *Directions in Psychiatry*, 21, Lesson 21.

Lindgren, K.N. & Coursey, R.D. (1995) Spirituality and serious mental illness: a two-part study. *Psychosocial Rehabilitation Journal*, 18, 93–111.

Lucas, W.B. (1993) *Regression Therapy – A Handbook for Professionals*, vol. 1 and 2. Deep Forest Press.

McClelland, D.C. (1988) The effect of motivational arousal through films on salivary immunoglobulin A. *Psychology and Health*, 2, 31–52.

McCullough, M.E. & Larson, D.B. (1999) Religion and depression: a review of the literature. *Twin Research*, 2, 126–136.

Mental Health Foundation (2002) *Taken Seriously: The Somerset Project*. Mental Health Foundation.

Miller, W.R. (1998) Researching the spiritual dimension of alcohol and other drug problems. *Addiction*, 93, 979–990.

Montgomery, H.A., Miller, W.R. & Tonigan, J.S. (1995) Does Alcoholics Anonymous involvement predict treatment outcome? *Journal of Substance Abuse Treatment*, 12, 241–246.

Morehouse, D. (1996) *Psychic Warrior: The True Story of America's Foremost Psychic Spy and the Cover-Up of the CIA's Top-Secret Stargate Program*. St. Martins.

Murray, C.J.L. & Lopez A.D. (1996) The global burden of disease. In *A Comprehensive Assessment of Mortality and Disability from Disease, Injuries and Risk Factors in 1990 and Projected to 2020*, vol. 1. Harvard University Press.

Nisbet, P.A., Duberstein, P.R., Yeates, C., et al. (2000) The effect of participation in religious activities on suicide versus natural death in adults 50 and older. *Journal of Nervous and Mental Disease*, 188, 543–546.

Nowotny, K. (1995) *Messages from a Doctor in the Fourth Dimension*, vol. 1–6 (trans. O. Van Oppens). Regency Press.

Posadzki, P., Watson, L., Alotaibi, A., et al. (2013) Prevalence of use of complementary and alternative medicine (CAM) by patients/consumers in the UK: systematic review of surveys. *Clinical Medicine*, 13(2), 126–131.

Powell, A. (1993) The psychophysical matrix and group analysis. *Group Analysis*, 26, 449–468.

Powell, A. (1994) Towards a unifying concept of the group matrix. In *The Psyche and the Social World* (eds D. Brown & L. Zinkin). Routledge.

Radin, D. (1997) *The Conscious Universe*. HarperCollins.

Schaal, M.D., Sephton, S.E., Thoreson, C., et al. (1998) Religious expression and immune competence in women with advanced cancer. Paper presented at the 106th Annual Convention of the American Psychological Association, 14–18 August, San Francisco.

Stein, D., Witzum, E., Brom, D., et al. (1992) The association between adolescents' attitudes towards suicide and their psychosocial background and suicidal tendencies. *Adolescence*, 27, 949–959.

Swinton, J. (2001) *Spirituality and Mental Health Care*. Jessica Kingsley.

White, E. (2000) The BBC survey of complementary medicine use in the UK. *Complementary Therapies in Medicine*, 8(1), 32–36.

Woods, T.E., Antoni, M.H., Ironson, G.H., et al. (1999) Religiosity is associated with affective and immune status in symptomatic HIV-infected gay men. *Journal of Psychosomatic Research*, 46, 165–176.

World Health Organization (1992) *The ICD-10 Classification of Mental and Behavioural Disorders: Clinical Descriptions and Diagnostic Guidelines*. WHO.

World Health Organization (1998) *WHOQUOL and Spirituality, Religiousness and Personal Beliefs: Report on WHO Consultation*. WHO.

World Health Organization (2001) *Mental Health – A Call for Action by World Health Ministers. World Health Report*. WHO.

10

Consciousness That Transcends Space-Time: Its Significance for the Therapeutic Process

Psychoanalytical therapy is based on a metapsychology that has remained largely indifferent to advances in science over the past 50 years. While metapsychology provides us with valuable therapeutic signposts, the study of the signposts seems to have become more important than taking the journey to new places. As a result, certain kinds of experience that patients bring to the consulting room are not always given the attention they deserve.

I want to describe a new frame of reference that has become available and that has profound implications for psychotherapy, and indeed for human relations in general. In the first part of the paper, I will set out some theoretical principles that may help to throw light on the discussion of clinical cases that follow.

Where is the Mind?

The assumption we usually make is that the mind is located physically somewhere behind the eyes and between the ears. This is not just because the brain resides there, but also because input from the special sense organs enters through peripheral apertures in the skull. Even if we question whether the mind is actually inside the head, we

First published as 'Consciousness that Transcends Spacetime: its Significance for the Therapeutic Process' in *Self & Society* (2003), 31, 27–44. Reprinted with permission of Taylor & Francis (http://www.informaworld.com).

do generally house it within the body. This sensed location begins when the baby puts its finger first in its own mouth and then its mother's mouth, registering the difference between the one-sided and two-sided sensations. Later, looking in a mirror, especially a full-length one, the child is amazed to see itself from the outside, and to be able to experience being both subject and object at the same time.

All this supports the common-sense notion that there is within each of us a subjective, inner world called 'me' and an objective reality 'out there' comprising everything and everyone else. The external world is assumed to exist independently, while consciousness, the self-aware function of the brain, is needed to illuminate it like a torch shining in the dark. To put it physiologically, the brain translates the vibrations which variously impact on our special sense organs into the perceptions of light, sound, smell, taste and touch. Integrating these sensations enables us to build up a picture of a solid and enduring external world.

This is the Newtonian world-view, where mathematical laws apply with exactitude to the relationships of objects located in a physical universe. It is also a world in which cause precedes effect and time is the axis down which the one follows the other. Furthermore, the second law of thermodynamics tells us that the clock is steadily winding down. All processes, large and small, must eventually submit to the arrow of time, which only flies in one direction – towards the heat death of the universe, calculated to occur in about 100 billion years' time.[1] From this physicalist perspective, we are nothing but players on the stage of life, seemingly arriving out of nowhere and going nowhere except into death. While we are here, we can witness the miracle of existence but there is nothing 'real' beyond the substance of the physical universe, of which our brains are a part.

In such a world, where does the mind fit in? The giants of the early Renaissance took a dualist position. René Descartes saw the mind as existing independently of geometrical categories and as evidence of the workings of God,[2] holding that without the soul there

---

1. Powell (1993).
2. Descartes' proof of God is ontological – that God's existence can be inferred from a 'clear and distinct' idea of a supremely perfect being. See Cottingham (1986).

could be no consciousness. Isaac Newton, too, was a deeply religious man, whose studies were profoundly shaped by mystical reverie. But during the Age of Enlightenment that followed, Newton's discoveries were used to promulgate the view that we live in an entirely mechanical universe, one in which God, if he had any part to play, was consigned to winding up the universe like a giant clock.[3]

Science based on material realism disposes of the Divine altogether. Consciousness is seen as a by-product of evolution, serving the needs of the 'selfish gene'[4] and nothing but a remarkable outcome of brain activity. The findings of positron emission tomography (PET) scanning, in which specific areas of the brain light up when different mental tasks are carried out, are widely taken to substantiate this view.

However, this is not the only way to understand what is going on. PET scans can be equally well be interpreted as correlation effects rather than consciousness itself being produced by the brain. Further, no one as yet has been able to explain how something non-material like the mind can be created by something that is material. While most neuroscientists hold that the answer will be revealed if we keep chipping away at brain function, there remains an unavoidable problem. The 'objective' world out there can only be known through the agency of the mind, hence through the lens of subjectivity. More than that, the advent of quantum theory in the 20th century has shed new light on this conundrum, for it would now appear that the seemingly solid and real objective world is actually created by consciousness. The world is not as it is, it is as we are! The whole thing is determined by the collapse of the wave function, about which I will be saying more.

Freud and Jung

Sigmund Freud's great discovery was to realize how much of perceptual reality is shaped by the content of our projections and to be able to trace their source. He showed that the mind is busy constructing

---

3. A facile conclusion that was a travesty of Newton's profound teleological thesis. See Davis (1991).
4. Dawkins (1976).

a world out of impulses, fears and desires, even though it may consciously know surprisingly little about them. While Freud was, as far as we know, unaware of the implications of quantum theory, he intuited what the new physics was later to reveal – there is no such thing as reality that stands apart from the observer.

At the same time, his early work, *Project for a Scientific Psychology*,[5] reveals that he aimed to make psychoanalysis a science and not surprisingly his aspirations were entirely in line with the prevailing mechanistic paradigm. Accordingly, psychoanalysis has been left with a concept of the mind that has shied away from the discoveries of post-Newtonian science. Yet the very language of psychoanalysis suggests we are dealing all the time with energies far more substantial than mere metaphors. For instance, therapists will speak of repressed anger that has instead been split off and projected (outwards, into a thing or a person). But what exactly is getting sent from A to B, and which passes from one object in space to another? How does 'anger' in some mysterious way get out from inside, across space and into another mind/body, often bypassing cognition such that the emotion disowned by the patient is experienced as something autonomous arising within the psyche-soma of the psychotherapist?

Carl Jung, in line with his sense of the deep connectedness between all things, postulated a greater Self that was unconfined by the personal. Throughout his life, he sought to accommodate supernatural and extrasensory phenomena and was intrigued by the psychophysical implications of quantum physics.[6] Now that quantum theory is beginning to make a wider impact, Jung's ideas, previously disregarded by much of the psychotherapy fraternity, are coinciding with advances in consciousness studies.

Delimiting the Mind

Psychodynamic therapies traditionally make certain assumptions about the nature of consciousness and its substrata, providing a rich

---

5. Freud (1895). Freud's major critique of religion is set out in *The Future of an Illusion* (1927) and *Civilization and Its Discontents* (1929).
6. See Hoeller (1982), Main (1997).

framework of meaning but circumscribing the field of exploration. In summary:

1. The mind has a conscious aspect, the waking state, characterized by a rich phantasy life, capacity for reflection and insight, ego-adaptive behaviour and creativity. No less important is the unconscious aspect of the mind, revealed in dreams and through the analysis of its defensive operations. In both cases, the search for meaning is confined to the narrative of this one lifetime, from birth to the present, extending, of course, to all the intimate and social relationships that have arisen.

2. The mind is the property of the individual, each person being regarded as being in possession of his or her own mind. Thoughts and feelings are communicated by means of verbal or non-verbal signals, coupled with the necessary capacity for empathic identification by the receiver.

3. It is, however, recognised that one mind can affect another in strange ways, especially with regard to unconscious processes. Psychoanalytic object relations theory describes this by way of a variety of metaphors, projection, introjection, splitting and so on.

4. The focus of work is on the analysis of unconscious projections through the interpretation of the transference.[7] Attempts by the patient to extend the relationship beyond the ambit of the transference are viewed askance and generally addressed by further interpretation of the transference.

5. Existential questions such as 'Why are we here?', 'What is it all for?', 'Is there any ultimate purpose?', 'Is there a God?', 'Is there more than this one life?' are explored in relation to defences against the pain of psychic reality and re-framed in terms of problematical personal histories. If not that, they are taken to be irreducible existential concerns beyond the scope of the therapy.

---

7. For the non-clinical reader: psychoanalysis encourages the emergence of unresolved childhood emotions that get projected onto the therapist, a process called transference. The therapist remains as neutral as possible in order to be a 'blank screen' for such projections. By means of interpretation, the therapist endeavours to help the patient to become aware of what is happening, and to 'own' the feelings instead of splitting them off and projecting them onto the therapist and others.

For the therapist to participate in any such wider discussion, there may be significant impact on the transference, as the therapist's personal inner world would be revealed. Nonetheless, the therapeutic situation is extraordinarily intimate and where the therapist is sensitive to such matters, the big existential questions will arise not infrequently. More than that, synchronicities occur that go way beyond what otherwise might be dismissed as mere coincidence. The section to follow begins with one such instance.[8]

Transcending Space and Time

I had been supervising a trainee psychiatrist with her first psychotherapy patient, a young woman I shall call Gillian. Gillian longed for closeness but was deeply mistrustful of intimacy. The therapy went well and after a few months, Gillian decided to track down her birth mother, whom she had never known. She followed up various leads only to discover that her mother had died a year or two earlier. It was a bitter blow but she took it well.

A couple of weeks later, my trainee attended for supervision. She seemed flustered and somewhat embarrassed. She said, 'I want to tell you something, you'll probably think it's stupid of me'. She went on to say that on the previous Sunday, which she had been spending at home with her family, she had suddenly experienced a terrible sadness. It came on inexplicably at three in the afternoon and she could not shake it off. Then at about six o'clock the feeling vanished as quickly as it had come.

On Monday, she had seen her patient Gillian, who told her that since the last session she had found out that her mother had been buried in a London cemetery and that on Sunday she had gone there to try to find her. For hours she had searched in vain but at three p.m., she found the grave and had spent the next three hours crying for the mother she had never known.

What are we to make of this? We could just call it coincidence, which pre-supposes that events are random and their concurrence takes place by chance. In the Western world, we view most of life in this way. In China, on the other hand, it has been a fundamental principle

---

8.   Case report also included in *Beyond Space and Time*, this volume.

of Daoism for two and a half millennia that all events everywhere are understood to be interconnected, down to the smallest detail – that all of us are participants in an ocean of the unseen, which moves us every bit as much as we like to think we move it. We may maintain the illusion of separateness but ultimately, the observer and the observed are one.[9]

Daoism holds that the more we set aside the strident imperatives of the ego, the more sensitive we become to the interconnectedness of all life. States of reverie, reflection and meditation in which the noisy mind is stilled, re-awaken our capacity to attune to the whole. A different order of consciousness becomes available. At its most perfect, it is known in the Buddhist and Hindu traditions as *samadhi*, a state of oneness beyond words, in which space and time dissolve.

Few psychotherapists would describe themselves as mystics. Yet maintaining free-floating attention by abrogating memory and desire, as Wilfred Bion advises,[10] brings us to the threshold of this unitive state of consciousness. There is a reversal of the usual figure/ground constellation and instead of the ego being to the fore, attention is given to the ground of being, something sensed rather than cognised.

In the case study just cited, could the close rapport between patient and therapist have brought into play an unusual sensitivity of the non-local kind, an instance of the so-called paranormal known as telepathy?

In the West, the scientific community is so wedded to material realism that parapsychological research has been largely treated with contempt. Nevertheless, experiments by J. B. Rhine at Duke University in the 1930s, using random controlled trials, paved the way for what is now a vast body of statistical evidence for the occurrence of extra-sensory perception. Clairvoyance, clairsentience, telepathy, precognition, remote viewing, psychokinesis and healing have all been subjected to experimental validation.[11] Looked at from the Newtonian perspective, these findings are profoundly counterintuitive. However, there are new scientific paradigms to which we can

---

9.   Guo & Powell (2001).
10. Bion (1967, 1970).
11. Radin (1997).

turn, starting with the discoveries of Albert Einstein, which serve to contextualise such findings.

Superseding the Newtonian World-View

In 1905, Einstein formulated the theory of special relativity. This theory was founded on two postulates, first, that all motion is relative and second, that the speed of light is always recorded as being the same. The theory says that if I as the observer were to watch you accelerate towards the speed of light, your clock would slow down relative to mine. Further, the length of your spaceship would progressively contract, while its mass would be increasing, until finally, since mass and energy are exchangeable ($E = mc^2$), if you went on to attain the speed of light, length would have contracted to a point while mass would have become infinite.

In 1917, Einstein went on to publish his general theory of relativity. He proposed that stars and planets, having mass, bent the very substance of space-time. Newton's famous apple falls to earth not on account of a mysterious force called gravity but because it rolls into the local space-time 'well' created by the Earth. Space tells matter how to move, while matter tells space how to curve.[12] This is a far cry from the world of our sense perception of stars and planets suspended motionless in infinite space.

Einstein was now in a position to consider what it would be like to be a ray of light passing from the Sun to the Earth. At the speed of light, length in the direction of travel shrinks to zero, as does time. Therefore, from the point of view of the light ray, it goes no distance in zero time. Without time and distance, the concept of speed is meaningless. It is only from our position as observers that light from the Sun takes around 8 minutes to travel the 93 million miles to the Earth. In other words, it is the very act of our observing this light ray (rather than 'being' the light ray) that draws it out into the dimensions we know as space and time. Space and time are thus not things in themselves but are 'created' by the observer.[13]

---

12.   A memorable observation attributed to the ground-breaking physicist, John Archibald Wheeler.
13.   Powell (1993).

According to current cosmology, we now have reason to believe that we live in a multidimensional universe. String theory suggests that our four-dimensional space-time unfolded out of a plurality of other dimensions, doubtless having very different rule sets from our own. Sub-atomic particles constantly flit between universes. In particular, the eleventh dimension is thought to be infinitely long but existing only about one trillionth of a millimetre distant from every point in our space-time. Within it may lie an infinite number of parallel universes.

If we take off our Newtonian glasses, we can see the mind in a new light. The brain, having mass, is anchored in local space-time but the mind, having no mass, experiences no such limitations. And since quantum physics deals with events in which properties of mass are negligible, it makes sense to go there for the next clue.

Mind and the Quantum Domain

In 1965, a landmark experiment in the non-local nature of consciousness was carried out.[14] Research on two pairs of identical twins showed that eye closure in one (stimulating alpha rhythm) instantly induced alpha rhythm in the brain of the other. Fourteen years later, research under conditions of sensory shielding was to demonstrate that the electroencephalograms (EEGs) of two people who were empathically attuned showed synchronisation, no matter that they were now placed in different locations. An evoked potential in the first subject's EEG, caused by a flash of light, instantaneously produced a transferred potential interrupting the alpha rhythm of the second EEG.[15] As yet, there was no explanation for such extraordinary findings, but in 1982 Alain Aspect demonstrated that photons can communicate instantaneously with each other regardless of the distance between them, provided that the particles were originally in a state of quantum entanglement. Instantaneous means just that – there is no signal travelling from one particle to the other even at the speed of light; the communication is *supraluminal*, transcending

14.   Duane & Behrendt (1965).
15.   Targ & Puthoff (1974).

space-time.[16] In 1992, further research on brain wave correlations between subjects showed that these effects also take place instantaneously, just as with photons.[17] So we can fairly say that in the fields of both particle physics and consciousness research, the conventional rules of space and time have been violated, indeed superseded.

This throws new light on research on identical twins, who necessarily begin life in a state of 'quantum entanglement'. Notably, such twins, even when reared apart, have been shown later to make many of the same life choices including career and to display the same personal preferences such as clothing or naming of children.[18] Genetic predisposition is hard put to account for such intricate correlations.

The Quantum Paradigm

Pivotal to quantum theory is the double-slit experiment, which shows that light behaves both as wave and particle depending entirely on how the experimenter proceeds.[19] Photons simply have no fixed objective status the way Newtonian physics predicts. This uncertainty characterises quantum mechanics. An electron does not 'hop' from one orbit to another around the nucleus like a spinning billiard ball, as once was thought. Instead, it exists in the 'virtual state' as a probability wave spread throughout *all of space*. The electron only manifests in its space-time location when a conscious observer makes the measurement. This is known as the collapse of the wave. Further, there is only a statistical probability that the electron will appear where you expect it to be. It may just materialise, however improbably, hundreds, thousands or even millions of miles away. And when it does so, it materialises in zero time.

Such fundamental non-locality reveals the breath-taking interconnectedness of the cosmos. The physicist David Bohm coined the

---

16.   See Merali (2015).
17.   Grinberg-Zylberbaum et al. (1992).
18.   Bouchard et al. (1990).
19.   For a clear, non-technical demonstration of the double-slit experiment, see: https://www.youtube.com/watch?v=DfPeprQ7oGc (accessed 26 February 2017).

term 'holoverse', about which he says: '...the entire universe...has to be understood as a single undivided whole...'.[20] Space and time are manifestations of what Bohm calls the *explicate order*, no more than one special case within a generality of underlying implicate orders that enfold. Stranger still, while the human mind as we know it requires to be enfolded in physical reality, at the same time it appears to enfold and contain the totality, just like a hologram.[21] This is known as a 'tangled hierarchy'.

According to the quantum physicist Amit Goswami, when consciousness collapses the wave function, mind and matter arise simultaneously as two sides of the same coin.[22] In doing so, the brain-mind combines Newtonian and quantum properties. Its classical Newtonian function generates the subjective world of sense perception that obeys the law of cause and effect, gives us linear time and provides us with memories, a personal history and a stable identity. This is contingent on the wave function collapsing in line with the maximum probability according to all the countless collapses that have previously taken place. The physical world has structural stability because the probability wave has been generated by millions of individual consciousnesses pooled together over time.

Nevertheless, since the wave contains, in potentia, all that was, is and ever shall be, there is in theory no limit to what is possible. For instance, we know that healing by remote intention, or prayer, really appears to work, as shown in replicated random controlled trials on recovery in intensive care units.[23]

We now have a paradigm that addresses the conundrum of mind/body dualism: no longer a case of *either/or* but *both/and*. Our universe started with the quantum entanglement we call the Big Bang, and since then everything (and everyone) is connected to everything and everyone else. When consciousness is brought to bear on the universe's inherent, entangled state, the wave collapses, breaking the entanglement and precipitating a physical reality composed

---

20.   Bohm (1980: 174).
21.   See also *Putting the Soul into Psychiatry*, this volume.
22.   Goswami (1993).
23.   Byrd (1988), Harris et al. (1999).

of time, space and objects with mass, including our brains. The mind, interleaving with the brain, bestows both personal consciousness (harnessed to identity) and transpersonal consciousness (unbounded by space-time). A small minority of people appear to be naturally gifted with extrasensory perception. However, when the customary flow of thoughts is stilled, as in meditation, or when the mind of the psychotherapist is freed from memory and desire, sensitivity to the transpersonal is enhanced.

Implications for Psychotherapy

I want now to look at how transpersonal aspects of consciousness can affect what goes on in psychotherapy.

Energy Depletion

Psychotherapists know well how exhausting some sessions can be, especially with depressed patients. From the quantum point of view this is not surprising. The empathic rapport sought by the therapist provides exactly the right conditions for quantum entanglement. Where there is an energy imbalance, the wave repeatedly collapses in favour of the patient's needs.

This is nothing new. In the practice of the ancient Chinese art of Qigong, it is common knowledge that a person whose energy or *qi* is depleted will latch onto someone with stronger *qi*.[24] Just as water flows downhill, the *qi* flows from high to low. Unless certain precautions are taken, the patient goes off with a spring in their step leaving the therapist drained.

At first sight, managing this would seem to be difficult to reconcile with the empathic receptiveness needed for therapeutic interaction. However, the transpersonal approach (and one used by most healers) is for the therapist to be mindful to conserve their own energy and instead to replenish the patient with energy or *qi* from the universal energy field. This is possible by means of visualizing

---

24.   Guo & Powell (2001).

oneself replenished by a down-pouring of light from above and beyond. Unlike the therapist's own energy reserves, the quantum field is without limit and all that is required to collapse the wave is a conscious thought.

Toxic Projection

Here, the therapist has to deal with something more damaging than energy depletion, namely the impact of negative projections, often intensified by the transference. Psychotherapists are trained to maximise their sensitivity to their patients, to take on board these projections, contain them, analyse them and then, hopefully, find a way to return them to the patient in a form that will assist with integration of the psyche. Yet few psychotherapists know about the need for psychic protection and without appreciating this, they put themselves at risk.

From the quantum point of view, there is no inside and outside; these are simply constructs of space-time. Projections do not actually 'travel' anywhere, for everything is already everywhere. Accordingly, the minds of therapist and patient share the wave function until collapse of the wave. When the patient goes in for splitting and projection, the wave will predominantly collapse in favour of the unconscious defence, resulting in the unwary therapist becoming a ready vessel for negative affect.

In healing and spiritualist circles, the need to safeguard one's health is well known. Failure to attend to this can cause anxiety and depression, as well as all kinds of somatic reactions: headaches, weakness, heart, chest, abdominal and pelvic symptoms. To avoid falling ill, healers invoke protection and there are many ways to do this, such as prayer, the invocation of angelic assistance or 'taking a shower' in celestial light. All 'thought forms' are regarded as having real (although subtle) substance and while even the most toxic projections can be viewed with understanding and compassion, it is not seen as helpful to 'contain' them at the expense of one's own health. Instead, they need gently deflecting away. One approach is to regard everything in the universe as having its part to play in the totality, so that when a negative thought form is received, it is sent off, always with love, to 'its rightful place in the universe', wherever that may be.

Altered States of Consciousness

In analytical psychotherapy, heightened or altered states of consciousness tend to be treated with suspicion. While pathology does need to be considered, from the transpersonal perspective there is another possibility – that a transformative change is taking place. When this happens, it is not something to be tackled reductively. Instead, the task is to explore how this new experience may be integrated and creatively managed.[25]

In the esoteric tradition, awakening to Oneness is the work of the upper chakras[26] (bodily energy centres). It is essential that the patient is securely 'grounded' through the function of the lower chakras, otherwise there is the danger of a psychotic reaction.[27] From the transpersonal perspective, the infant knows the embrace of the Divine[28] long before coming to be held in its mother's arms. Experiencing the greater whole is a realisation that transcends the sum of its parts and, as told by survivors of the near-death experience, the earthly parts never look the same again.

The Group Matrix

As a group analyst, I have been intrigued by the way group processes take place within a transpersonal matrix,[29] each group acquiring a unique energetic identity – a *morphic field*, to use Rupert Sheldrake's term.[30] Once established, the field sustains its energetic presence between group sessions as something alive and enduring for each group member.

---

25. See *The Unquiet Self*, this volume.
26. For further explanation of the function of the chakras, see *Varieties of Love*, this volume.
27. Nelson (1994).
28. The trace memory that possibly inspired Wordsworth to write: 'Our birth is but a sleep and a forgetting: / The Soul that rises with us, our life's Star, / Hath had elsewhere its setting, / And cometh from afar: / Not in entire forgetfulness, / And not in utter nakedness, / But trailing clouds of glory do we come / From God, who is our home' (Quiller-Couch, 1963). Jung likewise writes: 'Life is a touchstone for the truth of the spirit' (1926: 337).
29. Powell (1994).
30. Sheldrake (1999).

Every group has its own distinctive character, but all groups that are well-managed have one thing in common; the wisdom of the group proves to be greater than the sum of its individual members. Therapeutic groups instinctively take the form of the mandala, a circle symbolising the archetype of wholeness. The archetype invariably carries a charge; at different times a person may experience the negative pole, fearing to be swallowed up and to lose their identity, or be drawn to the positive pole, desirous of merging with, and being sustained by, the *mysterium tremendum*.[31]

As we oscillate between particle and wave, so to speak, the matrix of the group allows us to explore the richness of the figure/ground gestalt – at one moment with the group to the fore, and in the next, retrieving one's individual selfhood. Like a hologram, the group is a microcosm of the cosmic totality. With each successive collapse of the wave, there comes a new birth out of quantum entanglement.[32] As Buddhism teaches, in this way there arises a ceaseless renewal of consciousness.

I will now present a number of clinical vignettes illustrating how a range of problems may be addressed transpersonally.

THE TRANSIENCE OF DEATH

Joan came to see me after the death of her husband Ted, having nursed him through a long and debilitating illness. They had been together some 40 years and her loss left her stricken with grief. Each new day was a living nightmare. She continually felt Ted's presence around the house but it only brought her pain. Yes, it was possible that life after death continued in the same way, but how could that help her now?

I asked Joan if she would like to try to make contact with Ted in a way that might help bring her peace of mind. At my suggestion she shut her eyes, relaxed, and I encouraged her to 'find' Ted wherever he might be. After a couple of minutes, a faint smile played on her lips and I asked Joan what she could see. She replied that she could see Ted in his cricket whites playing cricket and looking very fit and happy. Then a look of deep sadness passed over her face. I asked whether she would like to speak with Ted and she nodded. So l suggested she now walk up to him and see what might happen. After a

---

31.   Otto (1926).
32.   For a brief explanation of quantum entanglement, see *Putting the Soul into Psychiatry*, this volume.

moment, Joan said that she was standing next to him and he had put his arm around her. What was he saying? He was saying 'Don't worry, everything is going to be all right.' I asked Joan to look around her. Was there anyone else present? Then she could see her deceased sister and parents smiling and waving to her.[33]

This short example, which can be interpreted in a number of ways, illustrates how our perspective changes when the larger frame of reference is experienced. There are beginnings and endings, yet they are felt to be part of a journey in which this existence is but one stop. It is not a question of denying loss, but integrating it into the timeless flow of life, as the next case illustrates:

SOUL AWARENESS
Carol's story had been one of terrible abuse and hardship and for many years she had taken refuge in alcohol. During the first interview, I encouraged her to look inside herself and tell me what she found there.

What Carol saw was 'her heart beating so hard it could burst'. What did she want to do with it? She put it to rest in a silk lined coffin, saying 'only death will bring it peace'. But then after a moment the heart transformed into a little whirligig of energy. It would not be trapped but flew about the room. So she released it and watched it fly away.

Images of the soul are incapable of death, for the soul is our personal quotient of divinity. But Carol was not ready or able to harness her soul for her own benefit. She did not take up the offer of therapy, which would have meant abstaining from alcohol.

Nearly 4 years later Carol came to see me again, in the meantime having faced up to her drinking.

This time, she went inside herself, into a dark cave, where she found a treasure chest. I asked if she could pick up the treasure chest and see if there was any way out of the cave. She put it under her arm and soon found an archway and went through. Now she found herself in a sandy desert, by a pool of water and some trees. She sat by the water, resting peacefully, and said with a sigh, 'This is for me!' (All her life she has rushed around trying to please others.) Did she want a drink?

---

33. This case study is also cited in *Soul Consciousness*, this volume.

She drank deeply of the cool fresh water. Now where did she need to go? She immediately found herself back home, still holding the treasure chest, studded with jewels and very beautiful. She placed it on the floor in the middle of the room. Following this session, therapy was offered and accepted.

Malevolent Energies

Janet, now in her mid-twenties, had been depressed for many years. Her problem went back to a boyfriend in her teens who had left her feeling badly abused. Soon afterwards she developed gynaecological symptoms, which she was now being told might require a hyster-ectomy. Along with her current physical symptoms, she experienced difficulty in allowing closeness and intimacy, although she very much wanted this.

I asked her to go within, 'scan' her body and tell me what she found there. Right away she described 'a nasty dark red thing' attached to her womb. I invited it to speak and it explained, through Janet, that it had been there since Janet was seventeen. It was belligerent and boastful, saying it had made her ill and wasn't finished yet – it would end up giving her cancer. Janet suddenly exclaimed out loud 'It's a demon!' I asked her if she wanted to work on freeing herself, which she was very keen to do. I suggested she visualise angels enclosing the demon in a bubble of light. At once it cried out in fear 'Stop, I'm going to burn!' So I exhorted it to go deeper and deeper into the dark-ness within itself. Could it see anything? After a little while it said with astonishment that it could see a light! A moment later it experi-enced being flooded with the light and far from burning, it cried out in wonder saying 'This feels so good, I feel so warm and nice!' Then it went on to say, with deep remorse, 'What have I done? I have caused such pain and misery!'

This transformation of energy, or of psychic structure, if you like, is characteristic of spirit release therapy.[34] We can take the demon literally to be an other-dimensional entity that attached when Janet was especially vulnerable, or we could see it psychoanalytically as a split-off condensation of pathological object relations. From the clinical standpoint, the task is to decide when to work for integration

---

34.   Baldwin (1992). See also *Psychiatry and Spirit Release Therapy*, this volume.

and when to go for removal. In Janet's case, the energetic complex was treated as a spirit attachment and released into the light.

THE PRESENCE OF THE PAST

Peter, aged 27, came to see me complaining of an acute and unaccountable fear of water. A good swimmer with no evident neurotic traits, he had been travelling on a small ferry when he developed a panic attack, with sweating, racing pulse and breathlessness. Peter had been looking over the side of the boat at the time and the thought came to him that if he were to fall overboard, he would be swept away and would drown. No one would ever know what had happened to him.

Going into Peter's personal history, there was no obvious psychodynamic trigger for this acute anxiety. I invited him 'to go back' to the moment when the panic began, closing his eyes and picturing himself right there, but this time letting himself imagine that he was falling into the water. Peter's body immediately began jerking and thrashing about. I said to him 'What's happening?' and he cried out, 'I can't get free, I'm drowning'. I then asked him to go back in time to just before this moment. He said despairingly, 'We've been rammed and water's coming in the boat'. Why can't you get free? 'I'm chained to the boat!' I asked him what sort of boat this was and he said, 'It's a trireme' (a warship used in ancient Greece).

I then took Peter forward again to the moment of drowning. His struggling movements became weaker and then he went limp. What is happening now? 'I'm leaving my body, I'm rising up through the water and I'm going higher, up into the sky'. What can you see? 'There's a bright light, I want to go there'. Before you leave, look back on this life you just lived and tell me about yourself and how old you are'. 'I'm 27' he said, and then the story emerged of a young man who had been captured in war and had spent the last 2 years as a slave oarsman on a Greek trireme. During a naval battle with the Persians, the ship had gone down taking all the slaves with it. The young man's wife and children would never know what had become of him.

By creating an 'affect bridge', as it is called, the visualisation had facilitated entry into what is commonly known as a 'past life'.[35] The therapeutic effect can be immediate and lasting. The process can be understood in different ways; as an actual 'other life' once lived; as

---

35. Woolger (1999).

cryptomnesia (the historical facts having been absorbed previously and now enacted like a psychodrama); or as information held in the quantum field, to which Peter happened to be susceptible. Since the quantum field is transpersonal, it is impossible to say whether the experience really belonged to Peter as an individual, or whether he gained access to a collective memory bank.[36] Perhaps this doesn't really matter, so long as he got the help he was looking for – relief from his unexplained fear of water.

The Aura of Love

Rosemary came to see me several years after her teenage daughter Tessa was involved in an accident that left her severely brain damaged and in a vegetative state. Rosemary felt deeply responsible for what had happened and she could not escape the torment of her guilt and grief, which visited her nightly. Neither could she bring herself to look at her once lovely daughter, who had developed severe contractures. 'I cannot bear seeing what Tessa has turned into,' she raged, after a rare visit to the nursing home.

I had been struck by a comment she made, that she dreaded going to see Tessa because as soon as she went near the room, Tessa, who normally lay silent and motionless, would start to make loud moaning noises. I wondered aloud if Tessa could somehow sense her mother's presence. At first Rosemary denied the possibility but then she broke down in tears.

How could we help Rosemary go back and face her daughter? Without this there could be no healing. I advised her when going into the room immediately to fix her gaze on Tessa's eyes, making sure not to look at her body while she approached her. We took plenty of time to rehearse this. When mother came for her next appointment, she told me she had gone right close up to Tessa, making sure to look only in her eyes. Tessa then stopped moaning. Rosemary found herself cradling her daughter and telling her that she loved her and would be coming again. One year later, Tessa was beginning to communicate with the help of a clock alphabet, was trying to crawl and was being assessed for surgery for treatment of her contractures.

Research by Valerie Hunt into the human bioenergy field (or aura) at the University of California, Los Angeles, has confirmed that we

---

36. Also known in theosophy and anthroposophy as the Akashic records.

are highly sensitive to changes in the auric field.[37] It behoves us as therapists to be mindful that the energy fields of the therapist and the patient are in contact even before the session begins.

I will finish these clinical examples with an event that could have passed for coincidence, yet which I felt to be more. Synchronicity is an uncanny blend of the subjective and objective, and makes a lasting impression. Bear in mind, too, that the term 'consciousness' as I have used it in this paper means far more than that we are sentient beings. Rather, I have attempted to draw a picture of the sublime connectedness of 'all that is', a unified life force that permeates the universe.[38] From time to time we are powerfully reminded of that unity, as illustrated in the following consultation:

An Apt Synchronicity

It was a warm summer afternoon. My patient, a young woman, had begun telling me apprehensively about her sexual problems. She longed to be able to surrender to her own desire for the man she loved, but for reasons that lay in her past, it seemed that she would never overcome her inhibitions.

At that moment, a bee flew through the open window and landed on the near corner of the small table that was placed between my patient and me. This was a queen bee, and she was not alone, for she was mating with the victorious drone. Oblivious of their surroundings, the bees made love – there is no other word for it – for the remaining 20 minutes of the session. Their delicate, sensual and rhythmic coupling had my patient and me lost for words. Nature was giving us a master-class on how to live in the moment and live to the full.

Living to the full means being willing to give up the hurts and grievances of the ego and instead, with the greater vision of the soul, find acceptance of what is, and forgiveness for what has been. Then we can declare, like Julian of Norwich 700 years ago, that '…all will be well, and all manner of things will be well'.[39]

---

37.   Hunt et al. (1977).
38.   Can there be a single person who has never gazed into the starry night sky in awe and wonder?
39.   Backhouse (1987: 56).

In Conclusion

I have aimed to show that physical birth and death are no more than punctuation marks in space-time, framing the multitude of intensely meaningful events that constellate what we call life.

On a note of caution, to escape into spirituality as a defence against the challenges of life would be as futile as plunging into carnal pursuits in order to evade the spiritual self. Daoism teaches that we stand poised between heaven and earth, with our feet on the ground and our heads in the sky. The view from up there is not to be missed, for the trials and tribulations of life are seen to be part of a greater whole. Yet the more that we live life to the full, the more we stand to gain, not least since we take all that we have learned with us elsewhere, as attested by survivors of near-death experience.[40] From the perspective of the soul, the greater the hardship, the more profound the spiritual challenge.

Psychotherapy aims to alleviate distress with insight and compassion, and is a vocation of the highest calling. Yet it would be hubris to suppose that we therapists have the measure of life in its infinite ramifications. Rather, we are there to help partner the psychology of the mind with the vision of the soul, so that each person may discover the best of who they can be.

References

Backhouse, H. (ed.) (1987) *Julian of Norwich: Revelations of Divine Love.* Hodder & Stoughton.

Bailey, L.W. & Yates, J. (1996) *The Near Death Experience.* Routledge.

Baldwin, W. (1992) *Spirit Releasement Therapy.* Headline Books Inc.

Bion, W.R. (1967) Notes on memory and desire. *The Psychoanalytic Forum*, 2, 271–280.

Bion, W.R. (1970) *Attention and Interpretation.* Tavistock Publications.

Bohm, D. (1980) *Wholeness and the Implicate Order.* Routledge.

Bouchard, T., Lykken, D., McGue, M., et al. (1990) Sources of human psychological differences: the Minnesota study of twins reared apart. *Science, New Series*, 250, 223–228.

Byrd, R. (1988) Positive therapeutic effects of intercessory prayer in a coronary care unit population. *Southern Medical Journal*, 81, 823–829.

---

40.   Bailey & Yates (1996).

Cottingham, J. (1986) *Descartes*. Blackwells.

Davis, E. (1991) Newton's rejection of the 'Newtonian world view': the role of divine will in Newton's natural philosophy. *Science and Christian Belief*, 3(1), 103–117.

Dawkins, R. (1976) *The Selfish Gene*. Oxford University Press.

Duane, T.D. & Behrendt, T. (1965) Extrasensory electroencephalographic induction between identical twins. *Science*, 150, 367.

Freud, S. (1895) Project for a scientific psychology. Reprinted [1966] in *The Standard Edition of the Complete Psychological Works of Sigmund Freud*, vol. 1 (trans. & ed. J. Strachey). Hogarth Press.

Freud, S. (1927) The future of an illusion. Reprinted [1961] in *The Standard Edition of the Complete Psychological Works of Sigmund Freud*, vol. 21 (trans. & ed. J. Strachey). Hogarth Press.

Freud, S. (1929) Civilization and Its Discontents. Reprinted [1961] in *The Standard Edition of the Complete Psychological Works of Sigmund Freud*, vol. 21 (trans. & ed. J. Strachey). Hogarth Press.

Goswami, A. (1993) *The Self-Aware Universe*. Putnam.

Grinberg-Zylberbaum, J., Delaflor, M., Sanchez Arellano, M.E., et al. (1992) Human communication and the electrophysiological activity of the brain. *Subtle Energies*, 3, 26–43.

Guo, B. & Powell, A. (2001) *Listen to Your Body: The Wisdom of The Dao*. University of Hawaii Press.

Harris W.S., Gowda, M. & Kolb, J.W. (1999) A randomised controlled trial of the effects of remote intercessory prayer on outcomes in patients admitted to the coronary care unit. *Archives of Internal Medicine*, 159, 2273–2278.

Hoeller, S. (1982) *The Gnostic Jung*. Theosophical Publishing House.

Hunt, V., Massey, W., Weinberg, R., et al. (1977) *Project Report: A Study of Structural Integration from Neuromuscular, Energy Field and Emotional Approaches*. Rolf Institute of Structural Integration.

Jung, C.G. (1926) Spirit and life. Reprinted [1952] in *C.G. Jung: The Collected Works*, vol. 8 (eds H. Read, M. Fordham & G. Adler). Routledge and Kegan Paul.

Main, R. (1997) *Jung on Synchronicity and the Paranormal*. Routledge.

Merali, Z. (2015) Quantum 'spookiness' passes toughest test yet. *Nature*, 525, 14–15.

Nelson, J. (1994) *Healing the Split*. State University of New York Press.

Otto, R. (1926) *The Idea of the Holy: An Inquiry into the Non Rational Factor in the Idea of the Divine* (trans. J. Harvey). Reprinted [2004], Kessinger Publishing Co.

Powell, A. (1993) The psychophysical matrix and group analysis. *Group Analysis*, 26, 449–468.

Powell, A. (1994) Towards a unifying concept of the group matrix. In *The Psyche and the Social World* (eds D. Brown & L. Zinkin). Routledge.

Quiller-Couch, Sir A. (ed.) (1963) William Wordsworth, 'Ode: Intimations of Immortality from Recollections of Early Childhood' (1804). In *The Oxford Book of English Verse: 1250–1900*. Oxford University Press.

Radin, D. (1997) *The Conscious Universe*. Harper Edge.

Sheldrake, R. (1999) *A New Science of Life – The Hypothesis of Morphic Resonance*. Park Street Press.

Targ, R. & Puthoff, H.E. (1974) Information transmission under conditions of sensory shielding. *Nature*, 251, 602–607.

Woolger, R. (1999) *Other Lives, Other Selves*. Bantam Books.

11

Psychiatry and Spirit Release Therapy

The therapy known today as 'spirit release' aims to treat possession states by freeing a person from the harmful intrusion of 'spirit presences' (entities). As such, it is largely dismissed by modernity as pre-rational and pre-scientific,[1] either a case of *folie à deux*[2] or else attributable to the excesses of an over-wrought imagination. Nevertheless, before dismissing the notion of spirit attachment and spirit release therapy as shamanic hocus-pocus, it may be helpful for mental health professionals to reflect on some of the assumptions that govern what is understood by 'reality' on the one hand and 'imagination' on the other.

The primacy of secular imagination arose during the Age of Enlightenment in Europe in the 17th and 18th centuries. Isaac Newton's description of a mechanistic universe was used to displace God from the centre of reality and put the human mind there instead. At the same time, René Descartes' two classes of substance, *res cogitans* and *res extensa* (mind and body) ushered in a dualistic worldview that remains with us to this day. Although never intended to be taken this way by either Newton or Descartes, reality is now broadly treated as something 'out there' in the sensorial world, where it can be studied with the exactitude of science. Imagination, on the other

Paper prepared for conference 'The case for spirit release therapy', held by Alternatives at St James's Piccadilly, London, 27 October 2003.

---

1. Ellenberger (1970).
2. The presence of the same or similar delusional ideas in two persons closely associated with one another, in this instance, practitioner and patient.

hand, is regarded as 'in here', something produced in the mind, itself the product of physical brain processes in ways not yet understood.

The view of reality as objective and enduring has been especially important to the practice of psychiatry as the branch of medicine dedicated to the study of mental illness. In line with the prevailing culture of material realism, there is fervent hope that one day mental illness will be entirely accounted for by brain mechanisms (and indeed consciousness too). Recent advances in the neurosciences such as positron emission tomography (PET) and functional magnetic resonance imaging (fMRI) scans are cited in support of this viewpoint. A good deal of the research into two major mental illnesses – manic depression and schizophrenia – has followed suit.

During psychiatric training, there is little time or opportunity to step back and question what is really understood by the twin constructs of imagination and reality. Neither, regrettably, is there much deep enquiry into what the concepts of mental health and mental illness really mean. Instead, the young psychiatrist is offered a (largely implied) blueprint of 'normality', one that does not help much when it comes to acknowledging and supporting patients whose experiences place them outside the consensus reality of society. Our culture is intolerant of eccentricity and idiosyncrasy. We may regard ourselves as a good deal more enlightened than our mediaeval forebears, but modern society applies all kinds of subtle pressure, one notably being to medicalise workings of the mind that we do not understand and cannot explain, especially when these workings challenge the consensus opinion that imagination and reality are two entirely different things.

Scientific Realism

If the material universe is taken to be primary and the mind nothing but a product of the brain, there can be no truck with such things as 'attached spirits'. How could there be a spirit without a body?

The scientific ethos of material realism is essentially atheistic and so there can be no place for God either, let alone angels and archangels, devils and demons.[3] Surveys carried out amongst psychiatrists

---

3. See Freud (1927) for a relentless critique of religion.

and psychologists have shown that only some 30% believe there to be a higher power or divine presence; the mechanistic world-view clearly wins the day. Yet even in our materialist, consumer culture, population surveys reveal that over 80% of the public continue to believe in a higher power.[4] Should this be put down to sheer ignorance and superstition?

The greatest scientists, Albert Einstein among others, have consistently shown awe and humility in the face of the unknown. They know that the light shone by science on the mysteries of the cosmos is like the illumination of a street lamp at night. Looking for one's lost keys around the lamppost is a good place to start, but not to end, the search. Indeed, to take the analogy a step further, we shall never know everything about the nature of that light source when we ourselves are obliged to use it to see what is going on. Unfortunately, the application of science to modernity, with its allure of technology and focus on material comfort, has resulted in an attitude of indifference to what may lie beyond that street light.

Science and Spirit

Over the past 50 years, a quiet revolution has been mounting a challenge to the conventional schism between mind and matter. The far-reaching implications of quantum mechanics have begun to be applied to the question of the fundamental nature of reality. Here are just a few of the thought-provoking implications.[5]

- There is no such 'thing' as objective reality, for what we deem to be 'reality' is created by our consciousness, including the universe of time and space in which we live as embodied beings.
- In turn, our universe exists in a multidimensional cosmos that itself transcends time and space. Everything is connected to everything else – a single unitary field – like one unimaginably vast hologram.
- The consensus reality that we humans share, the world of sense perception that has structure and stability, arises from what is

---

4. Larson et al. (2001).
5. See also *Putting the Soul into Psychiatry*, this volume.

understood to be repeated collapses of the collective probability wave. Nevertheless, each of us has the capacity to collapse the wave in a place of our own making.

- Out of the infinite quantum potentia, we each precipitate a unique experience of reality. No one person's reality is more or less 'true' than any other. However, living in isolation, which is characteristic of psychotic reality, can be a lonely and sometimes dangerous place. Yet the reality of a person who from the clinical standpoint is hallucinated and/or deluded is still entirely authentic.

Psychiatric Diagnosis and the Paranormal

How, then, should we decide if a paranormal experience, such as experiencing a spirit entity, justifies a psychiatric label? One way is to see whether the experience being reported enhances or disrupts that person's life. This distinction may not be easy to make, but the aim must be to find meaning and purpose in the crisis, with the chance of moving towards wholeness of being. This helps us to delineate between the spiritualist who is dedicated to helping others through making contact with the deceased, and a person whose life is blighted by the involuntary intrusion of voices. The phenomenology of such hallucinations may be identical (hearing a voice coming from 'outside' in the absence of any external stimulus) but the significance for health as opposed to illness is entirely different.

Psychiatry has begun to acknowledge this in a small way. In the *International Statistical Classification of Diseases and Related Health Problems* (ICD-10), the diagnostic manual used in the UK, there is now an entry (F44.3) for trance and possession disorders.[6] These are classified as disorders in which 'there is a temporary loss of both the sense of personal identity and full awareness of the surroundings; in some instances the individual acts as if taken over by another personality, spirit, deity or "force".' Most importantly, ICD-10 goes on to say that 'only trance disorders that are involuntary or unwanted, and which intrude into ordinary activities by occurring outside (or being

---

6. World Health Organization (1992).

a prolongation of) religious or other culturally accepted situations' should be included here.

In the equivalent American manual, DSM-IV[7] there is a new category (V-Code 62.89) entitled 'Religious or Spiritual Problem'. This category does not imply an illness but is drawing long-overdue attention to the patients' religious or spiritual beliefs.

A Place for Spirit Release Therapy

Here is a short case study, which demonstrates the transpersonal therapy of 'spirit release':

> A young woman I will call Jan came to see me feeling unwell and 'not herself'. She had been told she was clinically depressed; antidepressant medication had helped but she was still 'not herself'. I was struck by her use of the phrase.
>
> Going into the history, I learned that a few months before the symptoms began, Jan's friend had killed herself in Jan's home, having been staying there while my patient was away on holiday. By the time Jan got back, everything had been tidied up and the funeral had already taken place.
>
> Remembering how Jan had twice said she was 'not herself', I asked her if she had the feeling of someone else when she came back home. Jan replied that she hadn't wanted to mention it in case I thought she was mad, but every time she went into the house, she had the physical sensation that her friend was right there in the room with her.
>
> Taking this at face value, I asked if Jan would like me to invite the spirit of her deceased friend to the consultation to see if we could get some further clues. She was willing, so I asked her to close her eyes, tune in to her friend and try letting her friend speak through her.

---

7. American Psychiatric Association (1994). DSM-5 was finally released in 2013. The V coding remains the same, the entry stating 'This category can be used when the focus of clinical attention is a religious or spiritual problem. Examples include distressing experiences that involve loss or questioning of faith, problems associated with conversion to a new faith, or questioning of spiritual values that may not necessarily be related to an organized church or religious institution'. For an in-depth evaluation of ICD-10 and DSM-5 in this regard, see Prusak (2016).

Jan's friend 'came through' and went on to express deep regret at having taken her life. Suicide had solved nothing. She remained unhappy, lonely, and seeking comfort. I explained that staying on was having a bad effect on my patient, and was doing nothing for herself either. She apologised. 'If only I had known', she said, 'what I know now. I was facing the biggest challenge of my life and I went and messed it up. I feel even worse than I did before'. I said I was sure other opportunities would be given her. She was very relieved to hear this and we talked more about her hopes for another chance at life. When she said she was ready to move on, I asked her to look for the light. She exclaimed with a smile 'Yes, I can see it' and left at once. The moment she went, my patient felt the burden of oppression lift from her and it did not return.

Can such therapy ever hope to be recognised by mainstream psychiatry?[8] This might come about in two ways. The first would be consequent on a future cultural paradigm shift, recognising that our space-time dimension is enfolded by a multiplicity of other dimensions. It would require taking on board the evidence that consciousness is primary and not secondary to physical reality and that it is non-local, not being located within the brain but existing as a ubiquitous field. It would oblige us to acknowledge that beyond our space-time there are domains in which linear time does not exist, and that consciousness itself is eternal and infinite; in short, that human beings are nested within a living – some would say spiritual – cosmos.

Conventional science dismisses such views as heresy. Quantum physicists and cosmologists who have embraced these revolutionary implications have been mocked and pilloried by their colleagues, sometimes losing not only their grants but their academic posts too. The resistance to paradigm change is an age-old characteristic of the human mind, just as when Galileo discovered that the Earth went round the Sun and for his pains spent the last 10 years of his life under house arrest.

Any such radical re-think seems a long way off. As a species, we have not even been able to comprehend the essential unity of life on planet Earth, let alone grasp that space-time is enfolded within other 'non-physical' dimensions.

---

8.   See also *Mental Health and Spirituality*, this volume.

However, there is a second approach. It should be possible to accommodate spirit release therapy within mental healthcare by setting aside the ontological question, 'What is really going on?' and simply treating it as a psychological therapy appropriate for some patients in some circumstances. This approach has the merit of being pragmatic, for it has long been recognised that working with the beliefs of the patient brings the best results.[9]

When responding to a patient's belief that he/she is 'possessed', it behoves the psychiatrist to remember that all therapy takes place within belief systems that organise the interpretation of sensory data, how it is processed and the consequent subjective experience. For some people, the notion of spirit attachment (and release) comprises a coherent, explanatory model for certain experiences. Individual accounts support the therapeutic efficacy of spirit release in selected cases, although there are no research data that would satisfy the stringent requirements of evidence-based medicine.

For the clairvoyant medium, the presence of spirit attachment is self-evident. For the religiously inclined, there is a tradition of healing interventions – for example, the ministry of deliverance within the Christian church and the casting out of *jinn* in Islam. The sceptic will argue that even the best result using spirit release therapy does not verify the existence of attached spirits. Rather, it will be argued that we are dealing with a dissociative disorder and that the therapeutic interaction is taking place with a split-off aspect of the unconscious mind.

Are there other explanations? Medical science has been in the habit of putting the unexplained relief of symptoms down to the placebo effect[10] based on emotional suggestibility. Yet from the quantum perspective there is no such thing as 'the placebo effect', since mind and matter are two sides of the same coin.

The debate will continue. Nevertheless, as a therapy, it is not necessary to set out to prove or disprove the presence of entities. Efficacy can be demonstrated on the black box model of input, throughput and output, without knowing how it is achieved. However, what does

---

9. Frank (1963).
10. A medicine or procedure prescribed for its psychological benefit rather than for any physiological effect.

seem clear is that for spirit release therapy to work, it needs to offer a meaningful paradigm for both patient and therapist – one that has heuristic value as a psycho-spiritual tool.

Keeping an Open Mind

The last point I want to make is that Newtonian science is based on the dichotomy of either/or – for instance, an object cannot be in two places at the same time. However, the quantum universe knows no such limits. Technically called superposition, subatomic particles simultaneously exist and do not exist; they can be everywhere and nowhere, truly an Alice in Wonderland kind of world. Where space was once thought to be an empty vacuum, we now know it as the zero-point field, swarming with energies of unbelievable magnitude.[11]

Nature in her wisdom has shielded us from the impact of these energies, so that our personal, everyday consciousness can get on with raising families, holding down jobs, coping with our emotions and, if we have time to spare, puzzling over the nature and purpose of life. But when a person is in an altered state of consciousness, whether through psychedelic drugs, hypnotherapy, meditation, deep reverie or dreaming, they may find themselves in touch with very different worlds on the other side of a paper-thin veil.[12]

When someone has the misfortune to suffer from the disturbance of brain function we call schizophrenia, it seems very likely that the veil becomes porous to energies that were never intended to flood in. Likewise, when the emotions of the bereaved connect them to the energies of the deceased, we should hardly be surprised if communications arise that transcend space-time.

The unbounded nature of consciousness is a wonderful thing. Yet so is space-time, for without it our bodies would not exist and we would be deprived of the chance of growing in wisdom through facing the challenges of life. I would suggest that when our actions are occasioned by love and tempered with humility, we find ourselves aligned to the workings of the universe with a harmony that makes

---

11.   McTaggart (2001).
12.   Powell (2003).

us tolerant of prejudice and accepting of differences. I am sure this will give the best chance for spirit release therapy to find, in the fullness of time, its place as a recognised and valued contribution to mental healthcare.

References

American Psychiatric Association (1994) *Diagnostic and Statistical Manual of Mental Disorders, Fourth Edition (DSM-IV)*. APA.

Ellenberger, H. (1970) *The Discovery of the Unconscious*. Basic Books.

Frank, J. (1963) *Persuasion and Healing*. Schocken Books.

Freud, S. (1927) The Future of an Illusion. In *The Standard Edition of the Complete Psychological Works of Sigmund Freud*, vol. 21 (trans. & ed. J. Strachey). Hogarth Press.

Larson, D.B., Larson, S.S. & Koenig, H. (2001) The patient's spiritual/religious dimension: a forgotten factor in mental health. *Directions in Psychiatry*, vol. 21, lesson 21.

McTaggart, L. (2001) *The Field*. HarperCollins.

Powell, A. (2003) Consciousness that Transcends Spacetime: its Significance for the Therapeutic Process. *Self and Society*, 31, 27–44.

Prusak, J. (2016) Differential diagnosis of 'Religious or Spiritual Problem': possibilities and limitations implied by the V-code 62.89 in DSM-5. *Psychiatria Polska*, 50(1), 175–186.

World Health Organization (1992) *International Statistical Classification of Diseases and Related Health Problems, 10th Revision (ICD-10)*. WHO.

12

Varieties of Love and the Near-Life Experience

'I have estimated the influence of Reason upon Love and found that it is like that of a raindrop upon the ocean, which makes one little mark upon the water's face and disappears.'

Hafiz[1]

From the perspective of a psychiatrist trying to make sense of the human condition, I would like to venture some observations concerning the eternal subject of love, with regard firstly to psychological growth, secondly to spiritual development and thirdly to the consequences of living without it, resulting in what I call the 'near-life experience'.

Love would appear sometimes to be an antidote to falling ill and at other times an *agent provocateur*. Psychiatrists are happy to sanction certain kinds of love, a mother's healthy love for her child, for instance, or mature love between consenting adults. Unbridled passion, however, is more often looked on as a potential threat, since it drives people to behave irrationally, act compulsively and frequently to suffer its painful consequences. Mature love inclines us to the Platonic ideals of beauty, truth and goodness for they engender a wonderful, intuitive sense of wholeness. Yet such values are generally

Paper prepared for conference 'Beyond the Brain V – Healing, prayer and forgiveness: frontiers in consciousness research and applied spirituality', held by the Scientific and Medical Network, Canterbury, August 2003.

---

1.   Quotation from *The Garden of Heaven. Poems of Hafiz* (Bell, 2003: 23).

overlooked in the psychological literature, the more surprisingly so since losing track of them is a serious danger to mental health.

Furthermore, in society these values get confused with morality. Far from leading to wholeness, morals based on enforced codes of conduct usually result in misconduct. The clergy have sex scandals, politicians who are supposed to behave with sobriety get drunk, judges are caught speeding and police take bribes like the criminals they are supposed to be catching. Eventually the strain of being good defeats a person and most of us at some time will have said under our breath, 'There but for the grace of God, go I'. We are forced to admit that in everyday human life, for every expression of beauty, there will be found one of ugliness, truth is twinned with falsehood, goodness is the inseparable companion of evil and love is not a million miles from hate.

Soul and Personality

'I was dead, then alive.
Weeping, then laughing.
The power of love came into me,
And I became fierce like a lion
Then tender like the evening star.'

Rumi[2]

Wholeness begets all else. Definitions include 'unbroken', 'intact', 'entire', 'complete' and 'unity'. This is the language of the soul. All great music, literature and art reflect such transcendent reaching towards the greater whole, being both of the world and yet mysteriously beyond.

Whence does this impulse arise? The teleological view expounded by Aristotle is to regard the universe as striving towards its own 'final cause'. Just as the acorn is impelled to become the oak, so there is a design, a purpose and a movement towards completion in all things. These days, cosmologists similarly refer to the anthropic principle, arguing that the chances of the right conditions having emerged to support our human consciousness are so many trillion to one against that it must have been in the Grand Design from the outset.

---

2. Barks (1999: 134).

Science and spirituality converge in this quest for the whole – that which is ultimate totality and unity. The theoretical physicist Stephen Hawking, speaking of the search for a Grand Unified Theory, writes, 'If we find the answer to that, it would be the ultimate triumph of human reason – for then we would know the mind of God'.[3] While we are waiting – and it could be a long time – we do have that remarkable instrument of subjectivity, the self, which enables us to access and experience wholeness directly through prayer, contemplation, meditation and dreams.[4]

We have a natural inclination to personify God – but how else to describe the ineffable? In the Daoist tradition, the source beyond all duality (that which cannot be named but merely denoted as *Wuji*) was said by the sage Lao Tsu in the 6th century BCE to be 'the mother of ten thousand things'.[5] In the 5th century BCE, the Greek philosopher Empedocles was the first to describe the nature of God as a circle of which the centre is everywhere and the circumference is nowhere. Anselm of Aosta,[6] in his *Meditation Proslogion* of 1087 CE, spoke of God as 'that than which nothing greater can be conceived'. Throughout history, regardless of creed and culture, we find the same yearning for the transcendent, beyond the power of any Imago Dei to convey.

If we were to confine ourselves to looking at love in relation to this search for wholeness, what I call 'soul love',[7] we could happily neglect the shadow side of human nature.[8] However, we must admit that for much of the human journey, the ego's struggle for survival entangles love with manipulation, control and possessiveness. These base attributes of human personality[9] are bolstered by the ego's defence mechanisms.[10]

---

3. Hawking (1988).
4. See *The Unquiet Self*, this volume.
5. Guo & Powell (2001).
6. Anselm, later enthroned Archbishop of Canterbury, 1093 to 1109 CE. Anselm's ontological argument was later used by Descartes in his proof of the existence of God.
7. See *Soul Consciousness*, this volume.
8. Carl Jung wrote, 'Everyone carries a shadow, and the less it is embodied in the individual's conscious life, the blacker and denser it is' (Jung, 1938: 76).
9. Bailey (1947).
10. See *Psychosocial Implications of the Shadow*, this volume.

One specific defence I want to single out is known as projective identification. Emotions that are felt to be dangerous to the self are split off without being acknowledged as one's own, and instead are projected onto another – whether it be an individual, community or nation. This is commonly known as scapegoating. Projective identification allows for a sense of virtue and goodness since the fault invariably lies with the other. Group cohesion is thereby strengthened – nations go to war and pray to God for victory. The war against terrorism is a case in point – the USA may be more united but the world becomes the more divided.

Regrettably, we find a strange disjunction between the peace and wholeness for which the human soul yearns, and the behaviour of human beings, riddled with factions, splits and dualities of every imaginable kind.

Fear of Life

'Life is either a daring adventure or nothing.'

Helen Keller[11]

Consider the fate of the child born into such a world as ours. We start out in life suffused with soul consciousness, innocent and wondrous.[12] As long as we feel to be centre of the universe, joy and delight prevail. Then, with the advancing complexity of social relationships comes the painful recognition that others hold themselves to be just as important as oneself, others who may have no great interest in one's welfare and rather more power; so the struggle for survival begins. In a world largely indifferent to a person's future, the human ego is indispensable to survival, and determines the path that will shape the rest of things to come.

A question that faces each person as they grow older is whether to brave the storms of life or to find some safe corner in which to take shelter. Opting for safety should not be confused with the universal need for privacy of the self, which every human being needs in order

---

11. Keller (1946: 50).
12. See *The Soul of the Newborn Child*, this volume.

to function. I am talking here about feeling too vulnerable to the inevitable hurts of life to be able to risk venturing into life and love.

Deep exploration of such withdrawal reveals that behind the fear to love is a greater fear of losing the one you love. Alfred Lord Tennyson writes, 'Tis better to have loved and lost than never to have loved at all'.[13] Yet such a sentiment is for the brave of heart. The faint of heart would rather avow 'better not to have loved than to lose'.

Death by Degrees

'No one ever said on their deathbed, "I wish I'd spent more time in the office".'

Unattributed aphorism

It is an extraordinary irony that engaging fully with life means at the same time to wrestle with death. What we most fear is what brings our attention to life. As Samuel Johnson remarked, 'When a man knows he is to be hanged… it concentrates his mind wonderfully'.[14]

One way of seemingly evading death is to live an 'unconscious' life, a theme taken up in a number of fairy stories. In the tale of Sleeping Beauty, there is only one way to become conscious, which is to awaken to love. The prince's kiss arouses the princess to the joy of life and although the fairy story does not say so, to the fact of their mortality.

The outcome is frequently less happy in the real world. The child who is deprived of love and protection can be coerced to do just about anything in order to survive. Children abducted by guerrillas, for example, soon become as brutal as their captors.[15] To show, or indeed, to feel sensitivity is to risk being killed, for the child who exhibits such fear becomes a vessel for the denied, split-off and projected vulnerabilities of the others. Then the vulnerable individual must be destroyed so that everybody else can magically feel rid of their own weakness.

---

13. *In Memoriam A.H.H.* (1847), Canto 27 ([2007]: 116).
14. Boswell ([1992]: 205).
15. See Veal & Stavrou (2007).

In less extreme circumstances a 'false self' develops, whose function is to minimise the threat of loss. When emotionally uninvolved, the person appears to be independent, confident and self-reliant. However, when the yearning for a relationship is kindled and there is the prospect of real intimacy, feelings of insecurity arise – anxiety, possessiveness and jealousy, along with unrealistic expectations about the partner's availability. Unless the problem of the underlying insecurity is faced, a crescendo of mental pain will result in the person breaking the nascent bond and reverting to a state of familiar, but safe, loneliness.

Such people are sometimes called schizoid because they evince so few signs of emotion; yet still waters run deep. When detachment defences break down, there can be a fierce attack on the loved one or serious self-harm. I remember one patient who, in front of his wife in their home, stabbed himself in the chest and abdomen and collapsed in a pool of blood. He survived after heroic surgery. The couple came to see me together. The wife was convinced that now she could never leave – her husband's blood would 'always be on her hands'.

The Emotion of Love

'My life has been filled with terrible misfortunes – most of which never happened.'

Variously attributed

Western depth psychology has elaborated a comprehensive model of early emotional development. We understand a great deal about how the infant internalises the goodness of the caregiver, beginning with the first successful feed at the breast, so that the emerging self can be experienced as essentially good. The baby also has to learn to withstand pain and frustration, initially in the body and then in its rapidly forming mind. It must organise what psychoanalysis calls the 'internal object world', in which loving and hateful impulses co-exist. To begin with, they are widely split but with good parenting integration of the contents of the child's inner world is achieved and the child develops the capacity to cope with ambivalence. Learning to bear with conflicting emotions towards the one and same other is essential if future relationships are to withstand the storms of life.

A good deal of depth psychology is concerned with the outcome of this integration, which leads to the capacity to be able to experience genuine concern for another, even when a person's own needs are not being gratified. Relationships can then be reflective rather than reactive (impulse driven). Importantly, the way is paved for moving from the two-person relationship of (usually) mother and child to the constellation of father, mother and child. There is the opportunity to witness the exchange of love between parents and to discover the pleasure of giving love as well as receiving it; motherly and fatherly love can be tried, tested and internalised as attributes of the self.

For the emotionally secure child, engaging with siblings and then the wider world leads to the realisation that more can be achieved by cooperation than going it alone. The maturing young person is preparing for parenthood and Nature arranges the necessary pair-bonding through the experience of falling in love. Later will come the travails of parental love, including learning to love one's children non-possessively for who they are, and to refrain from burdening them with expectations based on unrealised parental ambitions. This is no small matter, requiring that the ubiquitous shadow aspect of the self is recognised and contained. The positive archetype[16] of the mother offers bountiful and unconditional love – the munificent breast – and instils joy and delight in life. Yet the negative archetype, if unchecked, will devour the child in the name of love, and inhibit its growth and development. The positive archetype of the father takes the child forward into the world and encourages great things. In its negative aspect, the archetype is painfully conditional, and ruthlessly demands obedience to the father's will.

Where the circumstances are favourable, from the best of motherly and fatherly love arises the discovery of delight in the child's own being. (This is not to be confused with selfishness, which is the very opposite, being a desperate attempt to fill an inner void empty of love.) Studies of child development show that when we grow up having been loved, we are able to love ourselves, and so find love for others too. Our capacity for empathy and altruism stems from having known

---

16. According to C.G. Jung, the term *archetype* refers to an inherited idea or mode of thought that has its source in the collective unconscious of humankind (Jung 1934: 76).

what it is to have been loved unconditionally.[17] The second commandment: 'Love your neighbour as yourself'[18] depends on this psychological fact. It also accounts for the surprising saying of Jesus, 'Whoever has will be given more, and they will have an abundance. Whoever does not have, even what they have will be taken from them'.[19]

Love that is anxiety-driven, that seeks to assuage the angst of loneliness and emptiness, always ends in tears, for insecurity and possessiveness will drive away the loved one. Yet once this is grasped, there is the possibility of going on to experience mature inter-dependence, with life-enriching concern and care for the chosen other. Such love deepens with time, since it does not constrain but enables each person to be true to themselves; in secular psychology, this kind of love is more or less the best that can be expected of an ordinary man or woman. Love is geared to the protection of self and family, and by extension, to the social community.

What of unconditional love? Jesus has this to say: '…Love your enemies, do good to those who hate you, bless those who curse you, pray for those who mistreat you. If someone slaps you on one cheek, turn to them the other also'.[20] He then drives the point home: 'And if you do good to those who are good to you, what credit is that to you? Even sinners do that'.[21] Here, psychological theory is obliged to make do with questioning the nature of altruism, for in the West a good deal of what passes for love is self-referential – such is the nature of the ego. Even when a parent dies in a fire rescuing their child, this can be construed as not so different from self-serving love, in that the ego is invested in the survival of one's own flesh and blood.

Spiritual Love

'I lost myself. Forgot myself.
I lay my face against the Beloved's face.

---

17. Where there has been a history of childhood neglect or abuse, the spiritual path can lead for the first time to the experience of being worthy of love.
18. Matthew 22:39. *The Holy Bible*, NIV.
19. Matthew 13:12. *The Holy Bible*, NIV.
20. Luke 6:27–29. *The Holy Bible*, NIV.
21. Luke 6:33. *The Holy Bible*, NIV.

Everything fell away and I left myself behind,
Abandoning my care
Among the lilies, forgotten.'

From Songs of the Soul by John of the Cross[22]

It is not always clear what a person means when they say, 'I love you'. Are there strings attached ('I'll love you if you love me')? Does it mean 'I need you in order to feel good/secure/valued'? What of the stage of ambivalence previously mentioned? Sometimes people hesitate to speak of love because it is supposed to be all sweetness and light, yet they know there is a dark side to it. Might it be more to the point if we could say to our nearest and dearest in the same breath, 'I love you *and* hate you'?

When the needs of the ego are transcended, the spiritual love that supplants it takes a very different course. Such love is moved by what is in the best interests of the other, the desire being not to cling but to set free. Concerning the self, no fear remains, for what is there left to take away? Ultimately, only a person's physical life, and to the spiritual master this is of little consequence. As Jesus put it, 'For whoever wants to save their life will lose it, but whoever loses their life for me will find it. What good will it be for someone to gain the whole world, yet forfeit their soul?'[23]

Dietrich Bonhoeffer, the German pastor who plotted against Hitler, was incarcerated in Buchenwald and then hanged by the Nazis in 1945, is reported to have said to his Gestapo interrogator, 'You can take everything from me but that which is most precious – my soul'. Finally, as he was being led away for summary trial and execution, Bonhoeffer quietly turned to his friends in prison and said, 'This is the end – for me the beginning of life'.[24]

Most of us are spared the kind of ordeal that would test us to the limit and so we cannot know the measure of our own spiritual fortitude. Exemplars of such courage and selflessness make evident that we are no longer dealing with a mere emotion. This kind of love would seem to have a different source and a different consequence

---

22. This version from Starr (2002: 25).
23. Matthew 16:25–26. *The Holy Bible*, NIV.
24. Bonhoeffer ([1953]: 181).

entirely. I shall be suggesting that far from being merely an emotion, such love expresses the nature of consciousness in the most sublime form of which we humans are capable.

We can be helped in our understanding of this by turning to a schema that had its origins in the East long before Western civilization was born.

The Chakras

'Whether the symbol of the circle appears in primitive sun worship or modern religion, in myths or in dreams, in the mandala drawn by Tibetan monks, in the ground plan of cities or in the spherical concepts of early astronomers, it always points to the single most vital aspect of life – its ultimate wholeness.'

Carl Jung (1964)[25]

The conceptualisation of the chakras is over 5000 years old and pivotal to the ancient healing tradition of Indian Ayurveda. Even today, the importance of the chakras as psychological archetypes holds true regardless of scientific proof of the subtle energies being postulated[26] or of their hypothesised relationship to the autonomic nervous system.

The word *chakra* comes from the Sanskrit for 'circle' or 'wheel', symbolising a whirling vortex that draws in the subtle energy of the universal energy field (or *prana*) and transmutes the energy into a form that can be utilised, in this case, by the human organism.

There are seven main chakras located in the mid-line, lying along a spinal meridian known as the *sushumna*, linked by two collateral channels, the *ida* and *pingula*, running along either side. The chakras represent foci of high-intensity energy, influencing both psychic and bodily functioning.

In health all the chakras are open, balanced and with no obstruction to the free flow of energy. Each chakra powers a layer of the aura (human bioenergy field), an energetic standing wave that encompasses and interpenetrates every cell of the body. As it radiates

---

25. Jung (1964: 266).
26. Nelson (1994).

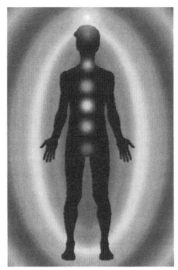

12.1 Illustration of the chakras and aura. Source: Pixabay.

outwards from the human body, it becomes confluent with the universal energy field.[27]

Telemetric research shows people to be extraordinarily sensitive to each other's energy fields,[28] as recorded in the account of Jesus' awareness of the woman who was healed of a blood disorder by touching his cloak ('At once Jesus realized that power had gone out from him. He turned around in the crowd and asked, "Who touched my clothes?"').[29] Similarly, 'hands-on' spiritual healing is carried out through making subtle adjustments to the auric field and the chakras.

Just as white light splits into the colours of the rainbow, each chakra represents an energetic differentiation of consciousness. Traditionally, they are each ascribed a specific colour refraction: red (the first or root chakra), orange (the sacral or second chakra), yellow (the solar plexus or third chakra), green (the heart or fourth chakra), blue (the throat or fifth chakra), indigo (the brow or sixth chakra) and violet/white (the crown or seventh chakra).

---

27. See Brennan (1988).
28. Hunt et al. (1977).
29. Mark 5:30. *The Holy Bible*, NIV.

- MULADHARA, the root chakra, provides the essential foundation for everything to follow. It anchors the self in physical reality. In the newborn, the individual self and the 'ground of all being' are as yet undifferentiated and the root chakra embodies the psyche of the infant in the physical world.
- SVADHISTANA, the sacral chakra, establishes the child's self-boundary. To begin with, wish-fulfilment and phantasy predominate. As the ego grows, mind and body differentiate. Duality arises and the emotions are born. Mental function is still concrete and pre-conceptual. At puberty, the chakra becomes genitally focused as the desire for sexual union arises.
- MANIPURA, the solar plexus chakra, is the furthest removed from the ground of all being. It mediates consensus reality, the collective consciousness on which society is based. Relationships are conflictual, love being characterised by need, possessiveness and insecurity, all hallmarks of ego-driven emotion. The mental and physical domains are widely separated, with abstract reasoning of the conceptual mind on the one hand and sense perception of the physical world on the other.
- ANAHATA, the heart chakra, lies at the midpoint between 'lower' and 'upper' chakras and here unselfish love makes its first appearance. The ego yields to a greater concern for all humanity. Compassion for the suffering of humankind, with an empathic outpouring of universal love, is represented by the Christ archetype.
- VISHUDDHA, the throat chakra, communicates spiritual will. The Higher Self or soul is expressed in grace, creativity, intuition and detachment from earthly goals – the Buddha archetype. By virtue of *knowing* as opposed to *believing* (gnosis rather than faith), the chakra manifests through spiritual teachings, sacred art or the most elevated scientific vision.
- AJNA, the brow chakra, sometimes known as the third eye, is the portal of the sixth sense, opening into the 'spiritual ground'. Ordinary consciousness is transcended and there is access to universal knowledge beyond space and time. Other-dimensional realities confer extra-sensory powers. Consciousness is no longer experienced as arising from the self. Together with unitive insight into the true nature of all things, it is the summit of attainment of the individual soul.

- SAHASRARA, the crown chakra, marks the return to the Source. The self is absorbed into the unity of spirit. Subject and object no longer exist and neither do space and time. The emotions dissolve into a state of is-ness, often described as perfect peace. All is One, as found in states of enlightenment or *samadhi*.

In Western psychology, there is very limited recognition of fifth-chakra consciousness (spiritual will) and regrettably, the characteristics of sixth and seventh chakra consciousness are generally taken to denote either religious or pathological altered states of consciousness. Yet to make sense of these chakras, we have to accept that any true description is beyond words – and thus beyond the reach of Western science. Lao Tsu, in the *Tao Te Ching*, says, 'Those who know do not talk. Those who talk do not know'.[30]

Working upwards from first to the fifth chakra, we find a broad correspondence with developmental psychology. The child is father to the man – the secure, happy child will grow into a confident and stable adult. Each consecutive chakra needs to be fully awakened, so that moving from ego-based concerns towards the spiritual life rests on a firm foundation. Sigmund Freud's contribution was mainly in the areas of chakras one, two and three, while Carl Jung's was to focus on the movement from chakras three to four and five, which he called the individuation process.

A good deal of confusion arises if it is not understood that the lower chakras have to do with personality and the higher chakras with soul. This confusion comes about because the undifferentiated nature of the first chakra, the 'no-self' of the newly born, looks at first sight like the mystical union of the seventh chakra with the spiritual ground. Similarly, the second chakra, where there is only partial differentiation between self and ground, may get confused with the sixth chakra, in which the limits of space-time are transcended. The third chakra, characterized by the striving of the ego for attainment, may similarly be compared to the fifth chakra, where there is an outpouring of creativity and will.

In each case, there is a crucial difference to be found in the relationship of 'earth' to 'heaven'. The first two chakras are rooted in the

---

30.   Feng & English (1973).

'ground of all being'. The young personality is forming and being prepared for the challenges of life ahead (sometimes referred to as the outward journey). This reaches its peak with the fully-fledged personality of the third chakra; we are pitched headlong into life to make of it what we best can. Then, with the opening of the heart chakra, we begin the return journey. The meaning of love profoundly changes as it becomes soul-centred. Thereafter, the task is to integrate life experience with spiritual reality, leading to wisdom.

Ken Wilbur calls the mis-identification of lower and upper chakras the 'pre/trans fallacy', since the lower chakras are implicated in pre-rational consciousness, while the upper ones are trans-rational.[31] The mystic with a stable sense of self who purposefully opens to higher consciousness is not to be confused with someone with a fragile self, vulnerable to delusions of an archetypal nature that can lead to a schizophrenic-type reaction.

Varieties of Love

'If I speak in the tongues of men or of angels, but do not have love, I am only a resounding gong or a clanging cymbal. If I have the gift of prophecy and can fathom all mysteries and all knowledge, and if I have a faith that can move mountains, but do not have love, I am nothing.'

1 Corinthians 13:1–2. The Holy Bible, NIV

First chakra love is primarily needs-driven, establishing in the first instance the infant's survival through taking milk from the breast, and subsequently, the motherly love that follows. This is the source of ontological security, first established through the rhythm and harmony of feeding on demand. From the 1920s, Dr Truby King, a widely esteemed paediatrician, argued that early training could impose desirable behaviour on children.[32] Mothers were instructed to follow a strict feeding regime, between times leaving their babies to cry lest it ruin the baby's 'independence'. King's regime was still influential in the 1940s and its effects are discernible to this day. This

---

31.   Wilbur (1980).
32.   King (1942).

and other disturbances of early child–mother bonding impair the function of the first chakra, leading later to a failure to feel 'grounded' in the body, and sometimes a vulnerability to psychosis.

Second chakra love is by its nature impulsive, unruly and inclined to phantasy. First making itself known in the toddler, it is passionate, unbridled and when frustrated, characterised by moodiness and tantrums. Teenage years are also dominated by the influence of this chakra – years that are idealistic, sexually charged and expressing the young person's emerging individuality. This love is of the still immature kind that says 'I love you *because* I need you'. It is essential that such volatile love be grounded in a stable first chakra so that it can build on a secure foundation of self-love. When stability is lacking, borderline pathology is sometimes evident, with transient hallucinations, disturbing Kundalini experiences[33] or dissociative states. Other distortions may arise across the whole gamut of neuroses, not least in the psychosexual arena.

Third chakra love is poised between the altruism of the fourth (heart) chakra and the self-absorption of the second chakra. At this level, the ego's power is harnessed to social ambition, sexual intimacy and finding a partner (often with the demands of family life). However, adulthood also means contending with the frustration and anxiety that life inevitably brings. Disturbances of the third chakra can lead to loss of control over alcohol, food, drugs or sex – attempts to quell feelings of emptiness and loss arising from disappointment in love. In the good outcome, the influence of the fourth chakra enables the third to relinquish its love of power in favour of the power of love that underpins healthy relationships. At the same time, the energy of the second chakra is increasingly harnessed to mature sexuality.

The fourth chakra holds the key to humankind's evolutionary potential. From here on, the meaning and purpose of love undergoes a profound change. Previous to this, in line with the dualistic nature

---

33. First referred to in early Hindu texts, Kundalini is experienced as an uncontrollable surge of energy accompanied by involuntary motor and sensory reactions and often in an altered state of consciousness. When sought through meditation, the aim is awakening to bliss. However, Kundalini can arise spontaneously, and in vulnerable individuals it can lead to a diagnosis of psychosis. See Sanella (1987).

of the world, the emotion of love has been coupled with its opposite pole, the emotion of fear. Since the lower chakras are required for the development of ego, love, longings and attachments inevitably carry a fear of disappointment and loss. Ideally, with the fourth chakra comes the first stage of the dissolution of ego and the transcending of personality – the Good Samaritan thinks only of how he can help, with no regard for himself.

Western psychology argues that the shadow must surely be in there somewhere, either repressed or split off and projected, as described earlier with projective identification. The esoteric view, however, is very different. Human consciousness is now awakening to love as the force immanent in all Creation. The ego and its fears are thereby transcended and insofar as it is still possible to speak of the concept of the shadow, it is found elsewhere in cycles of creation and destruction – on the grand cosmic scale, in the birth and death of stars.

When the heart is wide open to love, there is no longer the same shielding of the psyche by egoic structures and empathic sensitivity to pain can be overwhelming. In the practice of Tonglen,[34] Tibetan monks 'take in' the pain of life, transforming it through an act of healing into love that is sent out into the world. Someone who is not sufficiently mature or stable to cope with the inflow of pain can fall ill. It is therefore essential that the lower chakras are fully developed and engaged. As the Gospels make quite clear, there was nothing etherealised or 'ungrounded' about Jesus.

The fifth chakra is the seat of what is sometimes known as the Higher Self. This love, if we can but take heed of it, brings divine guidance to the unceasing drama of human life. As with the third chakra, there is a powerful outpouring of will, but now purely for the purpose of actuating spiritual love, for the benefit of humanity and indeed the whole world. Wisdom and equanimity are called for, otherwise a person may regress to the level of the second chakra, succumbing to grandiosity and the risk of breakdown.

Sixth chakra love is unattached to the human sphere, being absorbed profoundly in the primary nature of reality that transcends birth and death. This is the realm of extrasensory phenomena or

---

34. Rinpoche (1992).

siddhis. Adepts or practitioners of spiritual disciplines such as yoga or Qigong seek this level of consciousness, yet many people report occasional and transient breakthroughs of 'direct experience', especially when the mind is stilled.

The language of the seventh chakra is silence; there are no words or concepts to provide any kind of description. Where the base chakra is the starting point for the nascent human psyche, the crown chakra marks the absorption of the human psyche into the source of All That Is.

The seventh chakra has been likened to the seventh note of the musical scale. Some clairvoyants perceive an eighth chakra, reportedly eighteen inches above the crown of the head, which represents the first note of the next octave above. Octaves sound the same note, except that the frequency of the sound wave is doubled with each rising octave. It is humbling to remember that our space-time domain spans but one octave in a universe with many more notes than our senses can discern.

The Near-Life Experience

'...And the end of all our exploring
Will be to arrive where we started
And know the place for the first time'.

T.S. Eliot, from Little Gidding (1944)[35]

Every psychiatrist is confronted with people suffering from what I have called the near-life experience, in that they are not so much living as surviving. I have also observed that fear of dying is directly proportional to the sense of not having lived – the psyche knows there is a real danger of having missed the boat.

Esoteric wisdom teachings see the human journey as an opportunity for the development of the soul. I earlier described how the impact of trauma can cause a person to recoil from living to the full and instead to take refuge behind the barricade of ego defences. From this place of retreat, there can be no sense of adventure or

---

35.   Eliot ([1999]: 40).

discovery, only endless vigilance in the face of potential danger. As T.S. Eliot makes clear, 'to arrive where we started' does not mean treading a circular path, but seeing with new eyes in the light of the experiences that life has brought to us. For this to happen, we must equally bring ourselves to life.

In the parable of the talents[36] Jesus makes this point: the first of the servants, charged with investing his master's money in the master's absence, makes ten talents from the five he was given. His master is delighted, and is equally happy when the second servant makes four talents from two. However, the third servant who, for fear of losing the one talent he had been given, buried it in the ground to keep it safe, must bear the brunt of the master's wrath. The ego is deeply concerned with safety since it lives in fear of loss – loss of strength, of health, of relationships and of possessions. Most of all, the ego fears death. Being the psychological counterpart of the first three chakras, the ego is simply unable to comprehend the bigger picture in which a person feels to be part of, contributing to, and sustained by, a greater whole.

Spirituality, on the other hand, means *to belong to more than oneself.* It may be secular in kind, as when it is dedicated to humanitarian concerns, or sacred with regard to transcendent reality. Either way, however, the same joy is found in the well-spring of love that flows from selfless unity of purpose and in playing one's part the best one can.

The mundane struggles of life preoccupy most of us a good deal of the time. Nevertheless, as spiritual awareness grows – as the upper chakras open – a person will become aware of the vitality and power of love that transcends fear, including fear of death. This is the same love that is the hallmark of the near-death experience and which transforms the survivors for the remainder of their days.[37]

The advantage of looking at love in relation to the chakras is that we can see perfection in the design. We find a hierarchy of needs that transports the human soul from Earth to Heaven and this does not require us to wait for the resurrection. In the *Gospel of Thomas*, Jesus

---

36. Matthew 25:14-30. *The Holy Bible*, KJV. The talent was a unit of coinage used during the Roman occupation of Palestine.
37. Bailey & Yates (1996).

is asked about the Kingdom to come and replies, 'It will not come by watching for it. It will not be said, "Look, here it is", or "Look, there it is". Rather, the father's kingdom is spread out upon the earth and people do not see it'.[38] This is what the near-life experiencer finds so hard to recognise. Mired in the unhappiness of the past and constantly anticipating a fearful future, the beauty and majesty of the present moment passes unseen. Nevertheless, where there is the resolve, this developmental block can be overcome, for when we examine the nature of love revealed by the chakras in turn, we find that the journey through life is perfectly designed to allow for the unfolding of the psyche in its quest for self-realization.

Working With the Chakras

'Take hold tightly; let go lightly.
This is one of the great secrets of felicity in love.'

Alfred Orage, On Love (1924)[39]

No single chakra should be seen as more important than any other; each plays its part in the greater whole and speaking of 'lower' and 'higher' is merely a descriptive device.

The root chakra is the foundation of embodied life and all therapies must pay attention to the healthy emergence of the self from the ground of all being. The therapist needs to have the capacity to attune to the needs of the infant soul, for when this chakra is 'blocked', incarnation will have been tenuous and the life energy correspondingly depleted, with accompanying hesitancy and insecurity. Strengthening this chakra calls for unconditional love and recognition of the importance of 'grounding' with Mother Earth.

Second chakra love is demanding and needy and since the self is not yet developed, it requires meeting with loving but firm boundaries by the therapist, otherwise there may be impulsive 'acting out'. The patient needs help in learning how to accept and make do with

---

38. The Gospel of Thomas is one of the non-canonical gospels discovered at Nag Hammadi in 1945 and dating back to around 150–230 CE. See Meyer (1992).
39. Orage ([1998]: 17).

symbolic nourishment since the therapist is in no position to become parent or lover.

The third chakra is the domain of the untempered ego. Its hall-mark is the struggle of opposites: the conflict between greed and generosity, envy and gratitude, spite and kindness, hate and love. The danger lies in splitting and projection of the shadow, making the problem somebody else's fault instead of it being one's own. The person in denial of the shadow is frequently the most censorious, and at the same time no less fearful of being judged themselves. A rigid moral outlook may satisfy the demands of the super-ego but does not bring happiness. Yet when the shadow is owned and recognised to be part of the self, the wholeness that comes to be experienced puts the person in touch with the emotional world of others.[40] Then forbear-ance and consideration come naturally. Here is the opportunity for integration of the self and for healing of wounds. What enables such love and acceptance? This comes about with the help of the heart-centred fourth chakra. The ego is shown that compassion for the self and for others brings a greater happiness than sitting in judgement on all and sundry. Then the shadow can be seen as a gift, for acknowl-edging it as part of the self brings humility and tolerance.

The move from the third to the fourth chakra is one of the hard-est to make because the dynamic is always conflictual. Opening to the fourth chakra means moving beyond 'I love you because I need you' to 'I love you unconditionally'. For a person to overcome their ego anxiety and to let their loved one be free means that fear of rejec-tion and loss have to be faced. It is one thing trusting that love freely given will, in its own time and place, be returned in full; it is quite another to hold that in good faith when suffering the anguish and insecurity of third chakra love.

Sometimes a problem arises when the lower chakras are sup-pressed in an attempt to escape from the body and its emotional life. The self can become ungrounded and 'spiritualised', an inflation of the psyche that is both unstable and subject to spiritual pride. In contrast, true spiritual attainment is characterised by humility, together with a well-tempered and mature personality.

---

40.   Only the therapist who acknowledges their own shadow can help a client make peace with theirs. See *Good and Evil – a Psychiatrist's Perspective*, this volume.

For the purpose of this discussion, I am taking the upper chakras together because they present increasing refinements of the vibration of purely spiritual love. Rather than pathologise, it is surely time that Western psychology began recognising that these 'higher' states of consciousness have inspired the world's greatest religious, spiritual and shamanic traditions. They enable us to see beyond the bookends of our personal birth and death and to glimpse life on an altogether grander scale. Without the unitive vision afforded by this level of perception, the human species would seem to be stuck in a territorial mentality, which if unchecked in this age of global conflict, threatens the future of humankind.

Beyond Life and Death

'Do not stand at my grave and weep
I am not there. I do not sleep.
I am a thousand winds that blow.
I am the diamond glints on snow.
I am the sunlight on ripened grain.
I am the gentle autumn rain.
When you awaken in the morning's hush
I am the swift uplifting rush
Of quiet birds in circled flight.
I am the soft stars that shine at night.
Do not stand at my grave and cry;
I am not there. I did not die.'

Mary Elizabeth Frye (1932)

It may seem I have rank-ordered the chakras as though climbing the rungs of a ladder. However, all the chakras are intrinsic to the embodied psyche and need to work in harmony. Each one plays its part in equipping us to meet the developmental challenges that lie ahead. They also reflect the unique nature of the individual soul, for we arrive with different agendas and the tasks facing us are specific to our personal spiritual journey. All rivers flow to the sea, but each river must take its own course. The important thing is not to become snagged on an obstruction and of these, fear of life is the greatest. It is a great irony that fear of life leads to fear of death, while to embrace life is to make our peace with death.

As the river widens and we approach the unlimited ocean of consciousness, the upper chakras prepare us to take leave of the ego. Our egos usually get a bad press, yet without them there would be no means of transcendence, indeed no river to take us downstream. To the extent that we have been able to love wholeheartedly, we can plunge joyously and fearlessly into the ocean that awaits.

References

Bailey, A.A. (1947) *The Problems of Humanity*. Lucis Press.

Bailey, L.W. & Yates, J. (1996) *The Near Death Experience*. Routledge.

Barks, C. (trans.) (1999) 'Sublime Generosity'. In *The Essential Rumi*. HarperCollins.

Bell, G. (trans.) (2003) *The Garden of Heaven. Poems of Hafiz*. Dover Publications.

Bonhoeffer, D. (1945) *Letter and Papers from Prison*. Reprinted [1953], S.C.M. Press.

Boswell, J. (1791) *The Life Of Samuel Johnson*. Reprinted [1992], Everyman's Library Classics.

Brennan, B. (1988) *Hands of Light*. Bantam Press.

Eliot, T.S. (1944) *Four Quartets*. Reprinted [1999], Faber and Faber.

Feng, G.F. & English, J. (trans.) (1973) *Lao Tsu: Tao Te Ching* (section 56). Wildwood House.

Guo, B. & Powell, A. (2001) *Listen to Your Body: the Wisdom of the Dao*. University of Hawaii Press.

Hawking, S. (1988) *A Brief History of Time*. Bantam Press.

Hunt, V., Massey, W., Weinberg, R., et al. (1977) *A Study of Structural Integration from Neuromuscular, Energy Field and Emotional Approaches*. Rolf Institute of Structural Integration.

Jung, C.G. (1934) Archetypes of the collective unconscious. Reprinted [1959] in *C.G. Jung: The Collected Works*, vol. 9, part 1 (eds H. Read, M. Fordham & G. Adler). Routledge and Kegan Paul.

Jung, C.G. (1938) Psychology and religion. Reprinted [1958] in *C.G. Jung: The Collected Works*, vol. 11, Psychology and Religion. West and East.

Jung, C. (1964) *Man and his Symbols*. Reprinted [1968], Mass Marketing Paperbacks, Dell.

Keller, H. (1946) Faith fears not. In *Let Us Have Faith*. Doubleday.

King, T. (1942) *Feeding and Care of Baby*. Macmillan.

Meyer, M. (1992) *The Gospel of Thomas: Saying 113*. HarperSanFrancisco.

Nelson, J. (1994) *Healing the Split*. State University of New York Press.

Orage, A.R. (1924) *On Love & Psychological Exercises*. Reprinted [1998], Red Wheel/Weiser.

Rinpoche, S. (1992) *The Tibetan Book of Living and Dying*. HarperSanFrancisco.

Sanella, L. (1987) *The Kundalini Experience: Transcendence or Psychosis*. Integral Publishing.

Starr, M. (2002) *Dark Night of the Soul.* Riverhead Books.

Tennyson, Lord A. (1847) *In Memoriam A.H.H.* Reprinted [2007] in *Selected Poems: Tennyson.* Penguin Classics.

Veal, A. & Stavrou, A. (2007) Former Lord's Resistance Army child soldier abductees: exploration of identity in reintegration and reconciliation. *Peace and Conflict: Journal of Peace Psychology,* 13(3), 273–292.

Wilbur, K. (1980) 'The pre/trans fallacy'. *Re-Vision,* 3, 58.

13

Spirituality, Healing and the Mind

The words healing and wholeness share the same root. This reminds us that any discussion about healing has to address the longing for wholeness that has such universal appeal. Wholeness is the central archetype of humankind, symbolised by the mandala, a circle representing completeness, harmony and balance for both humankind and the natural world. Carl Jung, among others, paid great attention to the mandala. Within the circle is often found a quaternion of elements requiring synthesis, the healing of a dis-unity, which the circle embraces.[1]

In contrast, the approach of Western medicine is mechanistic, the term 'healing' referring to the repair of damaged tissues, as with wounds, burns or surgical incisions. As to mental healthcare, where it might be thought that the concept of healing would be helpful, the word is simply never used.

There is another term employed by Western medicine that betrays the same shift of focus away from healing. The word *pathology* derives from the Greek *pathos*, meaning suffering. Medical science has appropriated the word to stand not for *dis*-ease as something experienced, but to describe abnormalities of the structure and function of the body. This physicalist view of the patient has led to great attention being given to the car, so to speak, but not the driver.

Psychiatry has trodden the same path and has accorded neuroscience, which gives primacy to brain structure and function, a near-iconic status. When brain lesions (e.g. tumours) give rise to

First published in *Spirituality and Health International* (2005), 6, 166–172. Reproduced with permission.

---

1. Jung (1950).

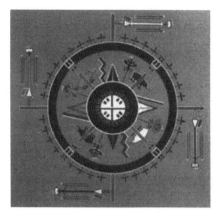

13.1. Sand mandala, drawn by a Navajo medicine man. It represents the internal balance that the ill person needs in order to achieve physical and psychological wholeness. The sand painting opens a connection to the spirit world. As the medicine man sings holy chants, the patient sits at the centre of the mandala facing East so that the spirits can bring healing agents and take away the causes of illness and imbalance.

abnormal mental states, we are indeed in step with medicine in speaking of pathology – in this case neuropathology. Yet even though most mental illness cannot be explained by physical, chemical, metabolic or hormonal influences, psychiatrists frequently refer to psychopathology (disease of the mind), justified on the grounds that the physical cause has yet to be elucidated or, failing that, to signify the extent to which an individual's thoughts, feelings and behaviour have departed from the consensus norm of society.[2]

The Healing Touch

'Diseases' are treated with specific remedies that at best may bring about cure; there are enough cures to disguise the fact that most diseases are chronic and cumulative, especially with ageing, and amelioration of symptoms is often the best that can be achieved. Yet 'cure' is a magical word, one that patients are as reluctant as their doctors to

2. Powell (2003a).

relinquish, for cure slays death, or at least promises to stay its hand. The objectives of cure and healing (wholeness) therefore lie on parallel continua:

Cure

PRESENCE OF DISEASE <--------------------> ABSENCE OF DISEASE
        (SYMPTOMS)   (SYMPTOM-FREE)

Healing

MINIMAL HEALTH   <-------------------->   OPTIMAL HEALTH
        (ILLNESS)   (WELLNESS)

Adapted from Swinton[3]

This raises the paradox that a person may have a terminal disease and yet be well, in the sense of health as wholeness of being. Health reflects the degree of adaptation to the conditions of life. This is why it is possible to speak of 'healing into death'. To face death peacefully and in repose, feeling that one's life was rich in experience and opportunity, that one made the best of it, that one has loved and been loved, and to be able to cherish such time that remains until taking leave of the world, is to die healed.[4]

Mental Health and Spirituality

Despite strong research evidence that spirituality and health are positively correlated,[5] spirituality has been regarded within mainstream medicine as largely irrelevant to the work of the clinical team. This is also true for psychiatry, not least because religious and spiritual themes have come to be identified with illness and viewed through the lens of pathology.

The psychiatrist, often beleaguered and trying to maintain an emergency service with pitifully inadequate resources, relies primarily on medication, secondly on social support networks and thirdly

---

3. Swinton (2001).
4. Kearney (1996).
5. Koenig et al. (2001).

on psychological interventions where deemed appropriate. Given that the psychiatrist is also three times less likely to hold a religious faith than is the patient,[6] it is hardly surprising that patients get little support for spiritual sources of comfort and strength. Sometimes the chaplain will be called in, but more often a patient preoccupied with religious or spiritual concerns will be advised not to dwell on such matters, or if suffering from a psychosis, will find those experiences dismissed as delusions or hallucinations. Despite this, there is evidence that up to a half of patients count their beliefs as very important in helping them get through their breakdown.[7]

The Spiritual Agenda

Across creed and culture, there is the belief that the soul takes a body for the purpose of incarnate existence. This is either a mass delusion, as Sigmund Freud would have us think,[8] or archetypal recognition of the soul's eternal nature, embedded deeply in human consciousness and undeterred by the prevailing culture of material realism.[9]

Different religions variously describe the journey of the soul, its passage through life and its final destination. Yet common to all, including many who do not belong to a faith tradition, is the belief that life is, by its nature, a profound spiritual challenge. Our emotions, which depend on our physiology as much as our consciousness, take us on a rollercoaster of joy and pain, delight and despair. The development of an integrated personality sustains us as we learn and grow. Through raising our level of consciousness, we become aware of the greater meaning and purpose of our lives. To suffer without finding meaning diminishes us, but suffering that holds meaning is a spur to growth. In the course of our soul-searching, we are beset by fundamental questions like 'Why am I here?', 'Why must I suffer?', 'What is the point of it all?', 'Is life just down to chance?', 'Is there anything beyond birth and death?' These questions can become crucial when the identity of the self breaks down and there is painful

---

6. Shafranske (2000).
7. Faulkner (1997).
8. Freud (1927).
9. See *Soul Consciousness and Human Suffering*, this volume.

loss of all that previously was familiar and reassuring.[10] If breakdown is to become breakthrough, a new sense of purpose – often a new goal – is needed for the shattered self to recover. The journey of heal-ing is a spiritual one and one that may involve taking a deep look at what really matters to a person in life.

It is remarkable that psychiatry resists this greater picture, since breakdown so often confronts people with deep existential anguish. Clearly, issues of personal identity, sexuality, family life, relationships and work all need to be addressed and for this we have a comprehen-sive bio-psychosocial model of development. Yet in the UK, as in many other countries, spirituality has been largely left out of the picture.[11]

The Consequences of Trauma

The first trauma a baby must endure is the birth process, following which – since anxiety, pain and frustration must arise from time to time – trauma is an inevitable accompaniment to life. The infant who is healthy and well loved can cope with these disruptions, but when love and care are in short supply, the trauma that began with birth is constantly re-activated and where there is cruelty and abuse, the effects on the child's personality can be catastrophic.[12]

To some extent, every emergent self is wounded along the way. When emotional distress becomes intolerable, ego defences are trig-gered.[13] Among these are repression, denial, splitting and projection. In the case of repression, the aim is to bury the source of pain, not unlike disposing of nuclear waste down a mineshaft. However, the same danger applies; the buried 'material' will eventually find its way to the surface, where the impact can be just as powerful 50 years on. Denial enables a person to strip an event of its emotional meaning, a pathological detachment that relieves pain at the cost of paralysing emotional responsiveness. Splitting relieves the psyche of the tension of holding ambivalent feelings – towards others and towards oneself.

---

10. Ulman & Brothers (1988).
11. See *Putting the Soul into Psychiatry*, this volume.
12. Kalsched (1996).
13. See *Psychosocial Implications of the Shadow*, this volume.

It often results in idealising the one we have chosen to rescue us (from ourselves), and denigrating the one who is perceived as having failed us. Projection entails discharging painful emotions into someone or something outside of oneself. Then it no longer feels to belong to oneself, but can be attacked without mercy in the other (the basis of scapegoating – hence the saying that inside every bully is a victim).

I outline some of these inner mechanisms to indicate that from an early age, we are busy defending our sense of self in a world that is frequently experienced as threatening and hostile, a stance some people feel obliged to take for the rest of their lives. Survival has been ensured but at a price since these defences work not by uniting the self but by putting up barriers against psychic pain. Consequently, there is a diminution of the deeper awareness that could otherwise bring insight and healing, which is to say, wholeness.

Overcoming Trauma

Finding wholeness of being is not something we can accomplish alone. For example, colic, chafing, hunger pains, colds and the like all threaten the nascent integrity of the infant psyche and thus are traumas in the making. However, the intimacy of love, and the sense of being safely held in the mother's arms, provide the infant with an experience of ontological security that becomes internalised.[14] Through this inward sense of containment and safety, the child is now learning to manage tension and distress without becoming traumatised, and this is the legacy of all good parenting.

A person who is experiencing a mental breakdown no longer feels 'held'. Rather, there is a painful sensation of the world falling apart, with nothing and no one to hold it together any more. The psychic pain can be so extreme that suicide sometimes seems to be the only way out. This is where psychodynamic therapy can help by offering a safe environment in which the patient can begin to recover the feeling of being held – the 'corrective experience'.[15] The therapist

---

14. See *Varieties of Love*, this volume.
15. Hartman & Zimberoff (2004).

comes to stand *in loco parentis* and what is known as transference develops, the patient bringing to the therapist their unresolved hopes, fears and needs, many of which have their roots in the distant past.

Together, therapist and patient explore how defence mechanisms have taken over at the cost of imprisoning the core sense of self and how these defences can be set aside. As the patient lets down their guard, emotional sensitivity is heightened, for the underlying pain has to be faced. This is done with the support and concern of the therapist much as a mother will attend to her child in distress.

Yet for a good many patients, if the frame of reference is confined strictly to psychological needs, progress will be limited. Spirituality *must* be ruled as admissible; otherwise, the soul – the archetype of wholeness known to every human being – gets left outside the door.[16] The soul itself may never explicitly be discussed but its qualities of generosity, forbearance, forgiveness and unconditional love need to be valued and affirmed by patient and therapist alike.

Love, Spirituality and the Ego

Being a good doctor is, at its best, a vocation prompted by love, although most doctors would not think of it as such. Moreover, this is not love that is ego-driven, for it arises from the soul. Characterized by compassion and humility, it forms a deep, unspoken bond between physician and patient. In the mental health profession, too, there are many with just this sense of vocation. How should people otherwise cope with the immense stress and palpable lack of reward?

The empathy natural to the soul comes from knowing we are like one another and that despite our many differences we belong to each other – just as quantum entanglement reminds us that we are waves of the same ocean.[17] When we understand this, we realise that we belong to life itself and this is to discover wholeness of being. Yet one wave is not exactly like another. We have individual selves, for which the ego is needed. Hungry for experience and for mastery of the world, the ego provides the locomotive power needed to meet the

---

16.   Powell (2003b).
17.   See *Beyond Space and Time*, this volume.

challenges of human life. Being dedicated to the survival of the individual self, the ego is disparaged in many spiritual teachings. Yet
trouble only arises when it behaves as master of the psyche rather
than its servant. Paradoxically, it is the ego's fear of illness, disability
and death that often prompts the most profound and soul-searching
questions about the nature and purpose of existence.

When we step back from the ego, the soul-centred perspective is
revealed and at once we become aware of a greater vision of life than
the ego can ever hold.[18] For many people, this vision is shaped by
religious belief. However, if we turn to reports of the near-death
experience, we find that no matter whether a person's background is
religious or non-religious, even though the content of the near-death
experience may be shaped by culture, its essence is the same: an overwhelming experience of being immersed in love so accepting and
without judgement that it is possible to know the worst about ourselves and still find healing and forgiveness.[19]

Fortunately, healing the psyche does not require such otherworld
excursions. However, if treatment aims merely to return the patient
to the same life circumstances that preceded the health crisis, the
result is likely to be further episodes of illness, for in its original
meaning of '*dis*-ease', illness is a warning that life is seriously out of
balance.

Soul-Centred Therapy

For healing to take place, it is important to be able to explore with
the patient, compassionately and without fear or prejudice, the areas
of conflict, inhibition, anxiety and fear that deeply affect a person's
well-being. The psychiatrist is used to taking a psychological history
just as the physician takes a medical history. Yet mental health professionals are not shown how to take a spiritual history, which can
be easily done and is often profoundly revealing of a person's values,
beliefs and concerns. For example, Koenig[20] suggests asking:

---

18.   See *The Unquiet Self*, this volume.
19.   Bailey & Yates (1996).
20.   Koenig (2002).

- Does the patient use religion or spirituality to cope with illness, or is it a source of stress?
- Is the patient a member of a supportive spiritual community?
- Does the patient have any troubling spiritual questions or concerns?
- Does the patient have any spiritual beliefs that might influence medical care?

These simple enquiries quickly open the way to deeper discussion if desired, with important implications:

1. The reductive/analytic questioning needed to explore the presenting problem is thereby nested within a unitive spiritual perspective.
2. It can be readily ascertained whether a person conceives of a greater (transcendental) reality. If so, issues of separation and loss, disability and suffering take on a new meaning.
3. The door may be open to working transpersonally,[21] using approaches in line with the patient's own spiritual beliefs. In the Judaic, Christian and Islamic faiths, for instance, the power of prayer may be harnessed.[22] Meditation, drawn from the Buddhist tradition, can form a valued part of therapy.[23] Belief in reincarnation, these days widely held in the West as well as in the East, allows for an exploration of karma and the possibility of healing through 'past life' therapy.[24] If a person complains of the presence of unwelcome spirit influences, spirit release therapy may prove to be an effective intervention.[25] Other times, in cases of abuse, for example, it may be appropriate to use a shamanic approach in helping the patient reclaim the soul they feared they had lost.[26]

---

21. The transpersonal has been defined as 'experiences in which the sense of identity or self extends beyond (trans) the individual or personal to encompass wider aspects of humankind, life, psyche or cosmos' (Walsh & Vaughan, 1993).
22. Perry (2000).
23. Kabat-Zinn (1990).
24. Woolger (1999).
25. See *Psychiatry and Spirit Release Therapy*, this volume.
26. Rutherford (1996).

How the therapist responds to the psycho-spiritual dimension of mental health problems depends on their training, skills and willingness to be engaged. At the very least, taking a spiritual history should be routine. Importantly, religious or spiritual prejudice in the therapist must be addressed in the same way that problems of transference and countertransference are identified in good clinical practice.[27]

In Conclusion

Where the therapist ensures that the relationship with the patient is honest and authentic, a contact is formed that deeply supports the patient in times of suffering.[28] The therapist need not be afraid of the love that is evoked, for this comes from the soul, which is the source of healing. Such love is as dispassionate as compassionate – contingent upon a source that transcends the best efforts of the ego. Deep in each of us, there is the desire to find happiness, fulfilment and love. No matter how wounded the psyche, the soul, albeit obscured by the pain and anguish of the ego, is nevertheless on hand and ready to bring healing to the broken heart.

Those of us engaged in mental healthcare can help to bring the soul into view and this is never more important than when the patient is mired in despair. Sometimes our patients mistakenly seek death as the means to ending their pain, not realising that what needs to 'die' is a life in which the ego holds them captive, leaving them feeling bereft of the love and wisdom on which to draw to see them through. Our task as doctors and therapists is to help them to discover that the healing of wounds does not have to wait on death. Rather, such healing can and should be at the heart of life.

References

Bailey, L.W. & Yates, J. (1996) *The Near Death Experience.* Routledge.
Faulkner, A. (1997) *Knowing Our Own Minds.* Mental Health Foundation.

---

27.   Larson & Larson (2001).
28.   See *Spirituality and Science* and *Mental Health and Spirituality,* both this volume.

Freud, S. (1927) The future of an illusion. Reprinted [1961] in *The Standard Edition of the Complete Psychological Works of Sigmund Freud*, vol. 21 (trans. & ed. J. Strachey). Hogarth Press.

Hartman, D. & Zimberoff, D. (2004) Corrective emotional experience in the therapeutic process. *Journal of Heart-Centered Therapies*, 7, 3–84.

Jung, C. (1950) Concerning Mandala Symbolism. Reprinted [1959] in *C.G. Jung: The Collected Works*, vol. 9, part 1: The Archetypes and the Collective Unconscious (eds H. Read, M. Fordham & G. Adler). Routledge and Kegan Paul.

Kabat-Zinn, J. (1990) *Full Catastrophe Living*. Delacorte.

Kalsched, D. (1996) *The Inner World of Trauma*. Routledge.

Kearney, M. (1996) *Mortally Wounded*. Marino Books.

Koenig, H.K., McCullough, M.E. & Larson, D.B. (2001) *Handbook of Religion and Health*. Oxford University Press.

Koenig, H.K. (2002) *Spirituality in Patient Care*. Templeton Foundation Press.

Larson, D.B. & Larson, S.S. (2001) The patient's spiritual/religious dimension: a forgotten factor in mental health. *Directions in Psychiatry*, vol. 21, Lesson 21. Available at: http://www.rcpsych.ac.uk/spsigarchive

Perry, J. (2000) *A Time to Heal: A Report for the House of Bishops on the Healing Ministry*. Church House Publishing.

Powell, A. (2003a) Psychiatry and spirituality – the forgotten dimension. Available at: www.rcpsych.ac.uk/powellarchive

Powell, A. (2003b) Consciousness that Transcends Spacetime: its Significance for the Therapeutic Process. *Self and Society*, 31, 27–44.

Rutherford, L. (1996) *Shamanism*. Thorsons HarperCollins.

Shafranske, E.P. (2000) Religious involvement and professional practices of psychiatrists and other mental health professionals. *Psychiatric Annals*, 30, 525–532.

Swinton, J. (2001) *Spirituality and Mental Health Care*. Jessica Kingsley.

Ulman, R. & Brothers, D. (1988) *The Shattered Self*. The Analytic Press.

Walsh, R. & Vaughan, F. (1993) On transpersonal definitions. *Journal of Transpersonal Psychology*, 25(2), 125–182.

Woolger, R. (1999) *Other Lives, Other Selves*. Bantam Books.

14

Death and Soul Consciousness

'If the Doors of Perception were cleansed, everything would appear to Man as it is, infinite. For Man has closed himself up, till he sees all things thro' narrow chinks of his cavern.'

William Blake, The Marriage of Heaven and Hell (1790)[1]

Given that this subject is only likely to attract people interested in what may lie beyond the physical world, I will be pursuing a number of strands of enquiry, each of which suggests that physical death, far from being the end of the line, is but a platform for changing trains.

I will begin with how I came to be interested in 'other worlds'. I hope to show how such intuitions and experiences can be reconciled with science, although not of the kind that was ever taught at school. Then, I will be highlighting some key areas of research into the survival of consciousness after death. I will conclude on a more personal note, with illustrations from past life therapy that have persuaded me that consciousness extends beyond the life one is experiencing right now.

First Enquiries

'We are perceivers. We are an awareness; we are not objects; we have no solidity. We are boundless. The world of objects and solidity is a way of making our passage on earth convenient… So, in essence,

Paper prepared for conference 'Beyond death – does consciousness survive?' King's College Hospital and Medical School, London, 2004.

---

1. Blake [2000].

the world that your reason wants to sustain is the world created by a description and its dogmatic and inviolable rules, which the reason learns to accept and defend.'

Carlos Castaneda, Tales of Power[2]

I was brought up in the Anglican tradition. My interest in 'other worlds', however, was fired by reading *The Tibetan Book of the Dead*[3] when I was 17 years old. The author, Walter Evans-Wentz, was a scholar and anthropologist who first brought the esoteric teachings of Tibetan Buddhism to the West. In this text, systematically described, I found an account of the *bardo*, the after-life realm, with clear guidance about what to expect. At the moment of death, a person would be drawn towards the clear light of absolute consciousness. But then, unless one's spiritual attainment had reached liberation from the cycle of birth and death, one would be pulled towards less brilliant but alluring colours, a kind of downhill slide leading to encounters with glorious and terrifying deities, and then, last of all, to the onset of sexual desire and the birth instinct, resulting in the next incarnation.

Another spur to my curiosity was coming across *The Doors of Perception*,[4] which described the effect of mescaline, a hallucinogen similar to lysergic acid diethylamide (LSD). I spent my last term at school in the chemistry lab trying to synthesize mescaline (with the bemused consent of the chemistry master). The experiment finally yielded a small flask of a dark oily concentrate, which looked and smelled so diabolical that I reluctantly poured it down the sink.

However, during the early 1960s, LSD could still be obtained legally from the manufacturers and so, while a medical student, I got hold of some and took it several times. With the astonishing dissolution of the ego that ushered in an ecstatic oneness with the cosmos, I found myself experiencing a reality in which consciousness traverses all sense of space and time. I did not know it then, but the effects of LSD were already being systematically researched by the psychiatrist

---

2. Castaneda (1974: 100–101).
3. Evans-Wentz (1927).
4. Huxley (1954).

Stanislav Grof,[5] who popularized the term 'transpersonal' and was pioneering the exploration of altered states of consciousness.[6]

The recreational drug abuse of the late 1960s led to LSD getting a bad name. Then in 1968, the anthropologist Carlos Castaneda published *The Teachings of Don Juan: A Yaqui Way of Knowledge*,[7] based on the fieldwork he undertook for his PhD and the first of an extraordinary series of books. Castaneda described being ritually inducted into the use of the hallucinogen peyote and its consequent effect on his life. There has been heated debate about the validity of Castaneda's account but nothing I read there greatly surprised me after my own experiences with LSD. Castaneda writes of the 'assemblage point', a somato-psychic point of attachment to our particular dimensional world, and how learning to move this point at will takes one into other worlds. He writes of watching his shamanic teacher and guide, Don Juan, pass out of this world by making such a transit when the time came to leave.

I will cite one more example, of the hallucinogenic vine ayahuasca, taken by Amazonian shamans to enter the spirit world. In *The Cosmic Serpent*,[8] anthropologist Jeremy Narby relates his own ayahuasca-induced experience, which suggested to him that in the altered state of consciousness it is possible to receive information directly from DNA. The Amazon Indians explained to him that they obtained their vast pharmacopoeia in this way by communing directly with the plants under the influence of the drug.

Such instances – and there are many more – challenge the rigid constraints of Western empirical science (the 20th century may prove to be the era in which material realism reached its zenith). Over the past 25 years, there has been a resurgence of scientific enquiry into the spiritual universe and the nature of soul consciousness, as evidenced by the Institute of Noetic Sciences in the USA and the Scientific and Medical Network in the UK.

---

5. Grof (1993).
6. See Bache (2000).
7. Castaneda (1968).
8. Narby (1999).

Medicine and the Physicalist Tradition

'The Universe is of the nature of a thought or sensation in a universal Mind.'

Sir Arthur Eddington[9]

'It is almost an absurd prejudice to suppose that existence can only be physical. As a matter of fact, the only form of existence of which we have immediate knowledge is psychic (i.e. in the mind). We might as well say, on the contrary, that physical existence is a mere inference, since we know of matter only in so far as we perceive psychic images mediated by the senses.'

Carl Jung[10]

Altered states of consciousness are one line of enquiry among many. It happened that my own researches started there. On qualifying as a doctor, I began to witness death, most of it traumatic. During failed cardiopulmonary resuscitation, I privately observed that a change would come over the person's eyes – they would seem to cloud over as though the life had gone out of them and when this happened, the person never came back. It struck me that the soul was no longer in residence.

The Concise Oxford Dictionary defines life as 'the condition which distinguishes active animals and plants from inorganic matter, including the capacity for growth, functional activity, and continual change preceding death'. Death is defined in turn as 'the final cessation of vital functions in an organism; the ending of life'. This is the verdict of the prevailing culture of physicalist science – one that sees death as the inevitable and final end-point of life. Nevertheless, to this day, many people with religious faith believe that physical death is no more than the end of bodily existence. Such trust is generally based on the idea that soul and body must be separate things. This dualist position is inimical to Newtonian science on two counts. Firstly, no one can explain how dualism actually works, since during life it would require a communication between mind and body that

---

9. Eddington (1938: 151).
10. Jung (1938: 12).

would violate the laws of conservation of energy and momentum. Secondly, the prospect of life beyond the grave is discounted by arguing that there can be no enduring identity if there is no brain. Based on such objections, reports of encounters with spirits and the like are dismissed as nothing but mental projections clothed in human form.

Quantum Cosmology

'One windy day, two monks were arguing about a flapping banner. The first said, "I say the banner is moving, not the wind." The second said, "I say the wind is moving, not the banner." A third monk passed by and said, "the wind is not moving. The banner is not moving. Your minds are moving".'

Zen parable[11]

The Newtonian revolution advanced the view that one could take a thing, dissect it, analyse it and so find out all about it. In the West, this view permeated the arts too, as illustrated in this short poem by Alfred Lord Tennyson:

'Flower in the crannied wall,
I pluck you out of the crannies,
I hold you here, root and all, in my hand,
Little flower—but if I could understand
What you are, root and all, and all in all,
I should know what God and man is.'[12]

The part is isolated from the whole. Yet we know now that there is no such thing as a closed system independent of the greater system in which it is nested (including in this case the mind of the poet). Flower and poem cannot be teased apart, any more than the reader, whose consciousness brings him/her into intimate relation with the poem. If we widen and deepen the vision we eventually find, as mystics have always known, the unity and indivisibility of all things.

---

11.   *Zen Buddhism: An Introduction to Zen* (Anonymous, 1959: 52).
12.   Nicholson & Lee (1917).

Thankfully, the canon of reductive science is counterbalanced by our instinctive, archetypal search for the living whole, the *anima mundi*. We go on wanting to know what happens to us when life is over, just as we want to know from whence we came. In the climate of material realism, such concerns are brushed aside since consciousness is held merely to be a by-product of cellular activity – coming from nowhere and going nowhere. However, astrophysicists who study the physical universe find themselves up against the same conundrum. Just what *was* there before the Big Bang? What *is* going to happen after the heat death of the universe in 100 billion years' time?

The big questions keep turning up at different orders of magnitude. This reminds us that the cosmos, physical and mental, is one coherent whole, a 'holoverse', as David Bohm put it,[13] so that the same configurations are bound to recur repeatedly, no matter where the spotlight is pointed. This concept is not new. It is fundamental to traditional Chinese medicine, which treats the human body as a microcosm of the macrocosm.[14] The part always contains the whole, as illustrated by the mapping of acupressure points on the ear.

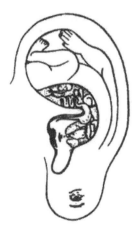

14.1 Acupoints of the body mapped on to the ear.
From Guo & Powell (2001: 8).

Fifty years before the invention of the hologram, Alice Bailey, endeavouring to bring the wisdom of the East to the West, wrote:

---

13. See Talbot (1991).
14. Guo & Powell (2001).

'Energy is now regarded as all that is. The physical manifestation is the manifestation of the sea of energies, some of which are built into forms, others constitute the medium in which those forms live and move and have their being, and still others are in the process of animating both the forms and their surrounding, substantial media. It must also be remembered that forms exist within forms; this is symbolized in the intricate carved ivory balls of the Chinese craftsmen, where ball within ball is to be discovered, all elaborately carved and all free and yet confined.'[15]

If a scale of magnitude is drawn between sub-atomic particles at one end to the known size of our universe at the other, we humans come halfway between the two. We can look in one direction reductionistically and in the opposite direction holistically. Particle physics has shown that matter is composed of energy, which manifests above a certain threshold as something solid and enduring. Yet on closer inspection, molecules dissolve into atoms that in turn dissolve into an array of particles mysteriously arising from the 'dark matter' and 'dark energy' that comprises 95% of the known universe. It is an ocean of energy so immense that the physicist Richard Feynman once remarked that one cubic metre would be sufficient to boil all the oceans of the world.[16]

Newton's laws deal with a mechanical universe situated in its own objective reality in which we observers come along and shine our torches on what was already there. What we illuminate is unmoved by our scrutiny and when the torch goes off everything remains just as before. On the other hand, quantum mechanics tells us that what we call objective reality does not, of itself, exist. There is no world of things out there that exists independently of consciousness. Rather, it is consciousness that brings about what in quantum physics is known as the 'collapse of the wave function'. From a quantum realm of infinite possibilities, the collapse of the wave precipitates the parameters of space-time and all it contains, including us.[17] Mind and matter are simultaneous products of the collapse of the wave; two sides of one coin, they cannot be treated independently of each other.

---

15. Bailey (1934: 81).
16. McTaggart (2001: 24).
17. See *Beyond Space and Time*, this volume.

There is nothing permanent about the physical reality that arises with the collapse of the wave; all matter is simply a temporary energetic structure vibrating with the life force of the cosmos. Like the *ouroboros*, the ancient symbol of the snake swallowing its own tail, the cosmos is engaged in an eternal dance, the part endlessly dissolving into the whole and the whole endlessly manifesting in the part. In this cosmology, complex life forms like us have a special role to play in the great scheme of things. Because of our faculty of self-awareness, we go about creating consciousness, just as consciousness creates us. We are involuntarily participants in what is called a 'tangled hierarchy'.[18]

The physical substance of the universe furnishes us with brains to mediate the thoughts, feelings and memories that comprise the ego. However, where the personal and temporal interleave with the transpersonal and infinite, we know intuitively that we are eternal beings. This is the nature of 'soul consciousness'.

Time and Eternity

'Time is what keeps everything from happening at once.'

Ray Cummings (1923)[19]

No physical matter can resist the arrow of time. In accordance with the laws of thermodynamics, all forms, organic and inorganic, invariably succumb to entropy.

At other times energy is massively concentrated, hence the singularity known as the Big Bang, which erupted from the quantum void, synthesising in the first few milliseconds all the matter that is now found in our universe.

In 1948, Thomas Gold, Fred Hoyle and Hermann Bondi came up with the steady state theory, which hypothesised that new galaxies continuously form to take the place of galaxies reaching the end of their lifespan. The theory was discredited, but it would now seem the problem was one of failure to appreciate the scale of things. Since the

---

18. Goswami (1993: 182).
19. Cummings ([2005]: 46).

discovery of super-strings, we know we inhabit a multidimensional cosmos resonating with infinite harmonies. Subatomic particles flit between universes, and it is inevitable that universes, too, come and go, as they arise, and are absorbed back into the quantum void.

Where there is consciousness, there is space. Where there is space there is movement and where there is awareness of movement there is time. Ego consciousness is grounded in the body and is thus bound to chronological time. Yet, for the soul, time has no fixed measure, as reported in states of enlightenment or *samadhi*, out-of-body experiences, near-death experiences and after-death communications. The information being relayed back is mediated by the mind/brain and so it can never have an independent status. No one can know what it is truly like after we die until we go beyond making the return journey but such evidence as we have suggests that space-time is fluid. Similarly, in what is sometimes called 'an awakening' or 'direct experience', space-time is transcended; past, present and future are one. Accessing other realms of space-time, such as during past life regression, reveals different 'rule sets' in which a person may find themselves stepping across into another life as though all the lives were arranged like so many spokes of a wheel around its hub.[20] In after-death communications, as with reported near-death experiences, travel takes no time (think yourself there and it is done) while communication with other souls appears to traverse space by means of direct thought transference.

Here in our everyday world, we regularly come across phenomena such as precognition, clairvoyance and telepathy that fly in the face of Newtonian physics. The evidence base is now well established and it is quite possible that in other worlds, this kind of communication may be the rule rather than the exception. Discussion of the quantum realm and other dimensions raises all kinds of paradoxes. Is there such a thing as free will, or is everything pre-determined, leaving us the illusion of freedom? We think we have choice; we deliberate and then decide on a course of action. Yet should the script already be written, we would still experience it *de novo*. Are we living in a virtual reality, like a cosmic computer game played by discarnate beings (ourselves?) in another dimension? Is there a multiplicity of

---

20. See *Putting the Soul into Psychiatry*, this volume.

virtual dimensions into which we venture? Not least, what about the anthropic viewpoint, which suggests that humankind is implicated in the emergence of a self-aware universe?

The physicist John Wheeler proposed the following thought experiment: imagine an observer some light years away from a quantum mechanical experiment. The experiment is carried out but the observer does not decide until later whether he wants to measure the momentum or the position of the particle released (according to quantum theory, one cannot know both at the same time). When this decision is made, at some point in the future, it must retroactively determine the outcome of the experiment in the past. Could it be that the cosmos similarly observes itself, the emergence of consciousness retroactively determining precisely those initial conditions that millions of years later will allow its unfoldment?

While this may all seem far-fetched, closer to home, consider the recent study on the retroactive effects of prayer by Leibovici.[21] The medical records of 2000 patients with bloodstream infection between 1990 and 1996 were randomised in July 2000 to a control group and an intervention group. Intercessory prayers were said for the well-being and full recovery only for those in the intervention group. Length of stay in hospital and duration of fever were found to be significantly shorter in the intervention group than the control group. Leibovici, as a hardened sceptic, carried out this experiment tongue in cheek and no one was more surprised than he by his own findings.

Looking forward through time brings us to the body of evidence for precognition. Anecdotally, there is no shortage of astonishing predictions. It is well known, for instance, that Abraham Lincoln dreamed of his death shortly before he was assassinated. An event of interest to psychotherapists comes in Carl Jung's autobiography, *Memories, Dreams, Reflections.* Jung writes that Sigmund Freud was arguing with him about the validity of precognition:

> 'I had a curious sensation... as if my diaphragm... were becoming red-hot... And at that moment there was such a loud report in the book-case... right next to us that we both started up in alarm, fearing the

---

21.   Leibovici (2001).

thing was going to topple over on us. I said to Freud, "There, that is an example of a so-called catalytic exteriorisation phenomenon." "Oh come", he exclaimed, "That is sheer bosh". "It is not," I replied. "You are mistaken, Herr Professor. And to prove my point I now predict that in a moment there will be another loud report!" Sure enough, no sooner had I said the words than the same detonation went off in the bookcase... Freud only stared aghast at me. I do not know what was in his mind, or what his look meant. In any case, this incident aroused his mistrust of me and I had the feeling I had done something against him.'[22]

One-off events can always be discounted as chance. Yet now there are consistent laboratory findings, such as Dean Radin's studies of presentiment. Radin showed his experimental subjects a series of pictures flashed up in random order on a computer screen. Some pictures were soothing in nature, others violent or erotic. At the same time, he recorded the subject's electrodermal activity as used in the lie detector test. He found that subjects responded with increased arousal (increased skin conductance) when the picture was violent or erotic, which is hardly surprising. Here is the point, though – he found that this physiological change consistently takes place about one second *before* the picture actually appears on screen.[23]

Space and Infinity

'All real living is meeting.'

Martin Buber (1923)[24]

'... for meeting is not in time and space but space and time in meeting.'

Maurice Friedman[25]

I have dwelled on the subject of time because I have wanted to show how we allow chronological time to limit our view of reality. Now I

---

22. Jung (1963: 178).
23. Radin (1997).
24. Buber ([2000]: 26).
25. Friedman (1958: 66).

want to put the dimension of space to the same kind of test by looking briefly at telepathy and clairvoyance.

Telepathy means feeling, or sensing, at a distance. A commonly reported instance is to know who is on the line before picking up the telephone. Another is of suddenly becoming aware of the death of a loved one, even though he or she may be on the other side of the world – information that frequently comes in dreams.

The first systematic research on telepathy was conducted by Joseph Rhine at Duke University in the 1920s and continued for more than 40 years. Playing cards were used to see whether information could be transmitted from a sender to a receiver, and over thousands of trials, significant positive correlations were found.[26] Then, in the 1960s, dream studies carried out by Montague Ullman showed that symbolic imagery could be sent by the experimenter to the dreamer.[27] Meta-analysis of 25 studies showed a 'hit' rate of 63% (against the chance finding of 50%); statistically speaking, this gives odds against chance of millions to one. Other experiments employed the Ganzfeld technique of using sensory screening to filter out 'mental noise' in the subject and yielded even higher 'hit' rates, findings that have been replicated in a large number of trials.[28]

Clairvoyance, also called remote viewing, was the subject of a US military research programme, established in 1973 by Russell Targ and Harold Puthoff at Stanford University and funded to the tune of $20 million. Remote viewers have been shown to provide information about target locations at any distance when supplied with the coordinates of latitude and longitude. In 1988, the database of 16,000 trials was analysed with results showing a billion to one against chance.[29] Research linking space and time was carried out on similar lines at the Princeton Engineering Anomalies Research Laboratory, except that the viewer was asked to identify the target *before* the target was known to the experimenter. This might be an object, a

26.   Rhine (1964).
27.   Ullman et al. (1973).
28.   Honorton (1985).
29.   May et al. (1988).

drawing or a location. Odds against chance of a quintillion[30] to one were obtained.[31]

Lastly, there is psychokinesis or mind–matter interaction, more recently popularised by Uri Geller. Since Helmut Schmidt began studying psychokinesis in the 1960s,[32] research at Princeton has shown that by thinking 'high' or 'low', the experimenter can alter the mean value of numbers being churned out by a random number generator, an effect that becomes clearly discernible over thousands of trials.[33] It has also been shown that the field effect of group consciousness can influence random number generators. The trial of O.J. Simpson was watched by half a billion people live on television and as the verdict was announced, five separate random number generators at different geographical sites peaked simultaneously.[34]

Portals to Other Worlds

'This life's five windows of the soul
Distorts the Heaven from pole to pole,
And leads you to believe a lie
When you see with, not thro', the eye'

William Blake, The Everlasting Gospel (1810)[35]

I have introduced some features of quantum cosmology and paranormal research because they prepare us so well for the 'life beyond death' question. Once the concept of matter and consciousness unfolding together out of the quantum realm is grasped, the saying of Jesus 'My Father's house has many rooms'[36] speaks as much for science as spirituality, for ours is most likely one of myriad universes

---

30.   Quintillion: a billion billion or 10^{18}.
31.   Dobyns et al. (1992).
32.   Schmidt (1970).
33.   Jahn (1987).
34.   Radin (1997).
35.   Nicholson & Lee (1917).
36.   John 14:2. *The Holy Bible*, NIV.

materializing in accordance with their rule sets of space and time. The quantum realm may be thought of as giving rise to a multiplicity of universes in domains of space-time as illustrated, all of them being, in a sense, 'virtual realities' (although subjectively no less 'real' for that). At the same time, we should remember that all such concepts only take us to the threshold of supramundane reality and that what lies beyond remains ineffable.

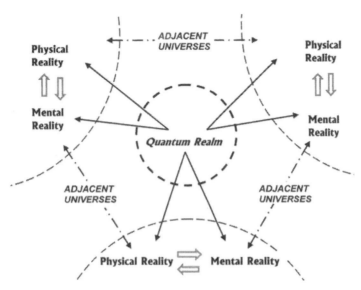

14.2 Representation of the 'multiverse'.

Quantum cosmology allows us to look at anomalous (paranormal) phenomena in a new way. We may simply be observing information transfer that takes place between adjacent domains, in our particular case the domain of the *bardo* or spirit realm and our own realm of space-time. When we set aside the limits of what Newtonian physics tells us is possible, a whole range of phenomena can be approached afresh; for example, mystical experiences, *psi* phenomena (psychokinesis and extra-sensory perception), near-death and out-of-body experiences, reincarnation, dissociative identity disorder and spirit release therapy, trance states, mediumship and healing, and past life regression.

The Journey of the Soul

'Death is a touch of the Soul which is too strong for the body.'

Alice Bailey[37]

There is general agreement as to what is meant by physical death. However, the notion of 'soul consciousness' is more arguable and so I will try to explain this further.

The word 'consciousness' derives from the Latin *com-scire*, words meaning 'together' and 'to know'. On the mundane level of reality, the accumulation of sensations, thoughts and feelings builds the awareness of a discrete self. As Theory of Mind has shown, we are also hardwired for the development of empathy – to be able to understand how others think and feel.[38] Notwithstanding the empathic bridge between self and other, the embodied mind still reflects separation of subject and object. However, consciousness in its highest reach transcends the personal, being unitary and indivisible; accordingly, the 'golden rule' of all the great faith traditions, to love one's neighbour *as* oneself, is to be taken literally, since transpersonally speaking, self and other are one. From this perspective, how might we distinguish between soul and spirit?[39] By spirit I mean the universal, sacred principle of consciousness, and by soul the unique expression of spirit in each one of us.

Throughout childhood and into adulthood, the developing ego energizes and drives us into the complex world of human relationships, with its desires, needs and attainments. Yet with the passing years, many people begin to seek an understanding of life that transcends the self-interest of the ego.[40] This is the work of the soul, symbolized by the heart chakra,[41] at which level spirit 'appears as an

---

37.   Bailey (1973: 78).
38.   Baron-Cohen (1995).
39.   These words have a common source in the Greek and Hebrew for breath, being *pneuma* and *neshana* respectively. The word 'spirit' derives from the Latin *spiritus,* again meaning breath, and refers to the vital and animating essence of all life forms. 'Soul' comes from the Old English *sawl*, and is usually taken to mean the spiritual or immaterial part of the human being that is immortal.
40.   See *Psychosocial Implications of the Shadow*, this volume.
41.   See *Varieties of Love*, this volume.

archetype endowed with supreme significance and expressed through the figure of the divine hero, whose representation in the West is Christ'.[42] All great spiritual masters serve humanity as exemplars of compassion and unconditional love. Even so, every human being who heeds the soul sets out on the same path.

Unlike the ego, which is rooted in the human lifespan, the soul, unfettered by the limits of human birth and death, journeys to 'many mansions'. We cannot help being curious about what kind of life after death we might expect. Near-death experiences go as far as the garden gate, so to speak, but never beyond. It is hardly surprising then, that after-death communications relayed by mediums clairvoyantly or through automatic writing, or 'past lives' and 'between lives' narratives elicited by hypnotherapy, meet with such interest. There is a burgeoning literature on the subject. What these many accounts hold in common is more striking than details of difference. From Swedenborg to Alice Bailey to Neil Donald Walsch,[43] the soul would seem to be endlessly engaged in the task of acquiring ever more learning and wisdom.

I remember sitting with a trance medium who 'brought through' a spirit presence identifying himself as Paul the Apostle. I wanted to know what Paul had to say about karma and the cycle of rebirth. He replied 'How typically human to suppose it all has to be worked out on Earth! Earth is where karma is accrued so that afterwards the soul can reflect on its deficiencies and spend as long as necessary making them good.'

In the following section, I will enlarge on some of the experiences that suggest the journey of the soul is a great deal longer than one short lifetime.

The Near-Death Experience

Much research has taken place over the 30 years since the publication of Dr Raymond Moody's book *Life After Life*,[44] a ground-breaking compilation of 150 case reports of patients who were resuscitated

---

42. Jung (1912: 413).
43. Swedenborg (1758), Bailey (1936), Walsch (1998).
44. Moody (1975).

following clinical death and which inspired subsequent research into the near-death experience. The extensive literature on near-death experiences[45] describes a sequence of events that, while shaped by cultural factors, carries the same core spiritual revelation and is strikingly consistent. Phenomena include awareness of floating above the body and looking down watching resuscitation being attempted, the experience of instant travel to other parts of the hospital or to home, including overhearing family and friends in other places, and entering a dark tunnel and being drawn towards a bright light. In the radiance of this light, there is frequently a dialogue with either a deceased relative or close friend, or a higher spiritual being. There may be a kaleidoscopic life review in which the whole of the life just lived, with all its deeds, both good and bad, must be faced. The judgement is entirely one's own, based on deep insight into one's past actions and their consequences. This life review would be unbearable were it not for the ambience of unconditional love and acceptance. There is awareness of a boundary that, once crossed, would mean no return. Because the experience feels so powerfully like 'coming home' there is usually great reluctance to return, but the person is told, or may decide, that an important life task still lies ahead. There follows a sudden and painful pulling back into the body with the recovery of consciousness.

Some scientists argue that what is being reported are the terminal throes of neural activity in a hypoxic brain. Yet these vivid and coherent recollections are quite unlike those of hypoxic or other organic conditions, which are fleeting and fragmentary. It has also been shown that the near-death experience occurs while there is no recordable electrical brain activity,[46] itself striking evidence for the non-local nature of consciousness.

Lastly, there is the spiritual impact of the near-death experience, leading to profound transformation of the psyche.[47] There is no subsequent fear of death. The survivor now knows beyond all doubt that the fundamental purpose of life is to give and receive love; all else pales into insignificance.

---

45. See, for example, Fenwick & Fenwick (1995), Bailey & Yates (1996).
46. de Vries et al. (1998), Parnia et al. (2001).
47. Morse (1992).

Reincarnation

The concept of reincarnation has been with us since at least 800 BCE. In Hinduism, it is believed that the soul transmigrates intact into another human or other life form, depending on the state of a person's karma. This is the cultural context in which young children, mostly in India, have astonished their parents by talking about another life previously lived, which was cut short – usually by some abrupt trauma such as an accident or murder. When taken to the former home, the child correctly identifies family members and recalls the circumstances of the death. Professor Ian Stevenson has painstakingly researched such cases, confirming that sometimes birthmarks found on the child correspond exactly to the bullet hole or wound on the murder victim.[48]

On the other hand, the Buddhist view is that individual consciousness dissolves away at death, leaving nothing but 'dispositions', which find their way back into re-birth as karmic intentions. Since according to Buddhism the spiritual goal is to transcend the ego in life rather than waiting for death, Buddhists are not very interested in the question of the survival of personal identity, since it is viewed as an ego-based aspiration.[49]

Can Buddhist and Hindu views be reconciled? This is possible if we do not insist on one cosmic reality to which everyone must subscribe. The way we 'collapse the wave' creates the world that we go on to experience, and thus the journey ahead is capable of infinite variety. The implication is enormous – think yourself into the future of your own choice!

Dissociative Identity Disorder and Spirit Attachment

Every psychiatrist needs to be familiar with dissociative identity disorder (previously called multiple personality), typically characterised by different parts of the psyche functioning independently and often unaware of the existence of other parts. This can result in

---

48. Stevenson (1966, 1997a,b).
49. Sumedho (1995).

the therapist striking up distinctive relationships with the various sub-personalities (or 'alters'), each of whom behaves like a person in his or her own right. People with dissociative identity disorder seek help because their lives become severely disrupted, since different alters have executive control at different times. Sometimes the patient suffers from periods of amnesia, coming round only to find a trail of chaos. Male and female alters co-exist, some prudish, others licentious, some dominant and others submissive. There is usually a history of severe childhood abuse and psychoanalysis holds that this early trauma has resulted in fragmentation of the ego, with disconnected sub-personalities developing from splits in the psyche. Therapy is arduous, addressing the defence mechanisms that have resulted in splitting and projection, and often sub-personalities refuse to be ousted, since it would be like involuntary suicide. Sometimes they can be helped to become aware of each other and to learn to live more peaceably together.[50]

Some transpersonal therapists consider that such problems may be the result of 'spirit attachment',[51] a split in the ego having opened the door to one or more intrusive entities that then take up residence.[52] Therefore, instead of aiming for the integration of autonomous psychic complexes, the purpose of spirit release therapy is compassionately to free the spirit entity to continue their journey to 'the light', very much as reported in the near-death experience.[53] These entities are understood to be the spirits of deceased persons, who have remained earthbound instead of continuing their soul journey. Such spirits are more likely to be confused and misguided than malevolent, sometimes not even realizing they are dead. The therapist can dialogue with them through the agency of the patient and obtain a personal history just as with any therapeutic consultation,[54] although

---

50. Phillips (1988).
51. As explained earlier, the term spirit is generally used to refer to the universal, sacred principle of consciousness, and the word soul to mean the unique expression of spirit in each person. However, spirit release therapists speak of 'earthbound spirits', perhaps because to use the word soul suggests embodiment in physical form.
52. See Sanderson (2003).
53. Powell (1998, 2002).
54. Crabtree (1985).

healers who are clairvoyant will 'see' and converse directly with the spirit presence.

The history of encounters with spirit is enshrined in age-old shamanic practices. In today's world, as well as guiding the process of spirit release, the therapist needs to explore the psychological status of the individual, since understanding how vulnerability arose in the first place will determine what further psychotherapeutic work may be needed to prevent relapse. Apart from childhood abuse, there may be a history of serious injury or illness (when psychic defences are impaired), excessive use of alcohol or drugs, or dabbling in the occult (e.g. using the Ouija board). Meanwhile, the Christian church works along similar lines with the ministry of deliverance. In the Islamic faith tradition, imams are authorized to cast out *jinn*.

On occasions, the therapist or priest comes up against an entity that seems truly demonic. 'Lesser demons' can usually be persuaded to talk, and on questioning will admit to never having been in human form. They may plague families for generations and relish creating fear, causing illness and sometimes destroying lives. The Bible states that when Lucifer was cast out of Heaven, he took a third of the heavenly host with him into Hell. Such 'demons' can be inveigled into looking into the depths of their own darkness, in the heart of which a light is discovered. Once this happens, there is an instant transformation, Satan's power is annulled and the demon is filled with remorse for its misdeeds. Such repentant 'fallen angels' are only too glad to leave for the Light. However, 'greater demons' show no remorse and can become violent. Few people, whether priest or lay practitioner, have the spiritual authority to deal safely with such possession states.

The phenomenology of spirit attachment highlights contrasting world-views. In the 'developed countries', the spirit world is discounted as superstition. Yet quantum cosmology is positing a new kind of reality – one in which 'inside' and 'outside', 'mine' and 'yours' have no meaning except as signatures of local space-time.[55] The implications are far-reaching, throwing into question the nature of the consensus reality we like to take for granted, and on which basis science dismisses 'spirits' and the like as mere superstition.

---

55. See *Consciousness That Transcends Space-Time*, this volume.

Trance States and Healing

During the 15th and 16th centuries, association with the supernatural – what these days might be described as the paranormal – was
condemned in Western civilization by the clergy as heretical; over
50,000 people, most of them women, were burned or drowned as
witches. However, in the 19th century, trance states began to attract
wide interest. Spiritualism was afoot in England and the Theosophical Society was founded in New York in 1875. The codification by
Allan Kardec[56] of discarnate spirits through the work of mediums
provided the foundation for spiritism, a syncretic Christian religion
centred in Brazil, with around 1 million adherents worldwide today.
Contact with the spirit world was beginning to be seen as a force for
good, calling on guides and benefactors in spirit to relieve pain and
suffering.

Trance healing, a cultural practice widely found in the Philippines
and South America but still performed worldwide, is carried out by
psychic or 'spirit surgeons', who perform surgical procedures while in
an altered state of consciousness.[57] Less contentious are 'hands-on
healing' and mediumship, supported in Britain by centres such as the
College of Psychic Studies in London and the Society for Psychical
Research, both active since the 1880s, and by healing organisations
such as the National Federation of Spiritual Healers.

Of note is the *Scole Report*,[58] published originally by the Society
for Psychical Research. A small group of researchers with respectable
scientific credentials regularly attended home séances held by spiri-
tualists, two of whom were mediums. A wide range of paranormal
phenomena were encountered, including moving lights that passed
through solid objects, the touch and vision of 'disembodied' hands,
and movements of the table. Voices were not only vocalized by the
mediums but also picked up on audiotape in a recorder from which
the microphone had been removed. There were a number of 'apports'
or materialisations, including a copy of *The Daily Mail*, 1 April 1944,
reporting on the trial of the medium Helen Duncan. (Print analysis

---

56. Kardec (1852, 1874).
57. Chard (1992).
58. See Solomon (1999).

proved it to be an original, yet the paper showed no sign of having aged.) There were also images on unexposed film, including faces, hermetic symbols and poetry, including some by F. W. Myers, one of the now-deceased founding fathers of the Society.

This detailed study strongly suggested that the phenomena were not fraudulent but genuine. The problem is that people with extra-sensory perception need no convincing, since for them such manifestations are self-evident, while others, more sceptical, can never be persuaded. No one these days doubts the presence of X-rays or radio waves that exist beyond the spectrum of sense perception. Yet science remains deeply prejudiced against the evidence for paranormal phenomena. For as long as it does so, bodily death will be viewed as the end of life.

'Past Lives'

It is a psychological rule that the brighter the light, the blacker the shadow, wrote Jung.[59] Jung's researches into the nature of the shadow have helped us to understand this duality.[60] When the light shines from within, no shadow is cast and this, as I see it, is the true nature of soul consciousness. However, most of us are still in the kindergarten of spiritual learning, so I will conclude this account of death and soul consciousness with two of the 'past lives' I personally experienced when working with a transpersonal past life therapist and which illustrate what it is like to experience another lifetime. Here is the first one:

'I am on a boat smuggling brandy from France. It is profitable but dangerous work. My job is to get off as we round the point on the return journey, climb up the rocks and meet up with other villagers while the boat beaches in the cove. No one is there to meet me and I

---

59. Jung (1950: 318).
60. Jung described how humankind maintains its sense of goodness, what he called the persona, at the cost of getting rid of the unwanted aspects of the self, which he grouped together and called the shadow. He writes, 'Everyone carries a shadow, and the less it is embodied in the individual's conscious life, the blacker and denser it is' (Jung 1938: 76).

realise something is wrong. Then I hear musket fire down below. The militia have been lying in wait and are killing everyone on board. I run away. Soon I am in a valley strange to me. I know I cannot go back. I am full of remorse. I will never see my mother and father again, or my sweetheart. In order not to starve, I become a highway-man. One day I stop a stagecoach and find a row of muskets pointing back at me. The militia take me to a judge who finds me guilty to be hanged. The next morning I am put on a cart and driven to a gibbet by the roadside. They put a rope round my neck and drive the cart away. I am hanging, I can't breathe, I feel myself choking. I am dying.

Now I am floating up. I look down and can see myself hanging there. I watch the birds peck out my eyes. Then they cut me down and throw my body into a pit of lime. I want to leave this awful place but I can't.'

Here the therapist interjects, 'Look around and see if there is anyone to take your hand and help lead you away from here'.

'No one comes. I am filled with remorse for my wasted life. My family was poor but loving and had I not been greedy I would be with them now.'

The therapist speaks to me again, 'Look up and see if you can find a light somewhere'.

'I look up and far, far away there is a tiny point of light. I feel a great longing to go there. I call out, "God forgive me for what I have done" and immediately I soar upwards into the light and it is all over.'

This particular 'past life' left a strong impression on me. What did I learn? Every action has its consequence and it really is possible to throw away the gift of life for a moment's greed.

Sometimes the opportunity for reparation comes in the *bardo* or spirit realm, as in this second account:

'I find myself in Nantes, France, in the 15th century, a miller by trade with a wife and two small children. There is a civil insurrection going on at the time. One day, without warning, I am dragged out of my home by soldiers and taken to the local prison on a trumped-up charge of treason (supplying grain to the rebels). A military tribunal summarily pronounces me guilty and I am thrown into a dungeon.'

As a 'past life' is experienced in real time, the therapist moves the subject back and forward through time, like running videotape, in order to reveal the whole life story. In this case, we kept fast-forwarding, year on year, but nothing changed. I stayed where I was in that wretched cell, in chains and alone. Finally, we moved on to the day of my death:

> 'My ankle iron has rotted my leg. I am feverish and dying. My last emotion before leaving the body is anger with my wife. During all those years, she has not once been to see me and I feel deeply betrayed. I carry that emotion with me as I leave my body and cross over into the realm of spirit.'

The therapist now put it to me that I might need to meet with my wife who had so heartlessly abandoned me. I agreed with bad grace, and waited there for her 'on the other side' to come across at the conclusion of her life.

> 'As soon as she catches sight of me, my wife runs forwards to embrace me lovingly. She tells me how she came to the prison day after day, year in, year out, imploring the guards to let her visit me, but that she was always turned away. When I hear this, my heart melts and my eyes fill with tears. I can see that my fury at abandonment, which had made my captivity infinitely worse, resulted from my lack of faith and trust in the goodness of love.'

What should I learn from this 'deep memory'? Keeping faith with the power of love in the face of implacable adversity is no small thing. I may have failed the test in that lifetime but I am being given – or maybe I should say I am giving myself – another chance.

Sceptics claim that 'past lives' are nothing more than the stuff of phantasy, which would be a legitimate psychological interpretation. However, the essence of quantum theory is not *either/or* but *both/and*. I do not reject the psychological view, yet bearing in mind the 'forms within forms' to which Alice Bailey refers, we may also be discovering that space and time are moveable feasts.

Whatever the ultimate nature of the experience I am describing, it had to be structured by my psyche. From the transpersonal perspective, can I really say that I personally 'lived' these experiences in other incarnations? Was I tapping into a quantum waveform that collapsed into those once-lived scenes based on sympathetic resonance? When we leave the body, who can say what is individual to each of us, or what becomes a collective consciousness? Hold up your hand with fingers spread and what do you see? Five fingers or one hand?

In Conclusion

I hope that the concepts I have presented and the experiences I have been reporting begin to sound as easy and natural as might arise in conversation between friends. I hope they will inspire some degree of optimism, for while death seen as an end holds no further meaning, death as a transition opens the door to new birth and new life.

References

Allen, R.E., Fowler, H.W. & Fowler, F.G. (eds) (1990) *The Concise Oxford Dictionary of Current English*, Eighth edition. Clarendon Press.

Anonymous (1959) *Zen Buddhism: An Introduction to Zen with Stories, Parables and Koan Riddles Told by the Zen Masters; with Cuts from Old Chinese Ink-paintings.* Peter Pauper Press.

Bache, C. (2000) *Dark Night, Early Dawn.* State University of New York Press.

Bailey, A.A. (1934) The nature of space. In *Telepathy and the Etheric Vehicle.* Lucis Press.

Bailey, A.A. (1936) *Esoteric Psychology.* Vol. 1. Lucis Press.

Bailey, A.A. (1973) *The Unfinished Biography.* Lucis Press.

Bailey, L. & Yates, J. (1996) *The Near Death Experience.* Routledge.

Baron-Cohen, S. (1995) *Mindblindness: An Essay on Autism and Theory of Mind.* MIT Press: Bradford Books.

Blake, W. (1790) The Marriage of Heaven and Hell. Reprinted [2000] in *William Blake, The Marriage of Heaven and Hell: A Facsimile in Full Color* (plate 14, p. 36). Dover Publications.

Buber, M. (1923) *I and Thou.* Reprinted [2000], Scribner Classics.

Castaneda, C. (1968) *The Teachings of Don Juan: A Yaqui Way of Knowledge.* University of California Press.

Castaneda, C. (1974) *Tales of Power.* Simon & Schuster.

Chard, L. (1992) *Dr Kahn: The Spirit Surgeon.* Elmore-Chard.

Crabtree, A. (1985) *Multiple Man.* Grafton Books.

Cummings, R. (1923) *The Girl in the Golden Atom.* Reprinted [2005], University of Nebraska Press.

de Vries, J., Bakker, P., Visser, G., et al. (1998) Change in cerebral oxygen uptake and cerebral electrical activity during defibrillation threshold testing. *Anesthesia & Analgesia,* 87, 16–20.

Dobyns, Y., Dunne, B., Jahn, R., et al. (1992) Response to Hansen, Utts and Markwick: Statistical and methodological problems of the PEAR remote viewing experiments. *Journal of Parapsychology*, 56, 115–146.

Eddington, A.S. (1938) Reprinted [2008] in *The Philosophy of Physical Science*. MacMillan.

Evans-Wentz, W.Y. (1927) *The Tibetan Book of the Dead*. Oxford University Press.

Fenwick, P. & Fenwick, E. (1995) *The Truth in the Light*. Headline.

Friedman, M.S. (1958) *Martin Buber: The Life of Dialogue*. Routledge and Kegan Paul.

Goswami, A. (1993) *The Self-Aware Universe*. Putnam Books.

Grof, S. (1993) *The Holotropic Mind*. HarperCollins.

Guo, B. & Powell, A. (2001) *Listen to Your Body: The Wisdom of the Dao*. University of Hawai'i Press.

Honorton, C. (1985) Meta-analysis of *psi* Ganzfeld research: a response to Hyman. *Journal of Parapsychology*, 49, 51–91.

Huxley, A. (1954) *The Doors of Perception*. Chatto and Windus.

Jahn, R. (1987) *Margins of Reality*. Harcourt Brace Jovanovich.

Jung, C.G (1912) The sacrifice. Reprinted [1956] in *C.G. Jung: The Collected Works*, vol. 5: Symbols of Transformation (eds H. Read, M. Fordham & G. Adler). Routledge and Kegan Paul.

Jung, C.G. (1938) Psychology and religion. Reprinted [1958] in *C.G. Jung: The Collected Works*, vol. 11: Psychology and Religion: West and East (eds H. Read, M. Fordham & G. Adler). Routledge and Kegan Paul.

Jung, C. (1950) Foreword to Moser: 'Spuk: Irrglaube Oder Wahrglaube?' Reprinted [1977] in *C.G. Jung: The Collected Works*, vol. 18: The Symbolic Life (eds H. Read, M. Fordham & G. Adler). Routledge and Kegan Paul.

Jung, C. (1963) *Memories, Dreams, Reflections*. Fontana Press.

Kardec, A. (1852) *The Spirits Book*. Federacao Espirita Brasileira, Departamento Editorial.

Kardec, A. (1874) *The Mediums Book*. Samuel Weiser.

Leibovici, L. (2001) Effects of remote, retroactive intercessory prayer on outcomes in patients with bloodstream infection: randomised controlled trial. *BMJ*, 323, 1450–1451.

May, E., Utts, J., Trask, V., et al. (1988) *Review of the Psychoenergetic Research Conducted at SRI International, 1973–1988*. Stanford Research Institute.

McTaggart, L. (2001) *The Field*. HarperCollins.

Moody, R. (1975) *Life After Life: The Investigation of a Phenomenon – Survival of Bodily Death*. Bantam Books.

Morse, N. (1992) *Transformed by the Light*. Piatkus.

Narby, J. (1999) *The Cosmic Serpent*. Orion Books.

Nicholson, D. & Lee, A. (eds) (1917) William Blake, The Everlasting Gospel. *The Oxford Book of Mystical Verse*. Clarendon Press.

Nicholson, D. & Lee, A. (eds) (1917) Alfred Lord Tennyson, 'Flower in the Crannied Wall'. *The Oxford Book of English Mystical Verse*. Clarendon Press.

Parnia, S., Waller, D., Yates, R., et al. (2001) A qualitative and quantitative study of the incidence, features and aetiology of near death experiences in cardiac arrest survivors. *Resuscitation*, 48, 149–156.

Phillips, R. (ed.) (1988) *When Rabbit Howls: The Troops for Truddi Chase*. Sidgwick and Jackson.

Powell, A. (1998) Soul consciousness and human suffering. *Journal of Alternative and Complementary Medicine*, 4, 101–108.

Powell, A. (2002) Quantum psychiatry: where science meets spirit. *Nexus*, 9, 51–55.

Radin, D. (1997) *The Conscious Universe*. HarperCollins.

Rhine, J. (1964) *Extra-Sensory Perception*. Bruce Humphries.

Sanderson, A. (2003) The case for spirit release. Available at: http://www.rcpsych. ac.uk/spsigarchive

Schmidt, H. (1970) Mental influence on random events. *New Scientist and Science Journal*, 50, 757–758.

Solomon, G. (1999) *The Scole Experiment: Scientific Evidence for Life After Death*. Piatkus.

Stevenson, I. (1966) *Twenty Cases Suggestive of Reincarnation*. University Press of Virginia.

Stevenson, I. (1997a) *Reincarnation and Biology: A Contribution to the Etiology of Birthmarks*. Vol. 1. Praegar.

Stevenson, I. (1997b) *Birth Defects and other Anomalies*. Vol. 2. Praegar.

Sumedho, A. (1995) *The Mind and the Way*. Rider.

Swedenborg, E. (1758) *Heaven and Hell* (transl. G. Dole). Reprinted [2000], Swedenborg Foundation.

Talbot, M. (1991) *The Holographic Universe*. HarperCollins.

Ullman, M., Krippner, S. & Vaughan, A. (1973) *Dream Telepathy*. Macmillan.

Walsch, N. D. (1998) *Conversations with God (Book 3)*. Hampton Roads Publishing Company.

15

Spirituality and Later
Life – A Personal Perspective

When I was asked to give this short paper at a psychiatric conference on spirituality and religion in later life, my first reaction was to say, 'But I only trained for six months in old age psychiatry'. Then I remembered that I am 60 years old, and that later life is already on me, so I felt I might be able to say something after all!

First, a disclaimer. Although I have had a strong interest in spirituality for most of my life, I do not see myself as having attained any special merit. For much of my life, my actions have been governed by the mundane preoccupations of the ego as much as moved by the soul.[1] I suppose the important thing here is to be honest and not to lay claim to any kind of superiority, or inferiority, come to that. These days, rather than compare myself to others, I prefer to listen to my conscience and like a compass that points north, I am usually shown the direction to take.

If it is our aim, the spiritual path takes us way beyond the realm of the physical world, but we must also keep our feet on the ground. We live in the era of the randomised controlled trial and there are times when this puts the practice of *ars medecina* sorely to the test. However, this problem is age-old and we have guidance from a

First published as 'Spirituality and later life – a personal perspective' in *The Journal of Holistic Healthcare* (2011), 8, 45–48. Reproduced with permission.

---

1. See Bailey (1942).

peerless exemplar.[2] The empirical, the objective and the rational are the currency of evidence-based medicine. Yet this does not mean that the subjective, the personal and the spiritual need be denied in either doctor or patient.

Interestingly, despite the prevailing culture of materialism and consumerism, the privilege of consciousness continues to drive *Homo sapiens* to try to make sense of our own existence and purpose. Richard Dawkins, the doyen of material realism, sees the advent of consciousness as nothing but the 'selfish gene' seeking an evolutionary advantage.[3] Others contend that consciousness is intrinsic to the cosmos itself, the human brain having achieved the degree of neurobiological complexity needed to attain the advanced status of self-awareness.[4] This is the perennial 'bottom-up' versus 'top-down' argument. Experimental science cannot answer this question, and so we are free to go looking for other kinds of evidence (people generally find the evidence that supports their preferred assumptions). Fortunately, whichever side of this argument you take, the spiritual impulse makes itself known just the same.

Any discussion of spirituality has to encounter the word, God, since the major faith traditions have need of this word or its equivalent to identify the source of 'all that is'. Some religions portray God with recognisably human characteristics. This can be understood from the 'bottom up' perspective as God construed according to a projection of the human mind, or 'top down', on the strength of our universe being structured holographically, in which case we really are made in the likeness of God's image – albeit through a glass darkly.

In the Abrahamic faith traditions, 'God' traditionally describes one absolute and supreme deity somewhere 'out there'. Heaven, therefore, had to be invented, so 'He' would have somewhere to live.

---

2. '… [the Pharisees]…came to [Jesus] and said, "Teacher, we know that you are a man of integrity. You aren't swayed by others, because you pay no attention to who they are; but you teach the way of God in accordance with the truth. Is it right to pay the imperial tax to Caesar or not?" They brought the coin, and he asked them, "Whose image is this? And whose inscription?" "Caesar's", they replied. Then Jesus said to them, "Give back to Caesar what is Caesar's and to God what is God's".' Mark 12:13–17. *The Holy Bible*, NIV.
3. Dawkins (1976).
4. Lorimer (2001).

Such a metaphysical theology is generally held to be incompatible with Newtonian science, leading to the view that belief in God is merely a psychological defence shielding us from the prospect of death and oblivion. Indeed, surveys show that only about one-third of psychiatrists believe there to be any kind of God, in contrast to the large majority of the general population.[5]

This is about more than theology, for as an archetype God springs up all over the place – in art, music, politics and even on the football pitch. All these activities can serve as 'religion' in the sense of the Latin root *religare*, meaning 'to bind (together)'.[6] In order to make sense of our existence, we cannot help but identify with meaning and purpose that includes us in a greater reality, conferring on each of us the experience of *belonging to more than myself*. This is the cornerstone of all spirituality, be it secular or sacred.

As we get older, secular spirituality frequently makes way for the sacred – but not always so. For example, the renowned philosopher A.J. Ayer, on surviving a cardiac arrest, said of his own near-death experience that he considered it to be a hallucination; his unswerving faith in logical positivism never faltered.[7]

In the search for a greater meaning and purpose in life, atheism (being itself a religion as defined above) is perfectly compatible with spirituality. Neither am I against reductive thinking, to which we are indebted for a good deal of our theories of developmental psychology and psychopathology. I would say, rather, that the spiritual impulse is manifest in the desire to imbue all life with love. In so doing, we come to know more of the whole – the other side of the coin to reductionism. Wholeness is healing – the root coming from

---

5. Shafranske (2000).
6. Definitions of religion extend to include 'an interest, a belief, or an activity that is very important to a person or group' (Merriam-Webster online dictionary, https://www.merriam-webster.com).
7. Ayer subsequently wrote, 'My experiences have weakened, not my belief that there is no life after death, but my inflexible attitude toward that belief' (1988). It seems that in the light of his near-death experience, Ayer was at least willing to own a very small degree of doubt. Ayer later speculated that if there is life after death (however unlikely) it would be more likely to take the form of reincarnation than resurrection.

the same word[8] – and to find healing, we have to engage fully with life and not shrink, as often we are tempted to do, from the adversities that must come our way.[9]

Fortunately, wisdom is not the prerogative of philosophers. We all get a little bit wiser each time we learn from experience and usually it is through our mistakes and misfortunes that we learn the most. The longer we live, the greater our capacity to see the error of our ways. However, we need not torment ourselves. What matters more is to put that understanding to good use in the future.

It is harder to admit our folly when young because the ego is still in the ascendant and does not like to think it gets things wrong. That is why we look for other people to blame, and do not spare them our judgements either! Yet the ego should not be censured, for in the first half of life our ambitions and goals are quite properly shaped by ego needs: the longed-for relationship(s), making a home, the desire to raise a family and the attainment of success at work. Then, and it usually comes as something of a shock, we find ourselves over the brow of the hill. Now we begin to see the cycle of birth and death in a new way. Life is so fleeting. How much more similar than different we all are with our hopes and fears! Everything we thought belonged to us turns out to be on loan – and a short-term one too!

Individuation, as Carl Jung calls it, has now started, setting everything against a backdrop of impermanence occasioned by the foreknowledge of death. This is not morbid thinking. Jung points out, 'It is just as neurotic in old age not to focus upon the goal of death as it is in youth to repress fantasies which have to do with the future'.[10] With individuation, the pull of the archetypes grows ever stronger. Again, in Jung's words:

> '...the archetypes [...] represent the life and essence of a non-individual psyche. Although this psyche is innate in every individual, it can neither be modified nor possessed by him personally. It is the same in the individual as it is in the crowd and ultimately in everybody. It

---

8. See *Spirituality, Healing and the Mind*, this volume.
9. In clinical practice, it is well recognised that while adversity can be a great teacher, too much stops a person from learning anything.
10. Jung (1934: 410).

is the pre-condition of each individual psyche, just as the sea is the carrier of each individual wave'.[11]

This shift is pivotal in determining whether a person is able to relinquish the strivings of the ego in favour of the greatest of all archetypes, the Self.[12] If so, there comes an acceptance of death, even regarding it as miraculous as birth. Otherwise, death must remain the dreaded spectre that will inexorably cut us off from all that we love.

People have different ways of preparing for the end of life. For some, acceptance is found in religious truths, doctrinal teachings and participation in liturgy. In my case, it has been important to bring together what I have personally learned about spirituality with my reading of quantum cosmology. This describes a universe that extends beyond time and space,[13] where all flows together in a vast ocean of consciousness and from which (I like to think) our souls venture forth into this phenomenal world of sense perception so that we can learn and grow through experience.

Nevertheless, death has aptly been described as the one appointment no one is in a hurry to keep. However well prepared we may think we are, coming face-to-face with dying is a profound existential challenge.[14] Unless we take flight in denial, we are painfully confronted with the big questions of life: Why was I born? What purpose has my life served? What have I left undone? What will happen to me when I die?

This is where trust in a Greater Design comes in.[15] Even to have glimpsed it dispels the spectre of meaningless existence. For the humanist, such meaning is furnished by a heartfelt contribution to humankind, be it family, friends or the wider community. Those of a

---

11. Jung (1946: 169).
12. Jung (1917) describes the Self as the totality of the whole psyche, conscious and unconscious, the latter comprising both the personal and collective (transpersonal) unconscious. Jung observes that 'The concept of the Self [...] embraces ego-consciousness, shadow, anima, and collective unconscious in indeterminable extension' (Jung, 1954: 108).
13. See *Beyond Space and Time*, this volume.
14. Even Jesus, on the cross, suffered this human anguish, calling out, 'My God, my God, why have you forsaken me?' Matthew 27:46. *The Holy Bible*, NIV.
15. The last recorded words of Jesus were, 'Father, into your hands I commit my spirit'. Luke 23:46. *The Holy Bible*, NIV.

metaphysical bent find their meaning in life, and death too, as a rite of passage to the life beyond.

Seeing the compass of life in one's middle years with new and sometimes painful clarity helps us understand why we were prompted to take one turning rather than another, and what the consequences have been. We see how our fears held us back, how pride leads to a fall, and how we were captive to our weaknesses. Indeed, depression can entrap a person in such memories; this is liable to happen when we are not able to recognize that every pitfall and reversal has been put there with unerring accuracy in order to face us with our worst fears and to teach us what we most need to learn.

We know from survivors of near-death experiences that the solution to all the travails of the ego is extraordinarily simple: to love without strings attached or expectations of reward. This is the nature of spiritual love and when we meet someone with it, we are instantly uplifted. Even though we may fall short, we can at least live with this aspiration.

Neurosis is a formidable obstacle to love, and psychotherapy aims to help the patient undo the tangle of feelings standing in love's way. Human solutions to human problems are generally a good place to start, for example, the oppressive influence of a punitive father that needs rooting out of the patient's mind. Yet in this case, there is often a serious further problem, for by means of projection not just the father but life itself is experienced as harsh and unloving. Once this projection is made conscious, the patient can be helped to distinguish between the personal and the universal. When life itself can be embraced, the nurturing archetype of the *anima mundi* – the soul of the world – is discovered alive and well.[16]

In soul-centred therapy, no matter how negative the picture might seem to be, the starting point is always the same: the therapist works to explore what the patient most deeply wishes they could express.[17] This leads a person – whether or not they are religious – to the soul, whose light may have become shrouded in darkness. Most often, there is found a longing to forgive, or be forgiven, to reach an understanding where before there was none, to be at peace instead of

16. See *Soul Consciousness and Human Suffering*, this volume.
17. Powell (2003).

in pain, or to tell someone you love them before it is too late. In later life, with time running out, the need is all the more pressing.

I have found that people close to death have two great fears – either oblivion or that judgement will be passed on them. When exploring this therapeutically, it can be helpful to find out what a person imagines life after death – if there should be such an existence – may be like. The scenario that presents itself is often poignant, for it turns out that rather than a void, there is often 'unfinished business' with kith and kin – feelings that are very much alive, and which it is not too late to share. As to fear of judgement, it is always possible to ask forgiveness, whether of the living or the dead, or of God.

Earlier, I mentioned the importance in mid-life of getting to grips with one's life story, not least to see what can be learned and how this can help in making personal choices yet to come. However, later life can bring another kind of profound realisation, one that is transpersonal. In the words of William Blake:

'To see a World in a Grain of Sand
And a Heaven in a Wild Flower
Hold Infinity in the palm of your hand
And Eternity in an hour...'

From Auguries of Innocence (1803)[18]

These lines of Blake's quicken the soul. We are made aware of the majesty of life that is revealed in the smallest detail when we stop and notice. Regrettably, we may discover how to live fully in the present only when we are reaching the end of life. It does not have to be so. In the Gospel of Thomas, when Jesus's followers asked him when the kingdom of heaven will come, He remarks: 'it will not be said, "Look, here it is", or "Look, there it is". Rather, the father's kingdom is spread out upon the earth, and people do not see it.'[19]

I want to conclude with what it means to me to have been a doctor for most of my lifetime. I am indebted to my patients for teaching me so much about myself. Having them share their greatest hopes and fears with me has been an enormous privilege. Our patients hold

18.   Keynes (1966).
19.   Bloom (1992).

up a mirror to us and if we choose to look into it, we are made aware that we are far more alike than different. In my efforts to try to help them, it turns out my patients have been helping me! Spirituality thrives on relationships, especially when the barriers are down, so let us ensure as doctors that we do not put barriers up. We can be certain of this, provided we give our attention not only to the head but also to the heart.

References

Ayer, A. (1988) Postscript to a post-mortem. *Spectator*, 15 October, 205–208.

Bailey, A.A. (1942) *Esoteric Psychology*. Vol. 2. Lucis Press.

Bloom, H. (1992) *The Gospel of Thomas: Saying 113*. HarperSanFrancisco.

Dawkins, R. (1976) *The Selfish Gene*. Oxford University Press.

Jung, C.G. (1917) The personal and the collective (or transpersonal) unconscious. Reprinted [1953] in *C.G. Jung: The Collected Works*, vol. 7: Two Essays On Analytical Psychology (eds H. Read, M. Fordham & G. Adler). Routledge and Kegan Paul.

Jung, C.G. (1934) The Soul And Death. Reprinted [1960] in *C.G. Jung: The Collected Works*, vol. 8: The Structure And Dynamics Of The Psyche (eds H. Read, M. Fordham & G. Adler). Routledge and Kegan Paul.

Jung, C.G. (1946) The Psychology of the Transference. Reprinted [1954] in *C.G. Jung: The Collected Works*, vol. 16: The Practice Of Psychotherapy (eds H. Read, M. Fordham & G. Adler). Routledge and Kegan Paul.

Jung, C.G. (1954) The Personification Of The Opposites. Reprinted [1963] in *C.G. Jung: The Collected Works*, vol. 14: Mysterium Coniunctionis (eds. H. Read, M. Fordham & G. Adler). Routledge and Kegan Paul.

Keynes, G. (ed.) (1966) 'Auguries of Innocence'. In *Blake: Complete Writings with Variant Readings*. Oxford University Press.

Lorimer, D. (2001) *Thinking Beyond the Brain*. Floris Books.

Powell, A. (2003) Consciousness that Transcends Spacetime: its Significance for the Therapeutic Process. *Self and Society*, 31, 27–44.

Shafranske, E.P. (2000) Religious involvement and professional practices of psychiatrists and other mental health professionals. *Psychiatric Annals*, 30, 525–532.

Index